Prac Place

CREATIVE AND CRITICAL REFLECTIONS ON PLACE

Edited by
Elaine Speight

Foreword by
Lubaina Himid

Foreword

LUBAINA HIMID CBE

On the 4th of March 1991 I moved to a house in Preston overlooking Avenham Park in which I have lived and made work for the past 27 years. There were a number of artists making a difference to the cultural landscape of the region then, but I could not find unsalted butter or smokey tea in any shop or on any market stall. I was more interested in the latter than the former, even though the date marked the day of a real commitment to living in the north of England and a realisation that talking to student artists all day was how I wanted to live my life and make my work. Since those days in the 1990s unsalted butter has appeared on more than one shelf and, sadly, a little too late for my addiction, lapsang souchong tea can at last be found all over the city.

In Certain Places, an art commissioning and research project based at the University of Central Lancashire and led by curators Charles Quick and Elaine Speight, emerged in 2003. Their aim was to examine how artists can contribute to the development of a city, through place-based art; an astonishing feat which has developed and grown, seeping into every corner of every decision about living here. However, a major part of their contribution to the critical discourse surrounding their work is Practising Place led solely by Elaine.

In early discussions together, more than a decade ago, she and I talked about social space, making space and debating space. We soon realised that in Preston these kinds of opportunities for artists to understand and develop deeper strands to their practice and to experiment with how to make work that could establish a place at the table in the wider conversations around cultural contribution just did not exist.

The Practising Place project understands that artists living and working outside the large metropolitan world centres have a huge contribution to make to the conversations which audiences urgently want to have. The artists involved have been given the chance time and again to expand their own ideas about both the special and the everyday, about the histories and the soundscapes of the lives the rest of us experience. The project is pivotal in that there is, at its heart, a genuine desire to listen to what artists think, say and do when asked dynamic, dense and intelligent questions by experts. Because the experts brought together by Practising Place, in dialogue with the artists, share a desire to delve deeper while sharing their discoveries, the project has changed lives. I have seen it and experienced it.

This may seem a simple and obvious strategy but only people who seriously believe in the power of cultural activism and who have a commitment to give artists agency could ever think of putting a project like this into the world.

This is a handbook.

Introduction

ELAINE SPEIGHT

This is a book of conversations about the meanings and production of place. Or rather, it is a collection of moments within conversations, which began a number of years ago and, in some cases, are ongoing. Such moments are expressed in a variety of forms: as visual essays, experimental texts, collaborative projects and transcripts of verbal discussions. Yet, each embodies a wider exchange between an artist and an academic from the humanities and social sciences. Fostered by the Practising Place project, after which this book is named, these discursive partnerships have entailed the sharing of knowledge, experience and enthusiasm for the study of place as a creative and critical practice. Through a focus upon common research interests, which span a range of themes, these dialogues have unfolded through face-to-face and virtual discussions, and have been made public through events. As such, the pages of this book provide a context for the latest iteration of these evolving conversations.

To describe a body of work as 'conversational', runs the risk of it being perceived as academically lightweight or professionally dubious. Contemporary forms of conversation resist the framework and focus of formal interviews or debates. Inherently tangential, they follow a more unpredictable path, full of detours, diversions and narrative loops, which occasionally lapse into awkward or companionable silences. Conversations meander, rather than march, and thus lack the institutional authority of more mainstream discursive forms. Yet its expansive and indeterminable nature is precisely what makes conversation so suited to interdisciplinary discourse. Geographer, Michael Dear, writes that 'the greatest enemy to academic creativity is disciplinary boundaries because they favor marginal advancements appreciated by relatively few specialists locked in disciplinary silos' (2011: 11–12). As a relatively non-hierarchical and inclusive form of communication, conversation creates a space for reciprocal and open expression, in which participants are able to 'venture beyond their disciplines and speak across boundaries in their respective tongues about matters of common concern' (*ibid*: 12).

The conversations in this project have unfolded over lengthy periods of time – almost five years in one case – and within a variety of public and private settings. Whilst the discursive process has taken a slightly different shape for different artist–academic pairs, each has begun by simply meeting for a chat, usually over coffee. Described by one participant as a type of 'research dating agency', these connections have, in the main, been brokered through the project. In each instance, the themes and concerns of the artist's practice provided the initial focus, with interlocutors selected via research or existing knowledge of their work. These initial encounters were usually three-way conversations, in which I adopted a role akin to that of a dinner party host, making introductions, highlighting commonalities and encouraging exchange. Generally, this preliminary meeting would be followed by one or two more over a number of months, with conversational threads picked up over email in the meantime. Through engaging with each other's work, participants began to formulate specific questions for their partner, moving the discussion on from the general to the specific, and gradually letting go of my conversational third wheel.

This practice of reading, writing, watching, listening and speaking was, to lift a phrase by contributing artist Joanne Lee, a way of 'keeping thinking in motion', through a productive to-ing and fro-ing. Inherently valuable as an intellectual process, this form of exchange also laid the groundwork for a series of public events, which formed a strategic part of the project. It is perhaps no surprise that Practising Place itself grew out of a series of conversations. These took place over a number of years between myself and fellow artists and curators in Preston, the city I returned to in 2005 to help develop In Certain Places – a programme of public artworks, interventions and events, which we invariably refer to as 'conversations with the city' (Speight 2014: 10). Our discussions concerned a particular observation: that there was important and interesting work being done by artists in Preston and similar communities about how we understand and interact with places; yet, for reasons of class and geography, such work receives scant recognition outside of its immediate locale. The programme of events, which combined individual presentations with an in-conversation format, was designed to address such issues of profile and visibility. Hosted in venues across the north and Midlands, it exported the work of artists from one city to another and, by theming events around specific place-related subjects, drew broader audiences than artists' talks typically attract. Rather than drawing discussions to a close, however, these events were the first step in a series of creative and collaborative projects, of which this book is the most recent part.

The 'practising' of Practising Place, refers not only to the work of artists, but also to the way in which each of us interacts with places as part of our everyday lives; how we contribute to their character and how they, in turn, shape ours. As such, many of the places depicted in these pages are sites of personal significance for the authors. Artist Jenny Steele talks about how her childhood visits to the Scottish resort of Stonehaven have influenced her practice, which celebrates the seaside's ambiguity as a place of 'reality and artifice... the everyday and escape' and seeks to capture the specific sense of place described as 'seasideness' by her co-author David Jarratt. Similarly, Joanne Lee recounts how her practice 'attends to the particular places' in which she lives and works, and draws connections between the rural setting of her formative years in County Durham and the untamed landscape of post-industrial Sheffield, where she lived during the late 1980s and has recently returned. Inevitably, the north of England emerges as a common theme throughout the book. Traversing a diverse landscape of libraries, holiday villages, oil refineries, working-men's clubs, areas of outstanding natural beauty, sabotaged footpaths, fracking sites and thriving seaside resorts, the chapters present the region as a contradictory and complex place. Unlike the boosterish rhetoric of the government's Northern Powerhouse agenda and the narratives of decline which it purports to remediate, this is a portrait of place informed by on-the-ground experience and emotional connections; the north as lived rather than looked at, as here rather than there.

The locations in this book are largely examined through what essayist Georges Perec termed the 'infra-ordinary' (2002) – the everyday and often overlooked details which inform our encounters with place. By attending to things such as urban noise, administrative boundaries, the surfaces of walls, ceilings and footpaths, litter, pylons and adverts, the authors connect us to places in ways which are instantly familiar. Yet, the significance of such ephemera is far from superficial. Ruth Levene, Ian Nesbitt and Bob Johnston discuss how getting 'up close' and 'listening to the landscape', in this case through walking within it, allows you 'to notice the small things, the incremental changes, the oddities', which create a 'tangible sense' of place. The cultural importance of such ephemera is further emphasised by Paul Wilson, who describes how the noticeboards of working-men's clubs can be viewed as performative spaces which, through 'a cacophony of individual notes' and voices, reflect the values of the organisation and 'act as a locus of community'. At the other end of the spectrum, David Jacques and Les Roberts's multi-layered reading of Stanlow Oil Refinery hauls us through the Earth's substrata and into the stratospheric network of global capital. Their description of the archaeology, wildlife and toxic emanations surrounding the refinery present it as a liminal, yet globally resonant site, and provide a glimpse of what geographer Doreen Massey called the 'place *beyond* place' (2007: 15).

Such close readings give rise to wider questions about our relationship with place. In their creative account of the Lake District as a holiday destination, Amelia Crouch and David Cooper explore how language mediates our relationship with the landscape, and the ways in which received notions of authenticity shape our experiences of it. Similarly, Rebecca Chesney and Rosemary Shirley critique the, often absurd, cultural tropes through which the countryside is romanticised and commodified. The shaping of places for economic gain or social control is a thread which runs through many of the chapters. Magda Stawarska-Beavan and James G Mansell, for example, examine 'the social functions of quiet' through an auditory portrait of Manchester's Central Library and a historical account of middle-class efforts to curtail and manage urban noise. Likewise, Emily Speed's playful interjections into Duncan Light's description of cities as 'continually used, shaped, made and remade, by a range of different groups', emphasise the contingent nature of urban spaces as sites of struggle between order and subversion. Ultimately, however, as her creeping vines suggest, such anthropocentric visions can only ever be fleeting; a notion which Victoria Lucas and Emma Fraser's flâneuse of urban ruins and virtual spaces would surely corroborate.

James G Mansell describes his collaboration with Magda Stawarska-Beavan as a practice of 'listening in two different registers'. Alluding to their shared interest in urban noise, this is also an apt description of this book. As philosopher Jean-Luc Nancy suggests 'communication is not transmission, but a sharing that becomes subject... An unfolding, a dance, a resonance' (2007: 41). Each author has played an equal role in this unfolding; offering up their work for consideration, whilst reflecting on that of their partner. The result is a collection of duets, which narrate what Amelia Crouch and David Cooper call the 'entanglements' of place in voices that variously question, respond, harmonise and deliberately interject. Yet despite their apparent cohesion, such collaborations have required an open mind and a willingness to take risks. Writer Rebecca Solnit describes how, whilst other disciplines aim to 'transform the unknown into the known, haul it in like fishermen', the role of artists is to 'invite in... the unknown' and 'get you out into that dark sea' (2006: 5). This distinction has been a source of anxiety for some artists who worried about how their work would translate into the language of academia, whilst academics not familiar with the processes of art have sometimes feared being swept out to sea.

The conversational format of this project has also been problematic at times. The informality of such an approach can make it seem less serious or important than more mainstream professional concerns, and it is a testament to the enthusiasm and generosity of the authors that nine of the original ten conversations have become chapters in this book. The intimate nature of conversation can also put it at risk of becoming insular and cliquey. It is surely no coincidence that the narratives on these pages largely reflect my own experiences of place, and a future project should invite less familiar voices to offer alternative accounts. For the moment, however, I hope that this book presents an interesting proposition for the study of place; one which is both critical and creative, foregrounds the vital work of artists and demonstrates the value of working across disciplinary boundaries. Above all, I hope that Practising Place inspires more polyvocal projects by demonstrating the vast creative potential of simply having a chat.

DEAR M (2011)
'Creativity and Place.'
In M Dear, J Ketchum, S Luria and D Richardson (eds) *GeoHumanities: Art, History, Text at the Edge of Place.* London: Routledge.

MASSEY D (2007)
World City.
Cambridge: Polity Press.

NANCY J (2007)
Listening (trans. C Mandell).
New York: Fordham University Press.

PEREC G (2002)
'Approaches to What?'
In B Highmore (ed) *The Everyday Life Reader.* London: Routledge. pp.176–8.

SPEIGHT E (2014)
'Subplots, Tactics and Stories-so-Far'
In C Quick, G van Noord, E Speight (eds) *Subplots to a City: Ten Years of In Certain Places.* Preston: In Certain Places. pp.9–13.

SOLNIT R (2006)
A Field Guide to Getting Lost.
Edinburgh: Canongate Books.

A Conversation About Forms of Inscription

Joanne Lee
/
Paul Wilson

Practising Place provided an opportunity for artist Joanne Lee and typography researcher Paul Wilson to expand upon previous conversations about shared research interests. Their in-conversation event, *Forms of Inscription: Surfaces, Patterns and the Typography of Place*, examined the relationship between communication, meaning and landscape, through a focus upon ephemera such as 'chewing gum constellations', fly tipping sites and the noticeboards in working-men's clubs. The following essay presents further reflections on the authors' individual research, which emphasise the importance of curiosity and close looking within their work and acknowledge the existing forms of creativity within everyday places.

This text is the consequence of one conversation which led to another. And then another. The ideas discussed here began with a chance meeting, sitting side by side during someone else's talk, and then shifted to something more formal where we ourselves ended up sitting and talking in front of an audience. The result is an essay structured to share the to-ing and fro-ing of conversation, through which a common set of five threads – North/east, Surface, Inscription, Tools and Amateur – act to shape the content as they reveal our shared interests and map the associations which connect us. Each stage and aspect of this quasi-conversational process revealed newer points of both similarity and difference, with sections written in relay and/or in response to one another. The five points of departure give a sense of shape and form to these words and, while they're the consequence of a loose plan, they aren't things to which either of us lay claim to ownership; instead they allow for an experiment in associative writing to take place which allows for two voices to orbit and pass each other.

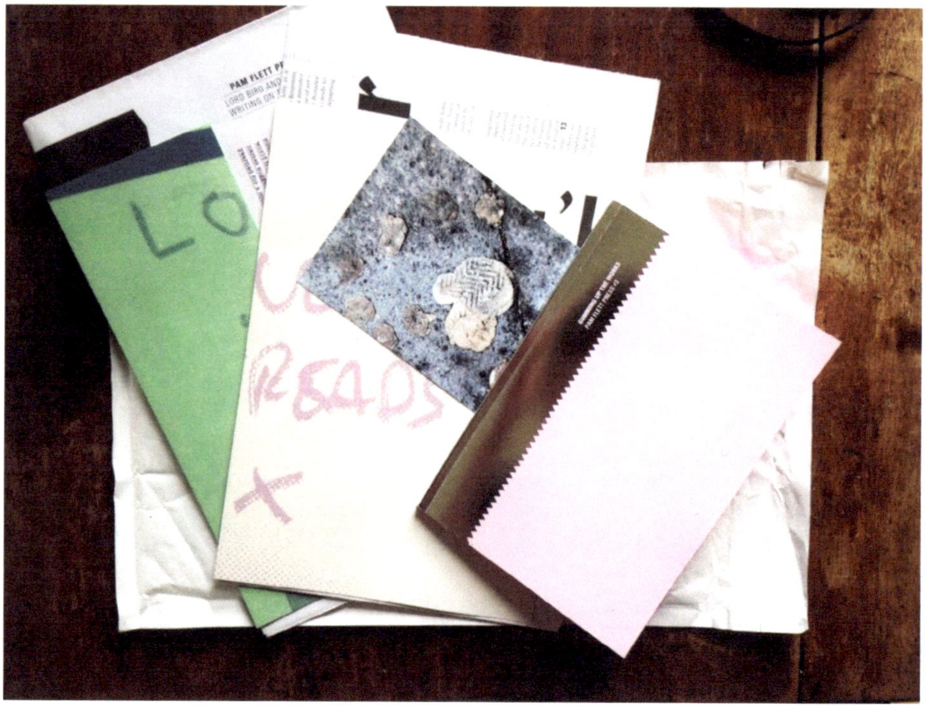

ESSAYING PLACE THROUGH THE PAM FLETT PRESS

JL An artist, writer and publisher based in Sheffield, my creative, critical practice involves the production of an independent serial publication, the *Pam Flett Press*. Realised in collaboration with designers at Sheffield collective 'dust', the project is about finding visual and spatial forms through which concepts of 'the everyday' can be analysed and enlarged. It attends to the particular places in which I live and work, which, for the most part, are in the north of England. Concerned about the ethics of travelling elsewhere to work site specifically, I have focused upon the places and communities immediately around me, encountering what is underfoot or close at hand.

I choose to work through what might be defined as an essayistic practice of writing and photography. The essay is, etymologically, a trial, test or experiment; it offers the scope to explore and wander critically and is a means of 'weighing up' the material I discover. Since the literary essay may accommodate digression and complexity, it can sustain different perspectives and multiple interpretations, whilst the photographic or visual essay can enable the divining of patterns and recurrences as well as noting distinctive or more unusual matters.

Through a purposefully superficial investigation, I pay attention to everyday surfaces and to the information inscribed there by people, machines, animals and plants. Such scrutiny as is paid to the explicit messages of graffiti, the tracks made by illicit off-roading or the imposing forms of pylons and other human structures extends to the more minute scale where mould and algae map the absence of human care, and discarded litter accrues in cracks and crevices.

The *Press* continues the tradition of pamphleteering and radical publishing into the 21st century, and its autodidactic, amateur approach – pursuing investigations according to curiosity rather than professional necessity – is intentionally distinct from that of much contemporary academia, whilst yet being a form of creative and critical research. It seeks to create a constellation of ideas and to enrich what can be thought of everyday things and places, keeping thinking in motion without the intention for there to be conclusive findings as a result.

MAKING COMMON: READING THE TYPOGRAPHIC CULTURES OF THE NORTHERN WORKING-MEN'S CLUB

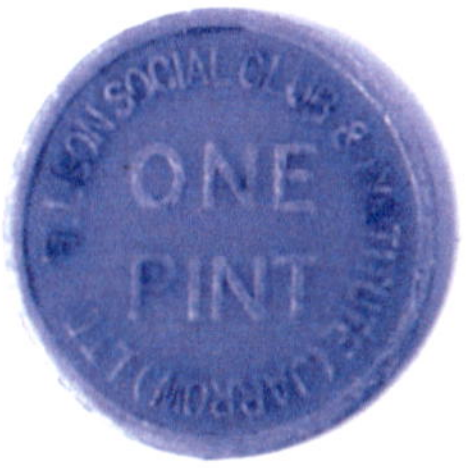

PW *It's no surprise that the words 'community' and 'communication' share a root and that their linguistic histories begin in the same place: with the Latin word 'communis' which translates as 'to share' or – when used as a verb – 'to make something common'. Communis has a range of potential meanings: a land that's held by many, often through tradition; a person not ennobled or privileged; and the ordinariness of everyday life.*

Each of these things – place, social class and class position and ideas of the quotidian – is at the centre of what I aim to discuss here. Each of these is underpinned by an ongoing and ever-present fascination with language in its broadest sense where I link technologies for making language with concepts and practices of writing, together with cultures of seeing and being seen.

The etymology of 'language' and 'landscape' (two other words at the centre of my interests) aren't quite so neatly linked, but they do offer further opportunities for reflection. 'Lingua', from tongue, clearly presents a phonocentric starting point: as it did for the earliest proponents of an ecology of verbal communication and visual language that in the beginning was... language. 'Land' is a word thought to originate in German and hints at ideas of belonging and a relationship with something ('that which something has to belong to'), while the suffix 'scape' is derived from the Old English 'sceppan' or 'scyppan' meaning 'to shape'. It has botanic, zoological and architectural uses relating to an unadorned stem or shaft; something reaching up from the ground towards the sky.

Similarly, language has a function of connection and of bringing one thing to another, together with its role in giving form to things: thought processed through an alphabetical lens. Perhaps this purpose isn't always aligned to a set of higher principles, and although language is by its very nature arbitrary, we can see letterforms as attempting to grasp something: an inherent meaning of language, perhaps, or some broader type of semiotic function.

Language clearly has many relationships with landscape. We see words in space – outside and within place – as objects or surfaces, or on objects and surfaces. And writing, arguably, happens on landscape, not simply as an alphabetic inscription but where ideas shape or reshape the visual appearance and spatial organisation of the environment itself.

Can a focus on the distinct typographic landscapes of the northern working-men's club give any insight into an idea of rules and how visible language is used to mediate relationships within the community of members? How does the typographic ephemera and its constituent narratives of place and association suggest a route to explore this under-discussed site of class experience?

NORTH / EAST

JL Growing up in County Durham in the north-east of England, I noted the particular concurrence of urban and rural, industrial and agricultural landscape. On its uplands, even amidst the designated Areas of Outstanding Natural Beauty and Sites of Special Scientific Interest, toxic lead spoil persists, whilst the remains of ruinous buildings and engineering designed to process the mined metal ore still stand out. Quarrying too has bitten rough arcs from the hillsides,

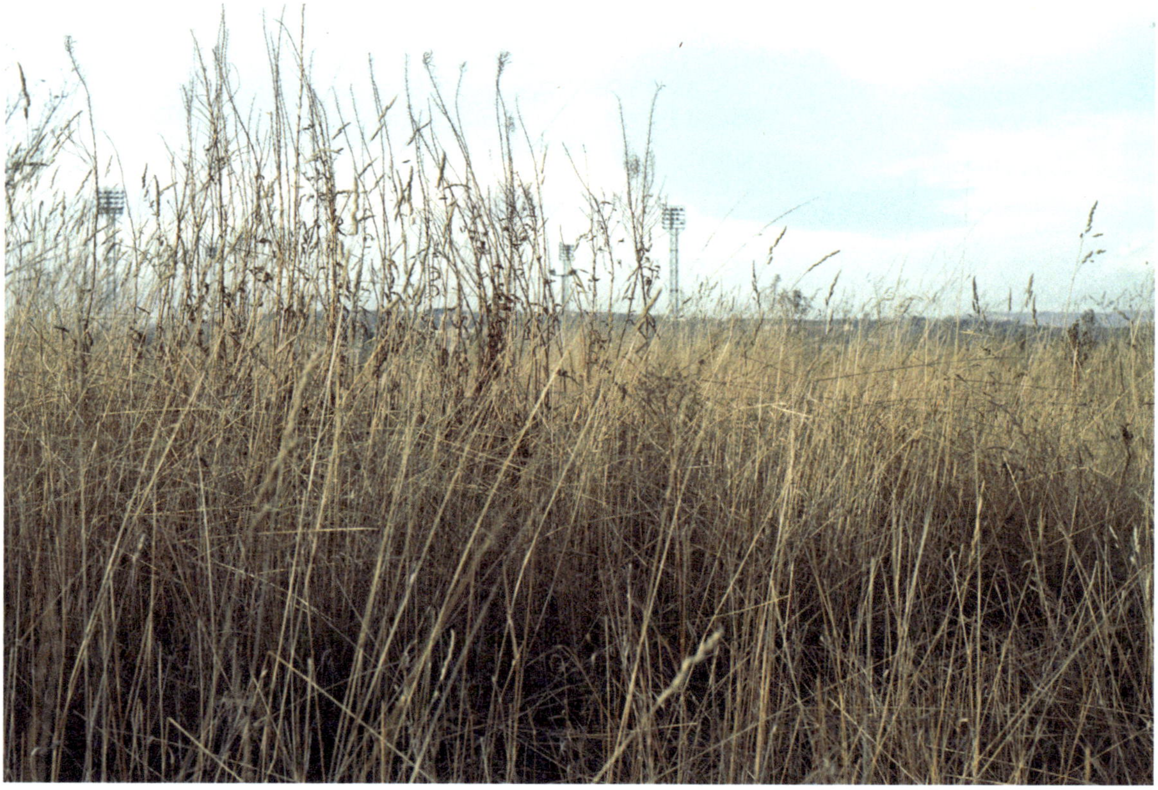

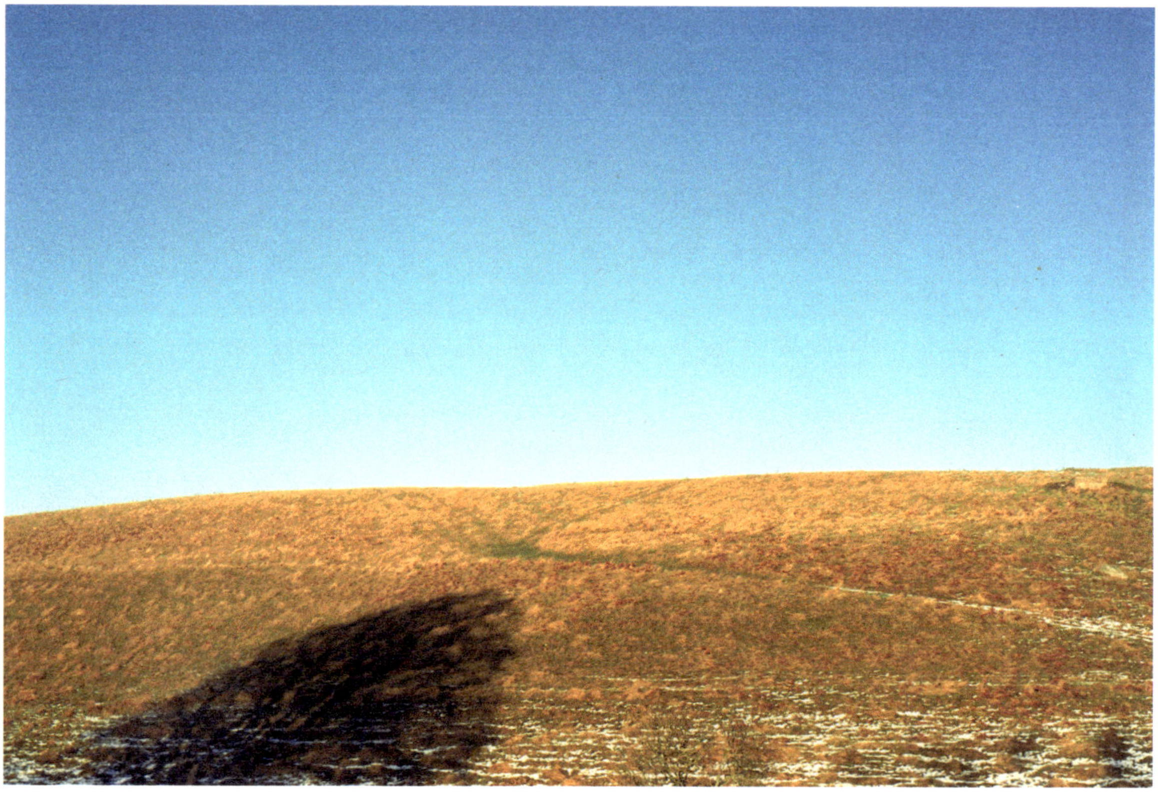

softened a little by the growth of colonising trees that found a roothold in the cracks and fissures, but still visible nonetheless. And with their old connection to the coal industry, the necessary proliferation of terraces or council housing for workers means that many villages remain ambiguously between town and country. Signs linger everywhere of the historical conjunction in this local economy between agriculture and the extractive industries.

When I reflect on the county in which I had my formative years, as well as centuries of mining for coal, iron, lead and minerals, and the quarrying of various types of stone, the landscape has been profoundly altered too by the construction of reservoirs that proliferate in the higher valleys: intended to gather water for industries further downstream on the Tees or Wear, they thus enabled the heavy industry that would manufacture products for worldwide export. It seems very often that the north-east is about what has been removed: the land is carved and incised on a grand scale for the benefits of those elsewhere. Robert Chesshyre characterised the north more generally as being where necessities such as coal, steel, cars, etc. were produced for the use and ultimate financial gain of those far beyond the region (1988: 47). In Ian Taylor, Karen Evans and Penny Fraser's *A Tale of Two Cities: A Study in Manchester and Sheffield*, the north is essentially to be 'defined by its subordinate and residual relationship to London and the South East', the places where real power is brokered (1996: 18).

Whilst it's common enough to hear a sense of 20th century ex-industrial sites as being considered 'fallen' landscapes (Kohl 2007: 97), to some eyes even the countryside itself – especially the moorland – was considered bleak rather than bucolic, with John Hillaby suggesting the peaty mud of the high Pennine Way to be like a slurry of manure (1968: 134). For J. B. Priestley, meanwhile, Durham 'did not seem an English landscape at all... You could easily imagine that a piece had been lifted out of the dreary central region of Russia or America' (1968: 335).

That one place might evoke another was played out when I moved to live and study in Sheffield during the late 1980s. The outer reaches of the city were increasingly derelict, and the Don Valley in particular was largely emptied by then of the steelmaking that had made its money and reputation; the ground cleared ahead of hoped-for redevelopment, expanses of wildflowers flourished behind the remaining walls and façades that replicated aspects of the rural Pennines from which I had come. The very vacancy and in-betweeness gave a feeling of possibility – that it was susceptible to becoming other, according to one's imagination. There is something here, I think, of Francis Spufford's sense that heading north is 'a journey into abstraction' because 'there's so much room to bring to it whatever you want to put in,' and that the very idea of the north is 'an endless argument between the real... and the dreamed' (Spufford cited in Armitage 1999: 225–6).

I want to think that the possibility to dream offers an opportunity for the north to offer a potentially critical position, somewhere quite other to and outside the dominant accounts emerging from the capital, the government and the City of London. In seeking alternatives and counter-narratives, I recall the assertion from artist/provocateur Bill Drummond (2014) that the proper position for artists to take is to stand on the edge looking further out. By investigating locations that trouble categories – the 'peripheral', 'residual', 'in-between' places – I want to provide different perspectives than the grand narratives of regeneration that figure in large-scale urban redevelopment, which sanitise our dirty, complicated past/present and miss opportunities for understanding the relationships between people and place.

PW *While the east can, for some, stand for lost causes (Sebald 2002: 159) it's at a periphery or at the furthest edge of peripheries where we confront a phenomenon that's set aside as being worthy of a certain kind of non-attention. The contemporary state of being of the working-men's club movement illustrates a problem for such places: too northern for the 'new' north which has emerged in the last 40 years and a reminder of a now-unfashionable idea of leisure practiced by a disappearing idea(l) of community.*

The club is a place most often associated with a particular image of 'northernness'. Its institutional identity is one often defined in and by an impression of its members: parochial, archaic, sexist and predominantly soaked in drink. Such an abstraction is defined by, and received through, media and forms the basis of a historically determined legacy further reinforced by an idea of a particular kind of north which is, in itself, part of a broader impression of a particular formation of class and community, their politics and culture.

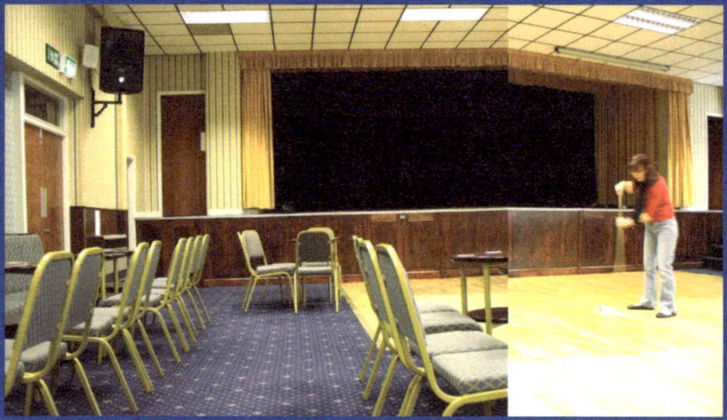

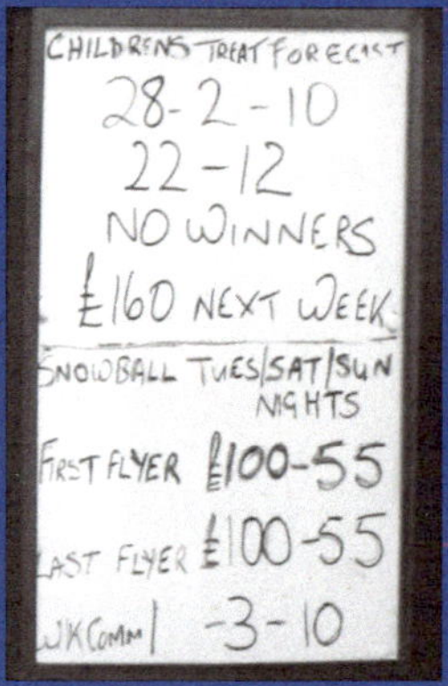
CHILDRENS TREAT FORECAST
28-2-10
22-12
NO WINNERS
£160 NEXT WEEK
SNOWBALL TUES/SAT/SUN NIGHTS
FIRST FLYER £100-55
LAST FLYER £100-55
WK COMM 1-3-10

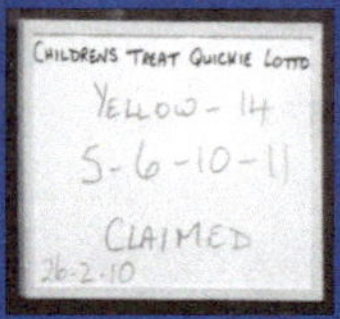
CHILDRENS TREAT QUICKIE LOTTO
YELLOW - 14
5-6-10-11
CLAIMED
26-2-10

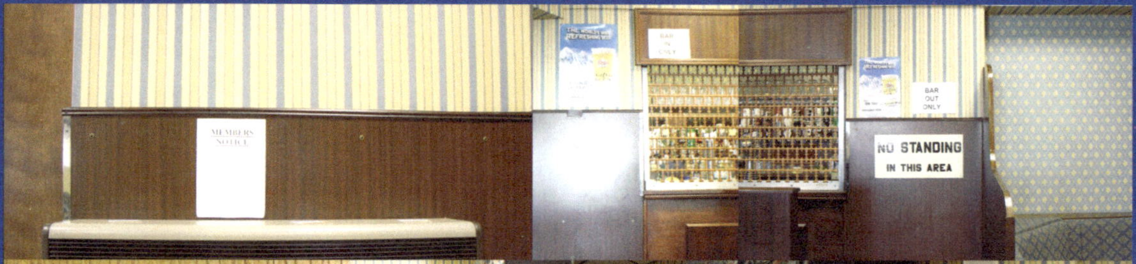
NO STANDING
IN THIS AREA

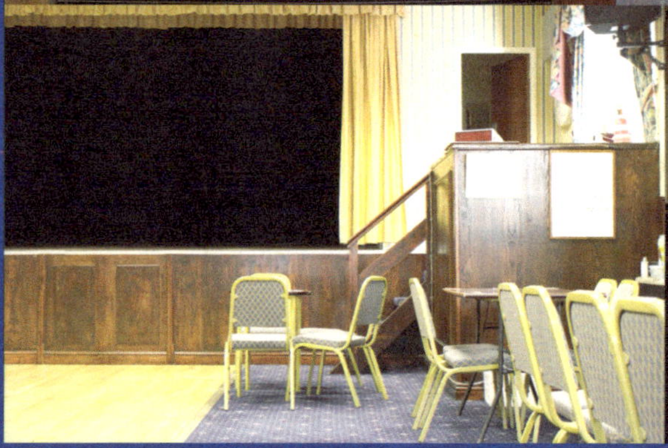

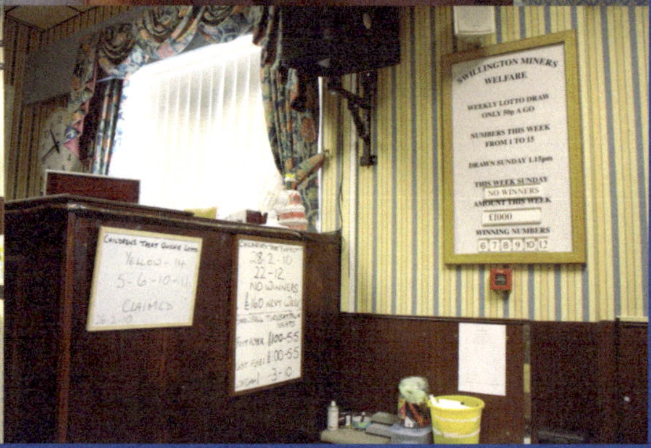

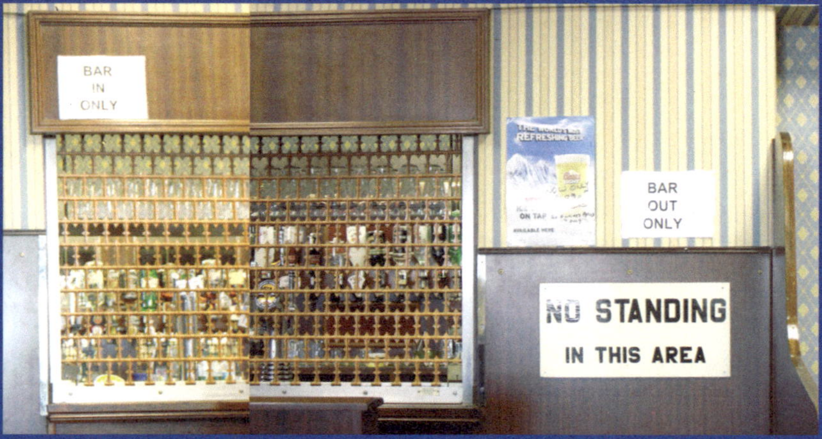
BAR IN ONLY
BAR OUT ONLY
NO STANDING
IN THIS AREA

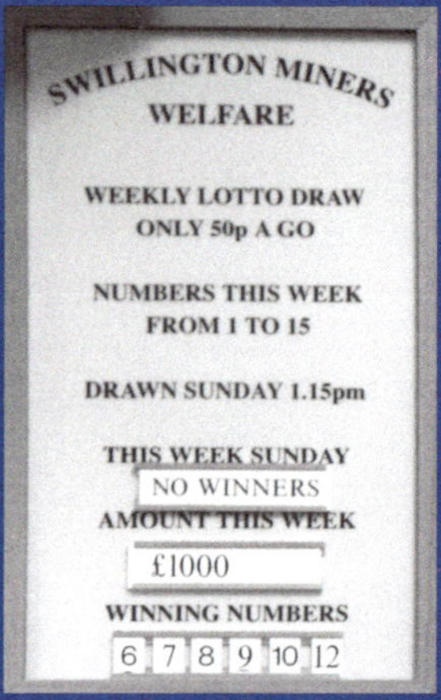
SWILLINGTON MINERS
WELFARE
WEEKLY LOTTO DRAW
ONLY 50p A GO
NUMBERS THIS WEEK
FROM 1 TO 15
DRAWN SUNDAY 1.15pm
THIS WEEK SUNDAY
NO WINNERS
AMOUNT THIS WEEK
£1000
WINNING NUMBERS
6 7 8 9 10 12

This becomes the dominant image of the club and of club life: perhaps playful in its intent (although this is up for discussion) but too easy to warp into something which is negative, damaging and, fundamentally, a caricature. Those impulses of betterment and association which constitute the organisational rules and objectives of 'Club Culture' are moved aside and replaced with something else which creates a morally amorphous reflection of behaviours, attitudes and manners and which acts to define a perception of the north which permeates future representations.

Typography often acts to mark place: it signifies, asserts, assists or alerts. Through visualisation, typography gives meaning to text. Typography is language transformed and occurs at a point where meaning can be clarified, developed, reinforced or challenged.

We can consider the connotative associations of type within the context of the visual culture of the northern working-men's club where, upon entry, there's a tendency to become over-sensitised by the semantic cacophony and an associative potential of visible language. A distinct form of typography and of typographic communication can situate communities within a particular place of their own. The noticeboards found in most (if not all) working-men's clubs have this function: determining the rules of engagement between a club and its members. How might what we read or what we're led to read in such places be affected by typographic design?

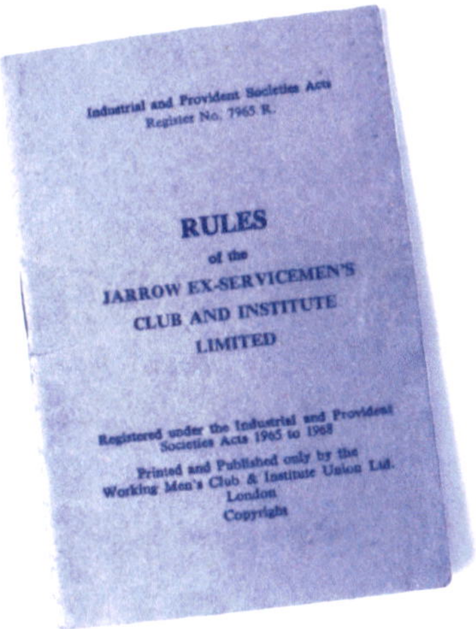

Clubs are fearsomely (albeit superficially) and predominantly spaces for speech, and those words often result in many and varied words upon words and signs which often make reference both to other signs and to other sources of authority. The noticeboards themselves are sites of a resolute graphocentrism, reflecting the organisational thinking present in such institutions where rules most certainly count. Founded in 1892 by the Reverend Henry Solly, the Club and Institute Union was for some time the largest private members' organisation in the world. During the heyday of post-war industrialism, clubs boomed for both economic and sociocultural reasons. Here was an institution tied tightly to industries of making, with professions and trades represented in acts of naming (of the clubs themselves) and where work and leisure (and living) was not easily separated. And these were places owned by members, with the relatively low membership fee granting access to, and the benefits of, a co-operative structure for shared economic ownership.

SURFACE

JL In getting to know a place through photography, I often want to press my nose right up against what I'm looking at. This should come as no surprise: theorist David Campany (2014) makes clear that, as a medium, modernist photography had a heightened interest in the surfaces of the world. When I dwell on surfaces – attending to ordinary floors, pavements, walls and ceilings – I hover close with the camera and the proximity has the effect of producing shallow depth of field. I have to breathe slowly so that a fractional change of position won't blur the specific aspect at which I'm looking. My attention becomes at an almost microscopic level: only a few centimetres at most are in focus and everything else slides into vagueness. When I'm finding where I am at, I am simultaneously getting lost.

Repeatedly walking Sheffield's Neepsend Lane, an urban thoroughfare offering a route for traffic heading between north and east Sheffield, I was often drawn visually to the colour and texture of the walls and pavement that made up the surfaces around me. In one memorable instance, I was pulled in by the pinkish-red paint covering the boarded-up windows of an old industrial building, but as I focused my camera, I noticed a pale line along the length of a brick sill and realised it was an accumulation of chewed gum, each piece fashioned into a neat ball. In this area where sex work is common after dark, the gum surely marked the passage of time for someone regularly waiting for trade. A different duration, that of slow looking, reveals different perspectives.

I return again and again to the words of Japanese writer Yukio Mishima: he asserted 'the profundity of the surface itself' (2003: 23). The historian Joseph Amato proposed that in order to understand modernity and our present, we ought 'to concentrate on surfaces' (2009: 2). I think of the wood, metal, stone, mineral, plastic, glass, natural fibres and countless

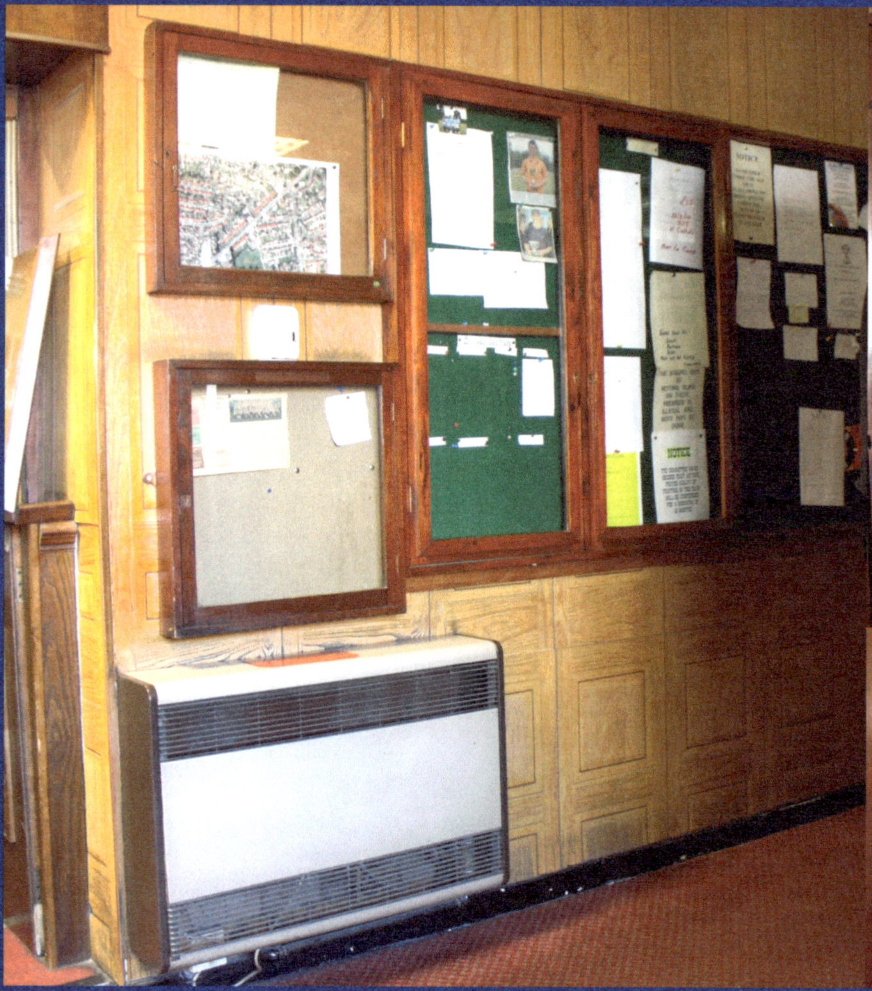

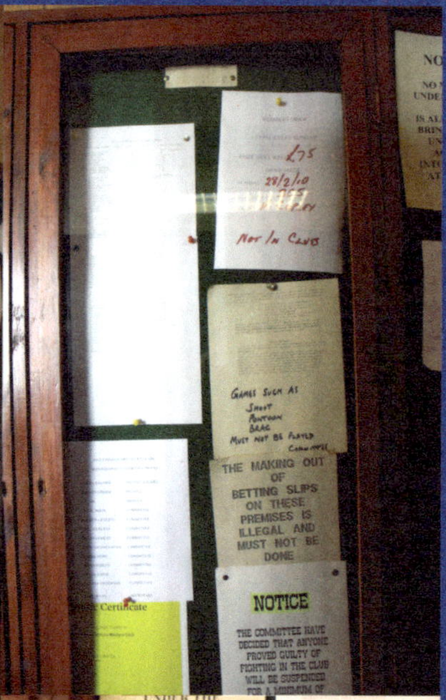
THE MAKING OUT OF BETTING SLIPS ON THESE PREMISES IS ILLEGAL AND MUST NOT BE DONE
NOTICE

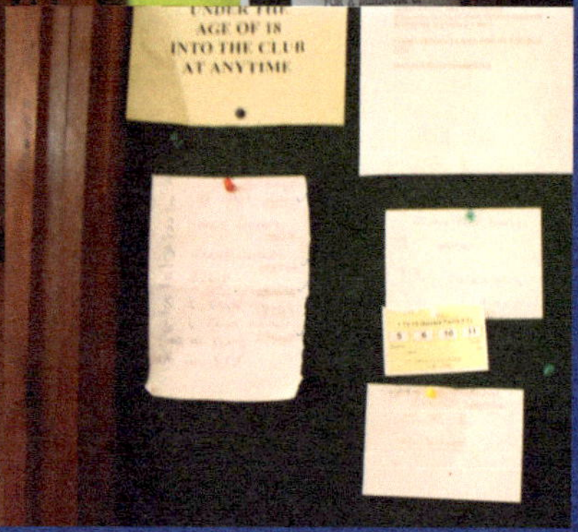
AGE OF 18
INTO THE CLUB
AT ANYTIME

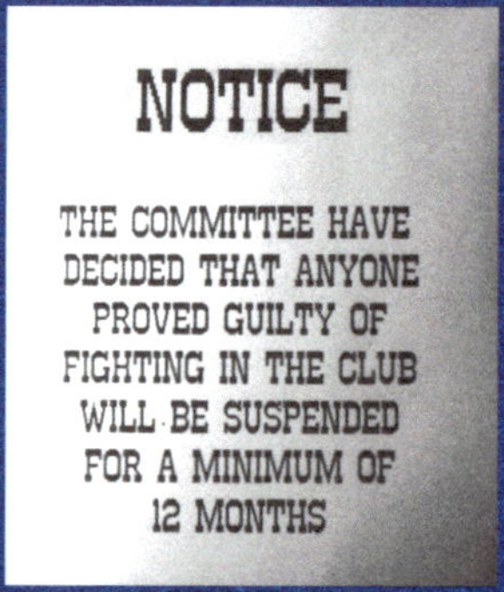
NOTICE
THE COMMITTEE HAVE DECIDED THAT ANYONE PROVED GUILTY OF FIGHTING IN THE CLUB WILL BE SUSPENDED FOR A MINIMUM OF 12 MONTHS

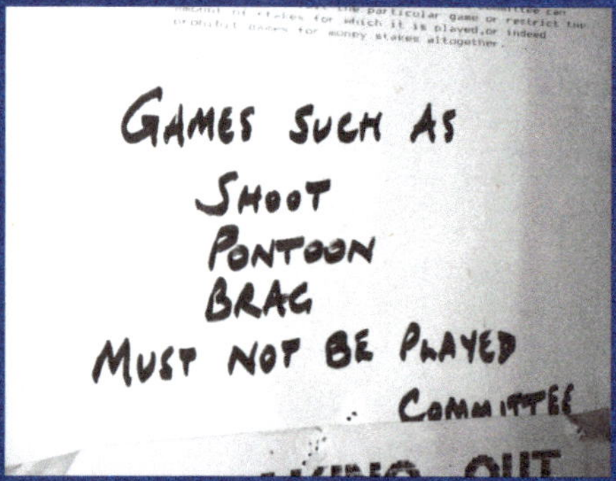
GAMES SUCH AS
SHOOT
PONTOON
BRAG
MUST NOT BE PLAYED
COMMITTEE

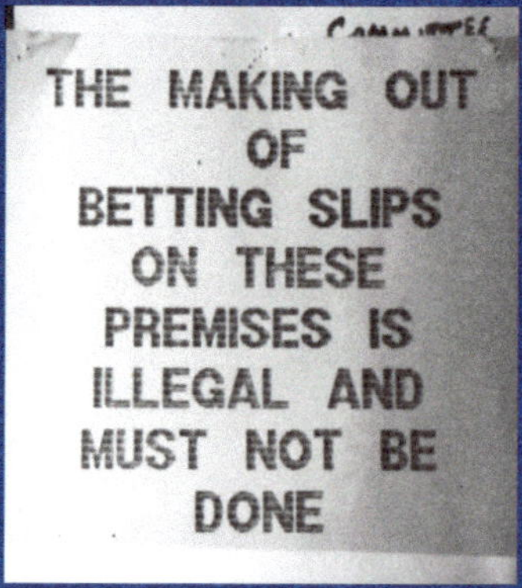
COMMITTEE
THE MAKING OUT OF BETTING SLIPS ON THESE PREMISES IS ILLEGAL AND MUST NOT BE DONE

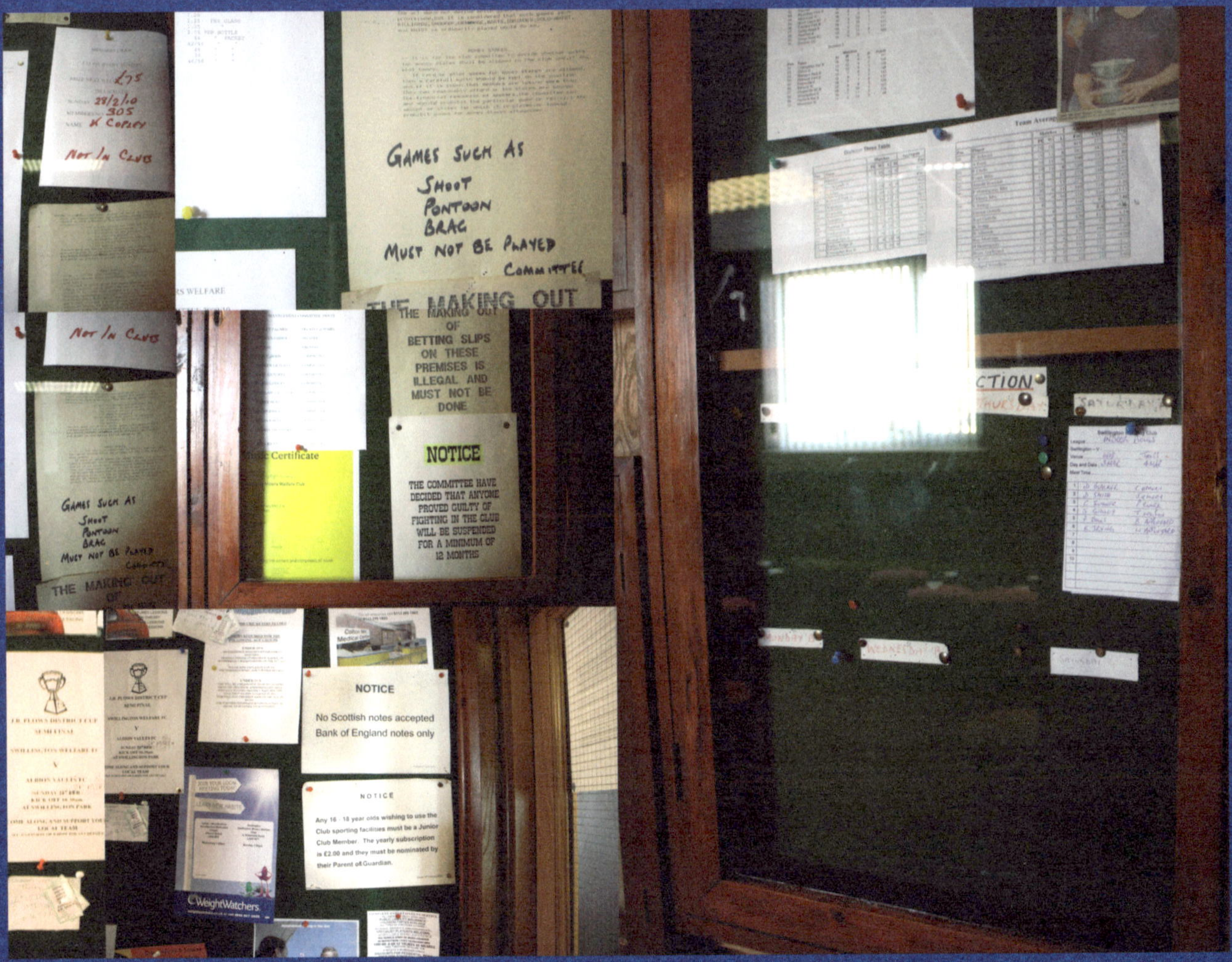

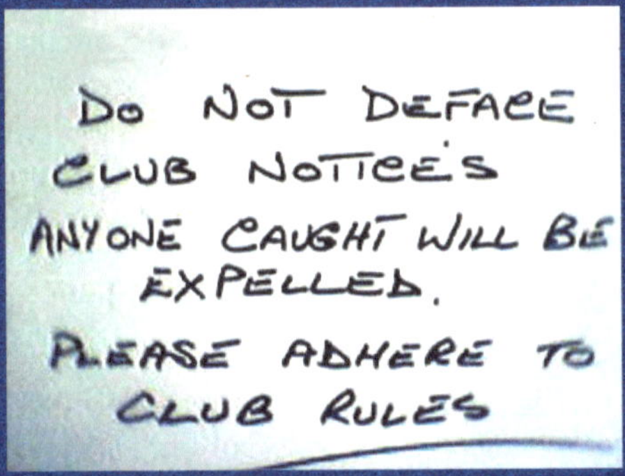

a a a and and and and as attached attested
appoints authority be be be be bear by
centre circle characters **Club** club club
committee committee committee custody
date device engraven have having in in in
in instrument is its legible Limited margin
members men- tioned name name **of** of of
of of of of of of officer on only or other
remaining resolution **Seal** seal seal seal
secretary secretary shall shall shall shall shall
shall signatures such **the** The the the the the
the the the The the the the the the the the
the the the the to two under upon used
whereof which which word words

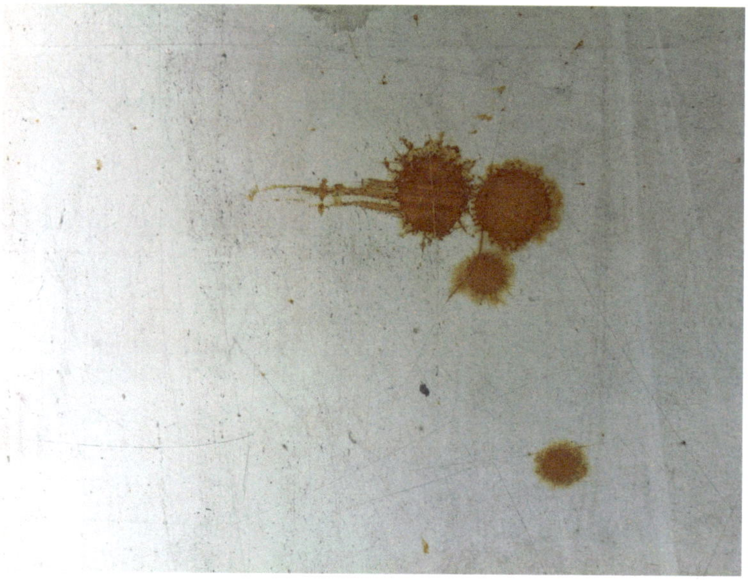

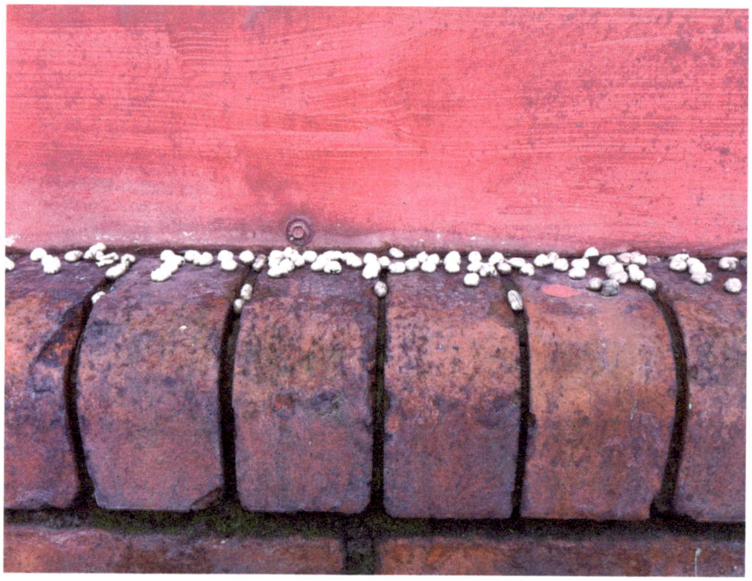

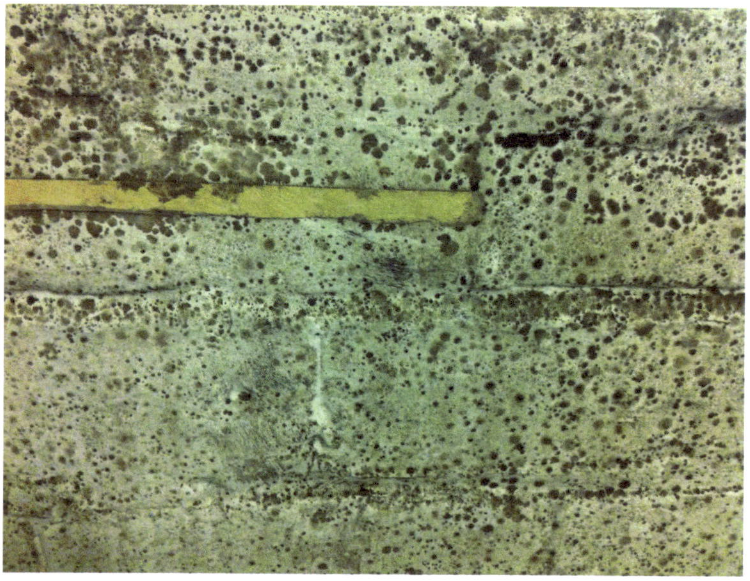

composites produced by people. I think of the process of that production. Materials are grown, quarried, dug, mined and drilled. Refined and extracted; spun and woven; melted and cast; modelled and carved; sawn and split; glued and screwed; polished and pressed. I think too how it feels to handle such matter in the making, and in our use, and when it is disintegrating through lack of care or purposeful disposal.

The surfaces in which I'm interested muddle the 'work' of human, animal and vegetable agents, as their forms and patterns echo, erase or overwrite one another. That this happens frequently in the vaguer areas of the north where land is less in demand and multiple histories sustain alongside the colonisation by other life forms is another reason why these complex sites draw me in.

PW *The leisure lives of the working-men's club members are played out on the noticeboards and across other inscribed surfaces of the club interior, alongside the associated typographical detritus of engagement with assorted leisure activities which is often found in their wastepaper bins. These surfaces become performative, a cacophony of individual notes, and act as a locus of community.*

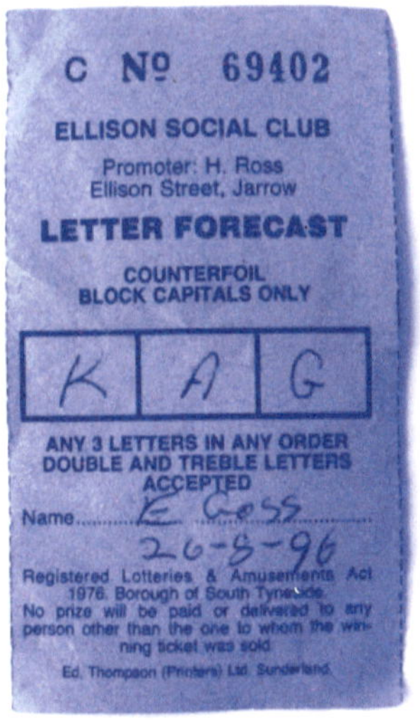

The institutional noticeboards are agents for typographic association: sites upon which association is played out and where scenes of embodied action exist upon a single surface (a substrate: a landscape), often as nested narratives (upon and within the noticeboard) and/or narrative as surface or surface as narrative where notices (and their messages) are piled alongside and upon each other, where we're able to make sense of a broader narrative told across their collaged whole.

From these we can see within club typography a need for order in response to the chaotic, disordered, everyday experience (of work and life), and through order there's collectivity and community (and anonymity). This is reinforced through a sense of belonging: of membership, exclusivity, association and participation, where club members are bound by a set of shared codes which, through forms of typographic expression, are made more explicit.

INSCRIPTION

JL Desire paths cross public spaces, cutting muddy lines into otherwise manicured grass, whilst illicit cut-throughs of private land inscribe paths where none are sanctioned. Off-road cars and motorbikes tear up amenity woodland and brownfield sites, finding routes around the barriers designed to prevent such activity.

As well as the official or vernacular signage, the notices forbidding, informing, inviting or naming, I attend to the informal messages left by those with something to say but nowhere else to say it and to the work of graffiti writers whose throw ups and tags punctuate walls and surfaces.

I notice the non-human marks: trees moved by the wind have scrubbed clean arcs in the dirt of old walls; heaped dog crap slowly disintegrates into mud; snails eat zig-zag trails into algae; mites feast on paperwork; fungus maps an inexorable progress across walls; rusty weals erupt from formerly sleek steel; and frost finds a way to crack open concrete. I have come to remark the overwriting of human traces by decay's relentless creativity. One thing encounters another, overwrites.

But in the north where the economy has so often stalled and reversed, palimpsests of what was before still remain, since the drivers to effect complete change are rarely powerful enough to sustain their intended projects. Multiple temporalities are present simultaneously, and the practice of reading the surfaces before me offers a way of attending and imagining.

PW *In his discussion of the 'text of landscape', Jonathan Smith describes landscape itself as embodying an act of inscription – both in terms of memorialisation and as a kind of writing: environment is 'concretized in the symbols of language' as a series of memorials, where 'gestures, which correspond to a sort of saying, are inscribed' (1993: 80). In Smith's terms, landscape is a text whose purpose is to 'write out' a moment on the surface of the landscape, often in an act of keep-*

ing something hidden. Likewise, Cosgrove and Domosh (1994) talk of a 'readerly' landscape, whose narrative presents itself for translation and transcription.

If we accept the notion that landscape might embody language, we can therefore embrace the idea that such linguistic expression will be in possession of qualities we can ascribe to typography – that these linguistic 'marks' affect and have impact upon their communication to a reader.

Typography is – fundamentally – a means through which meaning is added through a manipulation of the formal qualities of visible language. Whether through altering the appearance of individual letterforms or transforming their organisation, typography is embedded in and acts through text wherever we might encounter it.

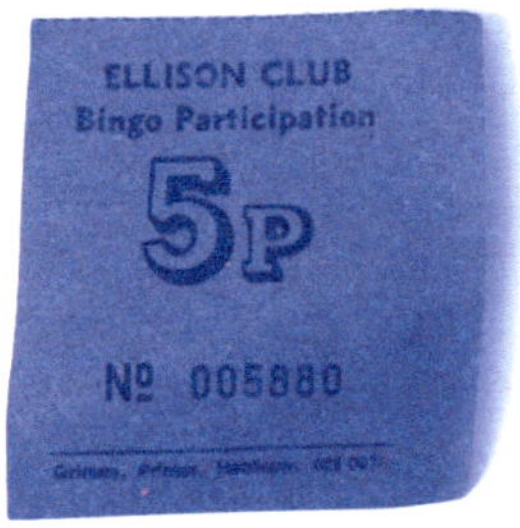

Tim Edensor has written of an urge to seek out what he called 'ghosts of place' (2005: 829): impressions left upon landscape and memory inscribed upon and articulated from the surface of a space. Again, making reference to writing, he describes this tendency for fixing and formation of narrative and our apparent desire for order as logocentric, or 'an inclination... to order the world aesthetically and epistemologically' (ibid). And, it can be argued, linguistically.

TOOLS

JL Whilst some of the pictures I take derive from an old East German 35mm camera, its build so tough that it can be dropped without significant damage, many of the photographs are made using my smartphone: since the mobile is so ubiquitous these days, few people even notice me taking pictures, which gives a certain licence I rarely felt with more cumbersome cameras. It's an old model that still functions well enough for my purposes, although its operating system can't be updated and several apps that others consider essential cannot now be installed as a result. I rather enjoy the creative constraints of this approach and it relieves me from the pressure to be constantly up to date with the latest stuff; its age makes it less likely to attract the eye of thieves as I wander the less salubrious places to which I tend to be drawn.

PW *Visual imperfection became a mark of xerographic reproduction, the grit or grain which – in the act of duplication – removed something from or degraded an original, prompting cultural expectations for the facsimile (although at odds with the dictionary definition). Whilst this perception of loss (of quality) is worth noting, something is added, here (via thing-power?) – an impression written on each copied page much like a stenographic watermark. For designers, such effects are often seductive in terms of their insinuation of a pre-digital era: of imprecision and unpredictability.*

Such tools – and their 'wetter' counterparts (the mimeograph and the hectograph) – were key to the establishment of alternative cultures of reading, writing and publication: the emergence of the fanzine gave the means for low-cost reproduction to enthusiastic amateurs passionate about their own interests to the point of obsession. Now, such tropes signify a visual culture of non-professional activities encompassing writing, design, manufacture and distribution. And now the photocopier occupies a position as cultural debris. Coveted by the aficionado of the analogue and redundant to the needs of a modern office culture, too bulky, too unpredictable – requiring far too much maintenance and, ultimately, out of time.

AMATEUR

JL Perhaps I prefer to use tools that are considered amateur because I don't want the distractions of technological gadgetry. I want to travel light and use as limited a means as possible to render the thing I have framed with my eye. I relish too what others might call a mistake or deficiency. Most photographers aim for high-resolution, pin-sharp imagery: if one reads the photographic press, whether analogue or digital, the discussion is always about what will deliver the best quality – the latest camera body or a better-specified lens, a certain film or superior digital-processing capability. I confess I have the opposite inclination. I love how light thickens or flares through cheap plastic lenses and colours shift unexpectedly so that everyday places are rendered different, dreamlike. This surely relates to that project of imagining otherwise for the north, of which I spoke earlier.

By consciously taking such an approach, I seek to adopt a position akin to Marshall McLuhan's description of the amateur as being anti-environmental, someone able to look askance at normal practice (1967: 93). Unconcerned with many of the markers of 'professionalism' by which others reckon a project worthy or successful, I think too of the late Mark E. Smith – always a lodestar for my investigations since

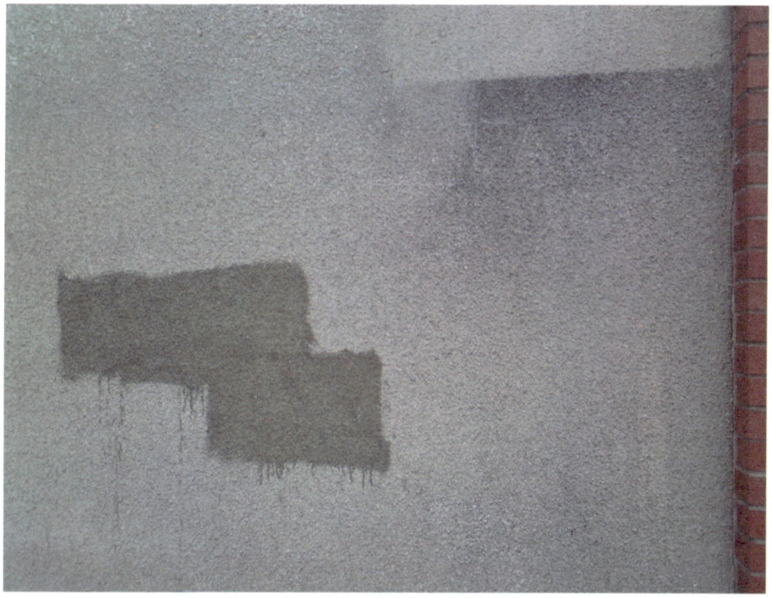

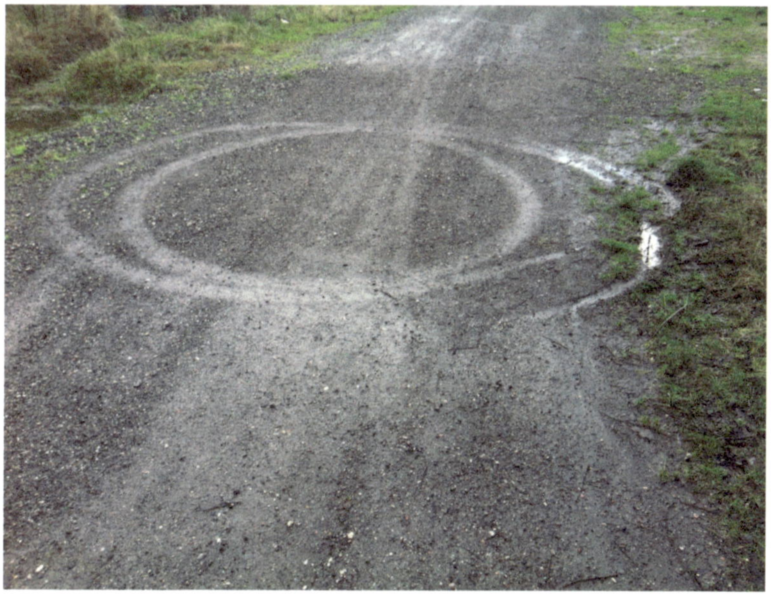

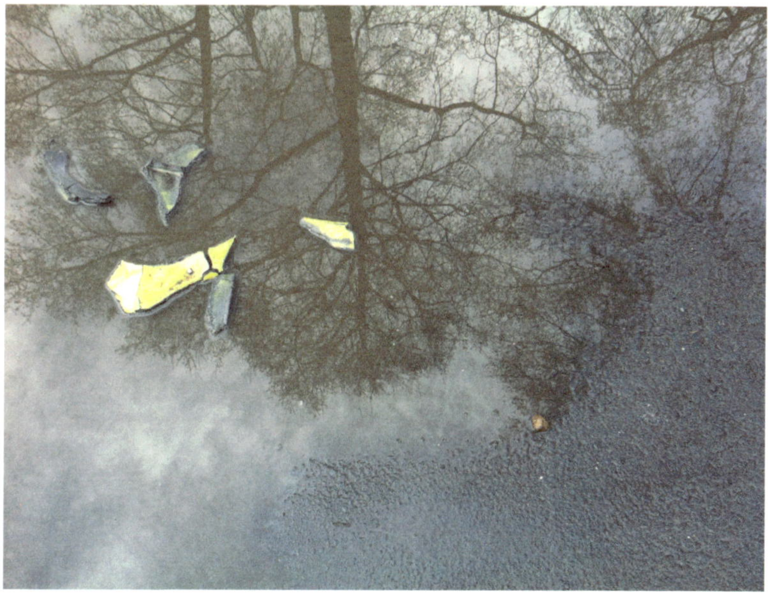

he so distinctively walked his own path – who often referred to his 'lay' ear as somehow offering a superior contribution to that of his band The Fall's actual musicians. I work to remember all this when I feel a meagre investigator, justifying my attention to the most seemingly unremarkable aspects of the world or looking too closely and too repeatedly at matters beneath the notice of most other photographers or researchers.

I want to assert the power in attending to minute, marginal, leftover things and places, and the value of sustaining a slow journey along a particular creative bearing.

PW *Baron Marcel Bich helped propagate a technology of writing which democratised and deskilled much of the craft of writing practices. The disposable ballpoint, whose design was actually created by László Bíró, stands out as one of a few technologies which challenge how and what we make (of) writing and give typography new objects through which new impressions of visible language can be made. The ballpoint pen responds to a need for writing situated very much in the everyday and helps shape those throwaway notes and messages which constitute the matter of pre-digital social connections (and much beyond).*

Our handwriting constitutes a particular kind of mark when so much technology acts to facilitate typographies which now seem to ape ideas of handmade. Typographer and founder of so-called 'Swiss Punk' design, Wolfgang Weingart, regarded his handwriting as an unstable medium, which seemed to actively resist any attempts to lazily frame it as being reflective of a fixed personality. Social media filters frame the addition of pseudo-written marks as a signifier of something, but they offer a contradictory impulse. Each keystroke replays the same glyph, frozen in one act of being written (or, in fact, drawn), but there is still some appeal if it means that I can write as another. Assuming such characteristics through easily downloadable fonts could lead to identity theft on an industrial scale.

Brian Stock's (1986) concept of a 'textual community' lets us think a little more about places such as working-men's clubs and their members and reflect upon the potential for texts to shape the meanings, practices and relationships found within particular communities determined by a particular set of words. Stock's notion of words as 'outer shaping devices' (ibid: 301) which work upon us with impact and effect is useful here: such words organise and mediate our social experiences, provoking or persuading some kind of response – our lives lived in accordance with words and shaping association and behaviour. A consequence of text and context.

These normative typographic practices appear (superficially) to reflect the intentions of Modernism. The visible language of the working-men's club, like those seen in the work of Modernism's early proponents, is a response to the sweeping changes brought about by industrialisation. The very notion of the industrial working class – and the working man (sic) whose needs the club would meet – is embodied in the philosophical shift which such pioneers of modern typography would aim to enact.

Typographic culture is by its nature dissociative: abstracting meaning from our sense-life. It sits above that which we experience directly, layering (visual) code upon (linguistic) code. It's also a force for association: again, Stock's idea of a community of text. Typography inhabits the sphere of material culture through an intention to both engage and communicate.

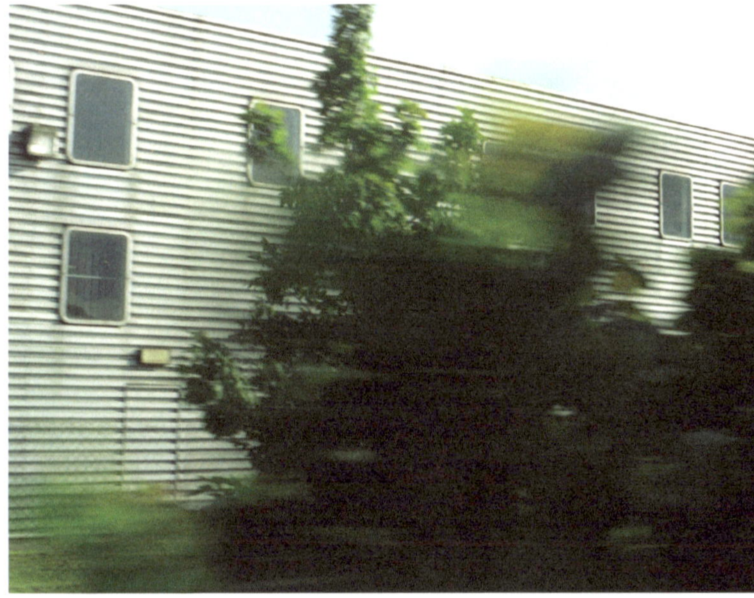

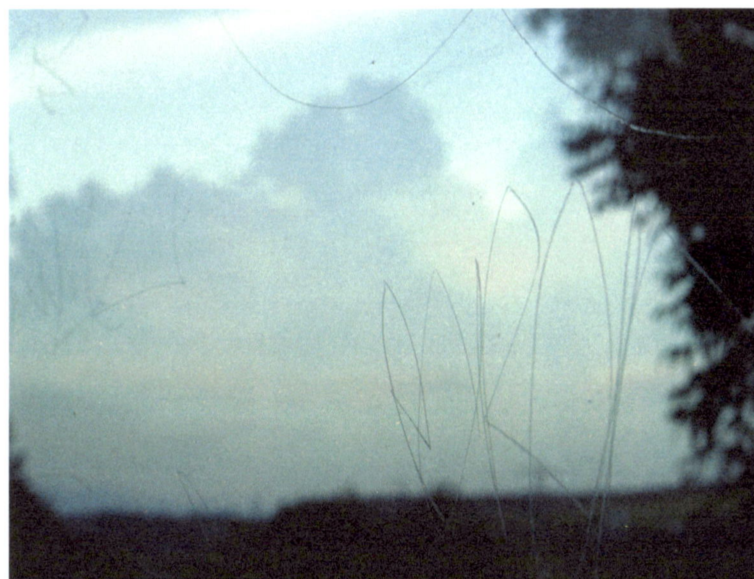

The essay begins and ends with our reflection on being situated at points of marginality – of being and working 'there' and of a kind of freedom which is made possible at such apparently unremarkable points in time and space. In this instance, our words and the images from the public talk with which they are further brought into relation only scratch the surface of the places and ideas with which we are concerned, but our investigation and dialogue sustains and echoes beyond these remarks.

We continue to work slowly, discovering the resonant complexities in the sites to which we have referred and the communities who make their marks therein. Like any conversation, we leave off for a while, with threads left hanging to be taken up at other times. Our concluding is temporary, a different kind of pause for thought.

AMATO J (2009)
'A superficial evocation of our times.'
Historically Speaking 10(4), 2–4.

ARMITAGE S (1999)
All Points North.
London: Penguin.

CAMPANY D (2014)
'Architecture as Photography: Document, Publicity, Commentary, Art.'
In A Pardo and E Redstone (eds) *Constructing Worlds: Photography and Architecture in the Modern Age.*
London: Prestel.

CHESSHYRE R (1988)
The Return of a Native Reporter.
London: Penguin.

COSGROVE D AND DOMOSH M (1994)
'Author and Authority: Writing the New Cultural Geography.'
In J Duncan and D Ley (eds) *Place/Culture/Representation.*
London: Routledge. pp.25–38.

DRUMMOND B (2014)
'Bill Drummond's 10 commandments of art.'
The Observer 15 June.
Accessed on 15·6·18 at: theguardian.com/culture/2014/jun/15/bill-drummonds-10-commandments-of-art-klf

EDENSOR T (2005)
Industrial Ruins: Space, Aesthetics and Materiality.
Oxford: Berg.

HILLABY J (1968)
Journey through Britain.
London: Paladin.

KOHL S (2007)
'The "North" of "England": A Paradox.'
In C Ehland (ed) *Thinking Northern: Textures of Identity in the North of England.*
Amsterdam: Editions Rodopi. pp.93–115.

MCLUHAN M (1967)
The Medium is the Massage: An Inventory of Effects.
London: Bantam Press.

MISHIMA Y (2003)
Sun and Steel.
Tokyo: Kodansha International.

PRIESTLEY JB (1968 [1934])
English Journey: Being a Rambling But Truthful Account of What One Man Saw and Heard and Felt and Thought During a Journey Through England During the Autumn of the Year 1933.
London: Heinemann.

SEBALD WG (2002)
The Rings of Saturn (trans. M Hulse).
London: Vintage Books.

SMITH J (1993)
'The Lie That Blinds: Destablising the text of landscape.'
In J Duncan and D Ley (eds) *Place/Culture/Representation.*
London: Routledge. pp.78–92.

STOCK B (1986)
'Texts, readers, and enacted narratives.'
Visible Language 20(3), 294–301.

TAYLOR I, EVANS K, FRASER P (1996)
A Tale of Two Cities: A Study in Manchester and Sheffield.
London: Routledge.

Oil is the Devil's Excrement: Hellmouth on the Mersey

David Jacques
/
Les Roberts

This essay presents ideas developed by artist David Jacques and spatial anthropologist Les Roberts, following their in-conversation event, *Liminal Landscapes: Assembly, Enclosure and the West Lancs Coast*. Premiering David's short film, *The Dionysians of West Lancs* (2014), the event explored the significance of 'liminal landscapes' as sites of political struggle and creative imagination. The following essay extends these conversations through a multi-layered reading of the estuary landscape surrounding Stanlow Oil Refinery on Merseyside.

The text is presented in dialogue with another short film by David, *Oil is the Devil's Excrement*, which can be viewed at practisingplace.org

We set you down, to care for us, Stanlow. So sang Andy McCluskey of 1980s synthpop group Orchestral Manoeuvres in the Dark about Stanlow Oil Refinery situated at Ellesmere Port on the Mersey Estuary in north-west England. And she does (care for us, that is). So much so it is as if we might happily abdicate any concern on our part and cruise along the motorways that flank its southern and western perimeters without the barest hint of a sideways glance; safely cocooned in the knowledge that our petrochemical desires are being amply fed. For the functioning addict, sustainability is a buzzword that speaks as much for the enduring vitality of the infrastructure that holds it all together ('it' here we can take as no less than modernity itself) as it does for the resources upon which it depends. It is only when we find ourselves spluttering to a premature halt, and the Ballardian chaos of the hard shoulder takes hold, that the sludge and seepage of a more primordial – *unrefined* – morphology excretes into view. They say that shit rises to the top, and this is shit of the foul-est provenance. For 'oil', indeed, 'is the Devil's excrement'.

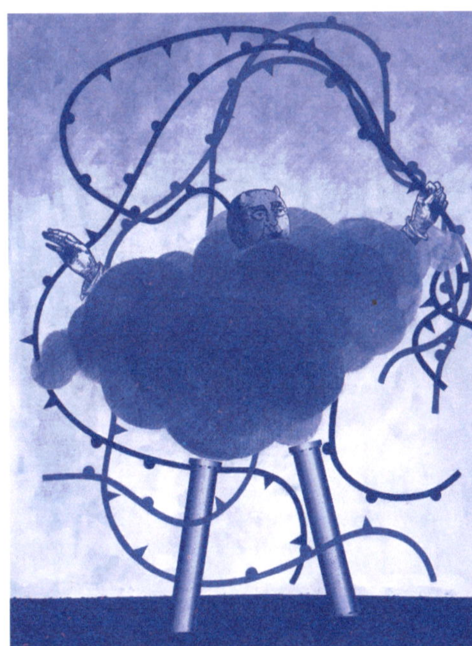

These apocalyptic words can be attributed to Juan Pablo Pérez Alfonzo, former Venezuelan Minister for Energy and founder of OPEC, the Organization of the Petroleum Exporting Countries, whose dying moments form the subject of an animated short by the artist David Jacques. The ideas and provocations proffered by the film, which we invite readers to engage with in tandem with this text,[1] provide the starting point for a conversation in which the aforementioned Stanlow quickly looms large, offering a ready-made locus of invocatory magic whereby oil, shit, death, putrefaction and topography intermesh to give rise to a further iteration of Alfonzo's feculent mantra.

Accordingly, our aim is to sketch the dovetailing of ideas and critical interventions that have sprung from our conversations around the politico-magical properties of oil, through reference to David's film and spatial anthropologist Les Roberts's explorations of Stanlow Refinery. While each of these trajectories represents a response to the same diabolical putrescence visited upon the dying OPEC architect, they also carve out their own singular yet intertwined pathways through the sump of critical terrain that probes oil's dark sentience and socio-political burden. In the hands of David, we plunge headlong into the defecatory slipstream, anointing ourselves by way of immersion and infusion in a substance whose alchemical power lies in its capacity to tap and drill deep into the geological bedrock of the human soul. Les, for his part, skirts the perimeter fences of an industrial colossus that dwarfs the surrounding landscapes as commandingly as it harbours and secretes a (death's) cargo that remains impenetrable: a secret that lies beyond the reach of those who can but yield to its gift.

Ten years from now, twenty years from now, you will see: oil will bring us ruin. Oil is the Devil's excrement.

Juan Pablo Pérez Alfonzo (1903–1979) died in exile, his legacy derailed by the loss of control over a global oil economy he sought to regulate through OPEC. An industry ultimately usurped by a raft of nascent oligarchies, hedging any accrued wealth and rendering their own citizens impoverished, prone to internecine wars and exposed to intolerable levels of toxic pollution. The final, totemic line of Alfonzo's prophesy invoked a cautionary saying, 'Oil is the Devil's excrement', which, paradoxically, originated with pre-modern native peoples. In effect, his claim brought to light the powerful emergence of oil tethered to capitalism and predicted a demise of mythic proportions.

Spurred by this mythopoeic frisson of death, oil, and excremental capitalism, David's film posits a symbolic portrayal of Alfonzo. He is envisioned through an interweaving of literary, scientific and

1. PRACTISINGPLACE.ORG

IMAGE BELOW: MAP OF STANLOW OIL REFINERY COMBINED WITH ANIMATION STILL FROM 'OIL IS THE DEVIL'S EXCREMENT', DAVID JACQUES, 2017.
OTHER IMAGES: 'A PSYCHOPOMP FOR JUAN PABLO', MIXED MEDIA ON PAPER, 76CM X 57CM, DAVID JACQUES, 2017.

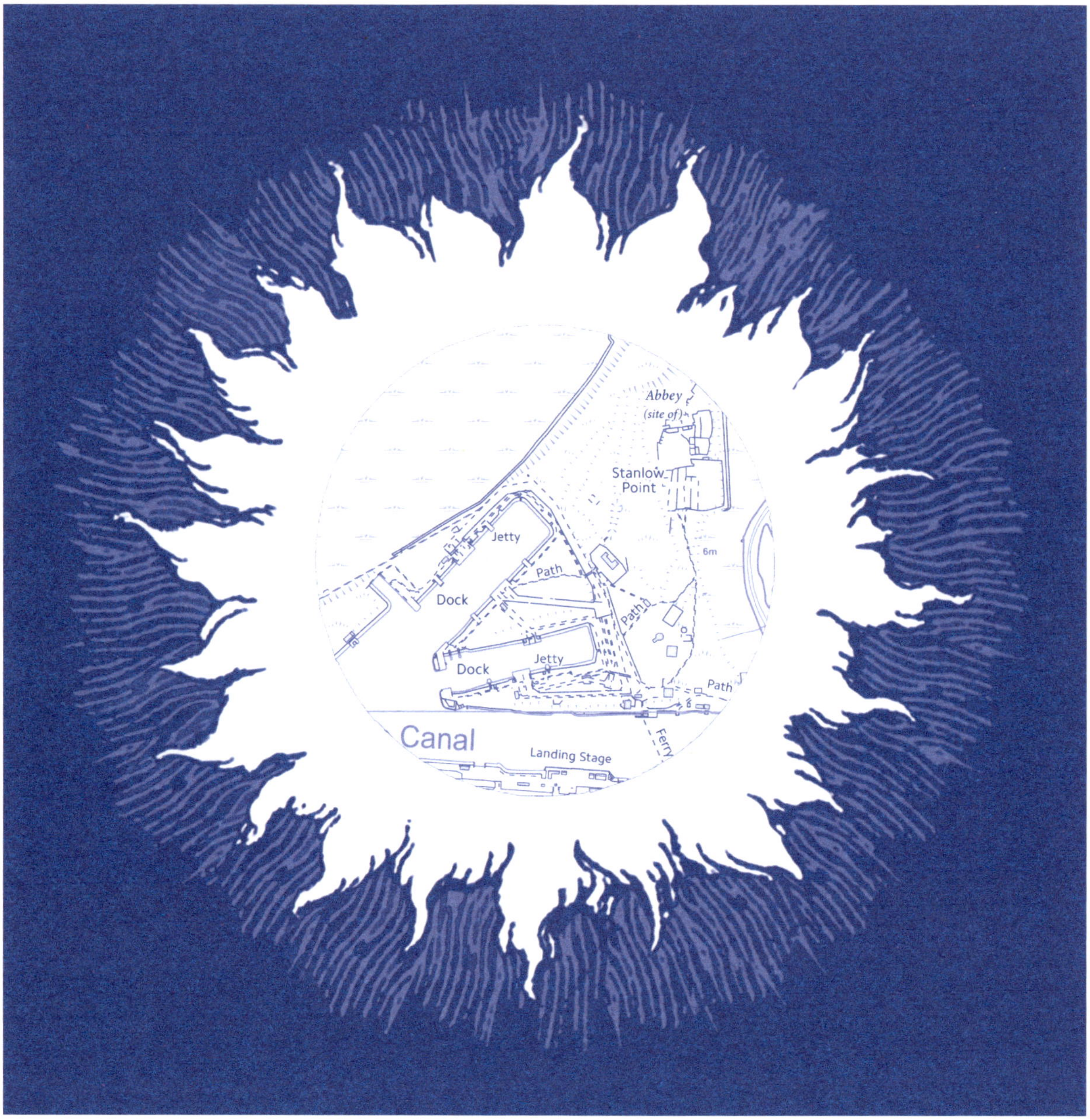

2. WEIRD FICTION IS A LITERARY GENRE COMMONLY ASSOCIATED WITH THE WORK OF WRITERS SUCH AS FRITZ LEIBER, EDGAR ALLAN POE AND HP LOVECRAFT. WRITER AND ACTIVIST CHINA MIÉVILLE DESCRIBES WEIRD FICTION AS THE 'INTERSECTION OF SF [SCIENCE FICTION], FANTASY, AND HORROR… [AND] OF THE TRADITIONS OF SURREALISM WITH THOSE OF PULP' (GORDON 2003: 357-8).

mythical threads, emanating from a series of historical registers. We engage with Alfonzo at the point of his death; he is about to confront 'the shadow within', to enter 'the dark night of the soul'. Terms, amongst others, that were advanced by Carl Jung as metaphors for the *nigredo*, the mediaeval alchemic process of putrefaction and decomposition – of realising 'black matter'. In his delirium, Alfonzo is visited by oil, revealing itself as a sentient entity (a trope previously played out through the genre of 'weird fiction')[2] and antagonised by a daemonic chorus who, in a rhythmic and skewed approximation of the 'heroic pentameter', narrate the doomed exile's fate. Ultimately, *Oil is the Devil's Excrement* concerns itself with the vagaries of an omnipotent petrochemical culture out of control and various competing state and corporate forces forever pitched at daggers drawn.

Void of a lingo but very clued in
The stuff of nightmares our shadowy kin
Dark fluidity expects from the ground
So absorb it all and pitch it around
A toast to the host the soon to be ghost!
Services rendered that proffered the most!
Our daemon chorus shall witness the dread
And marvel at claims of what he has said
And gasp at stories of what he has done
Matters no matter though after he's gone
But let's not forget his treacherous deeds
Those backsliding words that nobody heeds
For a puddled vision'ry oh so bold
Some unhinged sights are about to unfold

In 2012 nearly four tonnes of oil were sprayed into the air after a storage tank exploded at Stanlow Oil Refinery (which had passed into the ownership of Essar Oil just a year before). The subsequent drizzling of the surrounding area resulted in 7,500 gravestones in nearby Overpool Cemetery being covered in a film of oil and water. Later the same year a spillage of some five tonnes of oil ended up in the Manchester Ship Canal. Anointing the dead may not have been Essar Oil's expressed intention but the symbolism is certainly instructive when viewed through the prism of Alfonzo's daemonic chorus. The confluence of oil, steam and putrefying bones – *absorb it all and pitch it around* – finds its alchemical analogue in the *nigredo* recomposition of matter that gives up its ghosts in the fashion of an impending apocalypse. This is what gives Stanlow its air of imminence: as if it is always teetering on the brink of some calamitous event; an event destined to catch passing motorists – somnolent to the point of being automatons (like the driverless cars that will replace them) – blissfully unaware. But then alchemy and fossil-fuelled industrial modernity have long been curious and complicit bedfellows. Alfonzo's vision was a belated realisation of this: a demonic visitation that would come to haunt his final days.

In the early 1890s, the carving out of the ditch that would become the Manchester Ship Canal – a communication that was instrumental in the siting of the oil refinery (Britain's second largest) at Stanlow – threw up its own necrogeographical curio in the form of a skull unearthed at 'Frodsham Score' situated further upriver near the confluence of the Mersey and the River Weaver. On loan from the offices of the consulting engineer overseeing the dredging operations, the skull, upon examination, was estimated to be no more than 2,000 years old, but it lacked the requisite archaeological data by which to more accurately date the find. Save some 'red deer horns, and a canoe made in one piece in oak' (Spielmann 1891: 179) the excavation bore no traces of the human history that had given flesh and vitality to the life that once was. The oblivion that defined the skull's biographical origins had a geographical correlate in the form of the landmass of which Frodsham Score was now a part. Between the Ship Canal and the River Mersey lay what was now island topography comprised largely of salt marsh. This newly formed island stretches westward six to seven miles along the estuary foreshore from Frodsham to Ellesmere Port. Although the skull probably dates to a much earlier period, we could imagine all the same that the deceased had perhaps been a pilgrim bound for the Cistercian abbey at Stanlow Point on the northern flank of the island (or possibly a post-Reformation refugee heading for sanctuary in pastures new). Either way, the skeletal sludge that the Ship Canal navvies had scooped up was a constituent part of what is now liminal, isolated topography populated by none but the ghosts of the forgotten dead.

A chance then chief to knock off your meter?
Pleased to ignite and fire up your heater
Truss up and bury you deep underground
Matters whose matter then when it is found

If the Stanlow monks had been in the business of fending off the advances of the Devil then the proximity of the abbey ruins today – overshadowed, as they are, by the infernal megalopolis that is the refinery complex – tells a markedly different tale. The location of the former abbey at Stanlow Point, a promontory jutting out into the tidal mudflats of the Mersey and part of the larger island landmass severed from the mainland, is the site of two tanker berths that serve the refinery situated on the landward side of the canal. On a map of the site the two docks resemble the snapping jaws of a giant crocodile (*here be dragons...*) poised to consume the last remaining vestiges of the mediaeval redoubt. The site always had something of an on-the-edge (Roberts 2016) and desolate quality to it; a feature, of course, that drew the ascetically minded monks there in the first place. Writing

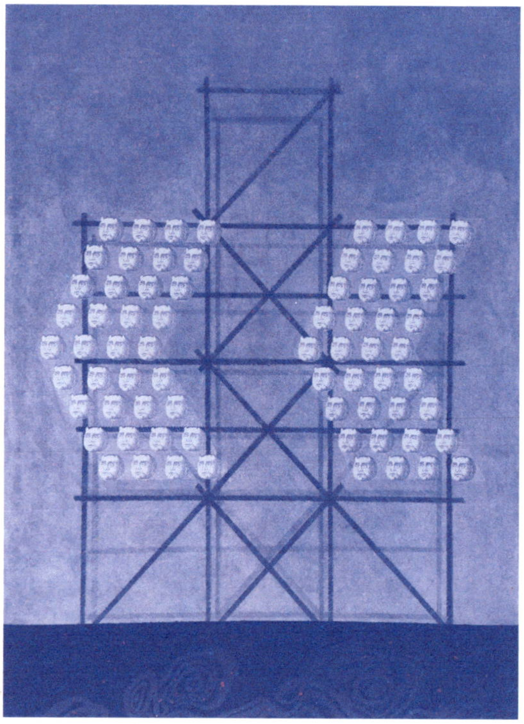

in 1816, the historian George Ormerod remarked that, 'Even at the present day, it is difficult to select in Cheshire a scene of more comfortless desolation, than this cheerless marsh' (in Ainsworth 2012: 17). Today's desolation is suffused with the sonorous hum of the leviathan that slumbers fitfully behind the wire meshing of its perimeter fortifications. Access to the island – necessarily discreet and covert on account of its annexation by the refinery – runs the risk of disturbing the sleeping giant and copping the full heat of its fury. Such a danger is compounded by the threat posed by jihadist terrorists purportedly targeting Western energy installations, which has, as with other of the UK's refineries, brought with it a tightening of security operations at Stanlow. The cowed supplicant who quickly skitters by will fail to notice neither the abundant signage pointing out that photography is prohibited nor the irony of a surveillant gaze in the form of the ubiquitous CCTV cameras dotted around the site, trained so pinpointedly upon them.

The finding of the Frodsham Score skull marked the point where the River Weaver, making a fleeting acquaintance with the Manchester Ship Canal, slips finally and unremarkably into the Mersey. Downstream, at the abbey's more sacral site of rested bones, here too a place of confluence: the Gowy, this time – a river which once upon a time 'came tumbling down in fury' to swell the rising Mersey (Young 1909: 69). There is not much in the way of fury that might characterise the Gowy today. As with much else that falls within the orbit of the refinery, the river is under its cosh. Shepherded discreetly through the oil installation, the Gowy exits by way of a syphon under the canal before joining the estuary via the island. The necrogeography of Stanlow's *zona pellucida* is, therefore, one in which a capillary meshwork of water channels has historically moulded a landscape that has either yielded to or subdued the vitality of human life it serves to sustain. The injection of oil's *dark fluidity* into this capillary system – whether symbolically in the revival of local industries or literally in the many documented cases of environmental pollution (Taylor 1991; ENDS 2015) – creates a toxic mix from which alchemical powers may be drawn and harnessed.[3]

Serving up this glorious atrophy
Must admit, we divined his malady
Blue dye and meds did enter this corpus
Pity it's time to render him porous
As enzymatic decomposition
Gives toxic and malodorous mission
With dutiful splitting of all proteins
Putrefaction will expose your unseens
Ever present, your deadly addiction
About to wrest your whole composition
These nocuous dregs best left well alone
About to rejoin and guide you back home

In *Oil is the Devil's Excrement*, a subterranean battle is waged between the *glorious atrophy* of the body and a diabolic life-force that pushes its way up through

3. IN LIGHT OF THE JUAN PABLO PÉREZ ALFONZO FOCUS OF DISCUSSION, IT IS WORTH REMARKING THAT A DIRECT VENEZUELAN-STANLOW CONNECTION CAN BE ESTABLISHED IN THE FORM OF AN OIL LEAK IN 1989, WHEN, UNDER SHELL UK'S WATCH, 150 TONS OF VENEZUELAN CRUDE OIL LEAKED INTO THE MERSEY ESTUARY FROM A FRACTURED PIPELINE SERVICING STANLOW REFINERY (SEE TAYLOR 1991).

the earth with *toxic and malodorous mission*. Putrefaction's slow and *enzymatic decomposition* of organic matter that history has vacated and left to decay gives form, over time, to the very stuff with which the re-animator (to invoke HP Lovecraft)[4] is able to ply his treacly trade. We observe the lateral, worm-like movement of a substance that embalms the bones of the dead in a sticky infusion; an incubus embrace from which no good can surely come. Alfonzo, not yet of the grave, has already begun to contemplate his resurrection. His vision of a zombie apocalypse fuelled by oil perhaps has already come to pass. Not so much the walking dead as the automotive dead. In his delirium, Alfonzo conjures a hell of his own making and it is this that Stanlow symbolically struggles to contain. When, having managed to keep a lid on things, the refinery is not showering the local cemetery with oil and steam, it is in the business of carefully regulated circulation and distribution. The fixer-in-chief. The manufactor of non-places (Augé 1995).

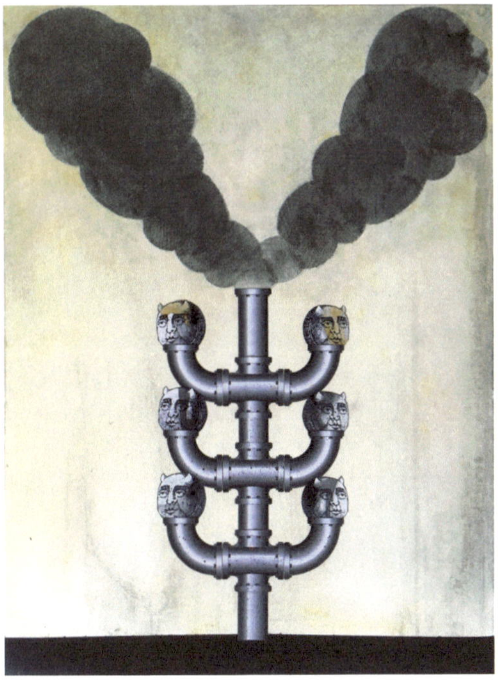

In *London Orbital*, Iain Sinclair makes literary capital out of the link between Bram Stoker's Dracula and Purfleet, a town in Essex situated near the M25 Dartford Crossing and site of the Count's English estate, Carfax Abbey. Remarking on the dominance of oil industry installations in the surrounding area, Sinclair re-imagines the Queen Elizabeth II Bridge over the Thames as a, 'ladder on which blood is turned into oil' (2002: 492) – the trafficking of one addictive commodity traded for that of another. Those who, by fate or design, become its carriers or consumers are enlisted into the burgeoning ranks of the undead: 'All that die from the preying of the Un-dead become themselves Un-dead, and prey on their kind' (Stoker, in Sinclair 2002: 493). The necromancer at large amidst the fringes of the capital is of a kind with those whose task is to administer the *nocuous dregs* that reanimate Merseyside's fallen pilgrims and set them on their strung-out path to nowhere.

Alfonzo's fevered departure from this world was quickened by the oily tide of a daemonic chorus which, by harvesting his tormented soul, would usher him into the next with the promise of eternal damnation. With its perpetually burning flare stack and air of infernal omniscience, Stanlow, like countless other refineries that service the insatiable global demand for oil, stands as a fiery symbol of profligacy and hyper-indulgence. It has always been ruin, not wealth, that the so-called 'trickle-down effect' has delivered with such ruthless efficiency; the hangover sweated out by those who made the revelry happen not those who it kept in drink. Economists' talk of a 'resource curse' or 'paradox of plenty' – an abundance of mineral or oil resources having a malign rather than beneficial economic impact – was exactly what Alfonzo so presciently divined back in the 1970s (Useem 2003; *The Economist* 2003). But the ruinous legacy of oil extends beyond that of a penurious slurry working its way deep into the folds and fabric of everyday social life. Its curse is one that cuts a wider and far deeper swathe through an urban and bucolic landscape from which its inhabitants have become evermore alienated. 'You can be sure of Shell' is the line that the oil giant has been peddling since the 1930s. Such was the surety of its environmental convictions (and corresponding insecurity with regard to its public image), that, in the 1980s, Shell ran an advertising campaign designed to showcase the capacity of its UK refineries to accommodate (and yes, who knows, perhaps even enhance) 'nature'. By promoting the petrochemical industry as a complementary rather than antagonistic presence in the landscape, Shell inadvertently conjures a 'hybrid socionatural' vision (Arias-Maldonado 2015: 2) where,

4. THIS IS A REFERENCE TO WEIRD FICTION WRITER HP LOVECRAFT'S SERIALISED SHORT STORY FROM 1921-22, 'HERBERT WEST-REANIMATOR'. THE TITULAR WEST IS A MEDICAL STUDENT WHO CONDUCTS EXPERIMENTS WITH HUMAN CORPSES IN A BID TO 'REANIMATE' THEM AND BRING THEM BACK TO LIFE.

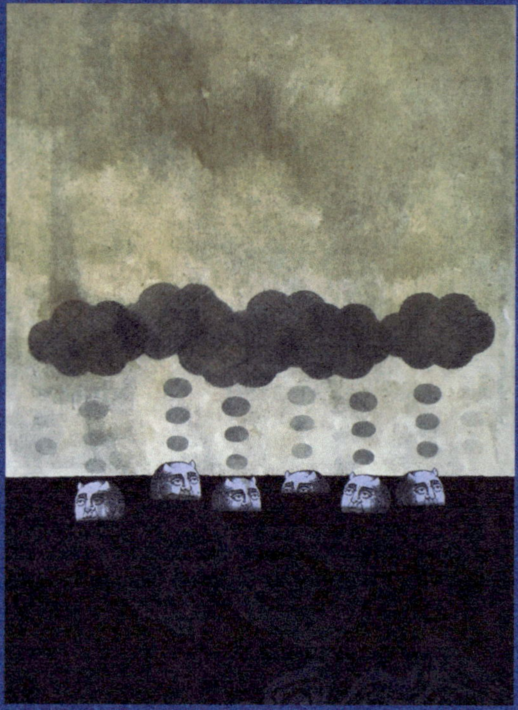
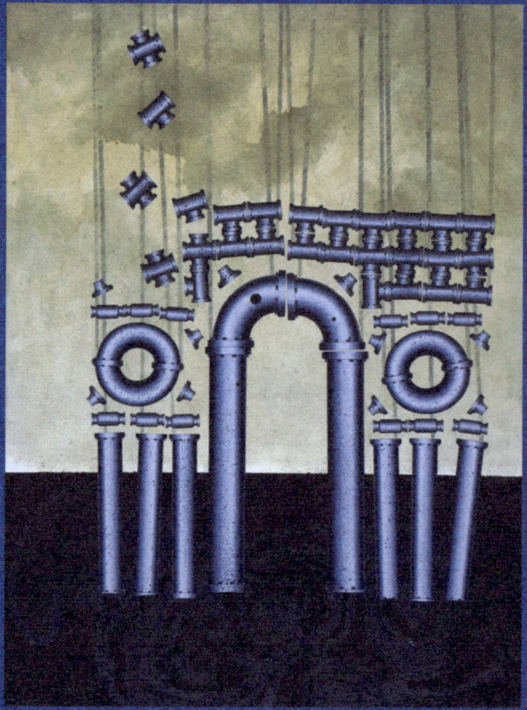
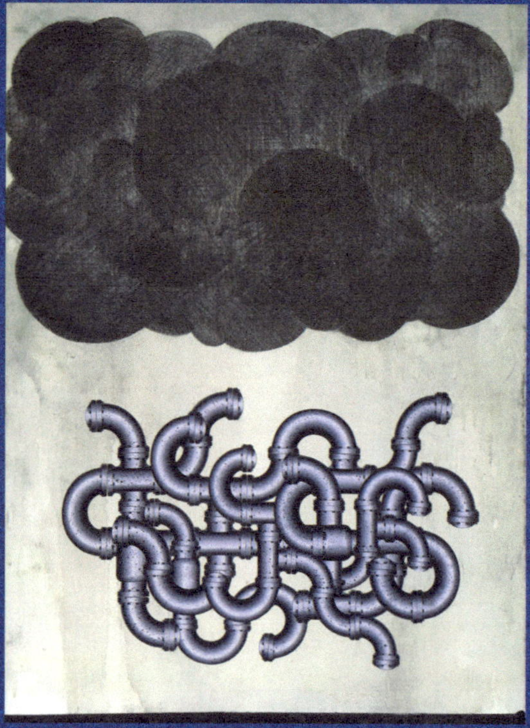
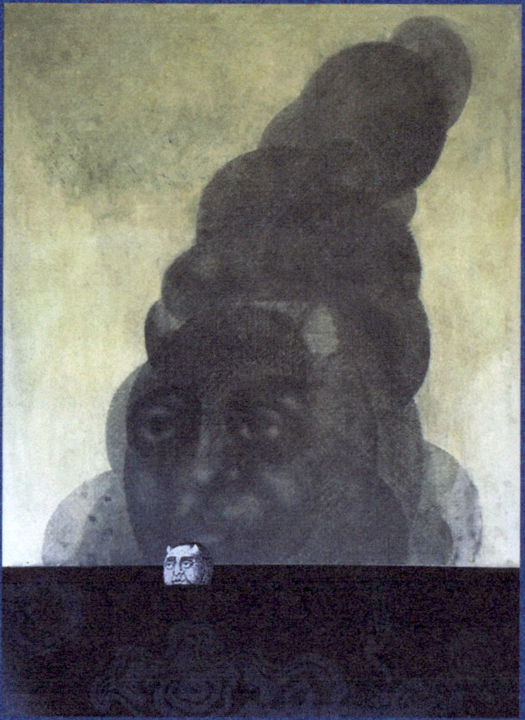

as with Blinky the three-eyed fish who swims in the polluted rivers and lakes near to the Springfield Nuclear Power Station in *The Simpsons*, references to the local fauna begin to invite suspicion where there might otherwise have been none.

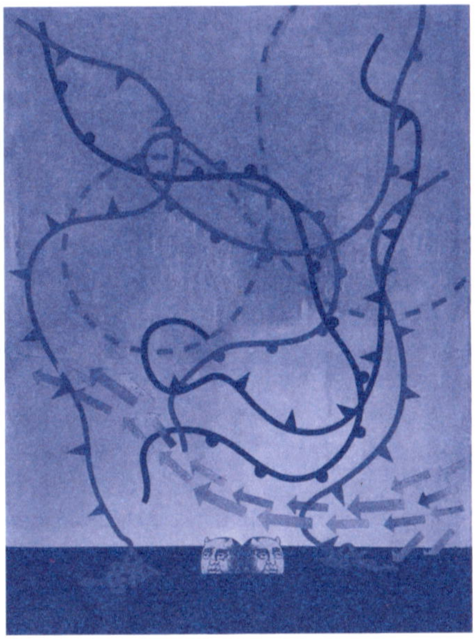

Patrick Wright cites the example of an advertisement in *The Guardian* from 1980 in which the image of a suburban fox in the scrubland adjacent to an oil refinery carries with it the slogan: 'A Shell refinery alive with wildlife'. The refinery in question is Stanlow (Shell being the owners prior to Essar Oil). One of Shell's 'environmental technicians' is quoted as saying: 'An oil refinery is not the first place you look for herons, or a marsh harrier, or a kingfisher, or a fox. Yet, strange as it may seem, the open spaces in and around Shell's Stanlow's refinery literally abound with wildlife' (Wright 2009: 55). And yet, given the marshy topography and wetland environment surrounding the Stanlow complex, the presence of a marsh harrier might not appear all that strange. The wildlife clings on despite, not because, of any nurturing qualities of the refinery, with which, like their human counterparts, they are required to negotiate by dint of necessity. The inherent liminality of the estuarine landscape is an explanatory factor in the siting of high-polluting energy facilities such as Stanlow (Roberts 2012: 104) not an ancillary by-product that enables local flora and fauna to flourish. For Shell's claim to have any kind of logical consistency, the only conceivable message being conveyed in the advert is one that upholds the aforementioned socio-natural hybridity thesis and the implicit embrace of a new anthropocenic vision of environmental sustainability, one that 'recognize[s] the primacy of human transformative powers' (Arias-Maldonado 2015: 6). As with the commonplace but no less arresting image of a bird hovering over the thermal-inducing lanes of a motorway, the depiction of wildlife apparently thriving within a synthetically generated microclimate is one that can be easily trumped by the carnage of a roadkill or oil-tarred avian apocalypse.

A pact with the devil is the abominable insight that befell the dying Alfonzo: a pact whose seemingly profitable advantage in the short term is countered by a perpetuity of hellish indebtedness. The weight of Alfonzo's burden was also that of a singularly Judaeo-Christian heritage: the antichrist as negation of all that bestows grace on a humanity that claws and scrapes its way towards a glimmer of redemption. Hailing, as he did, from Venezuela, Alfonzo would have been all too aware of the cultural particularities attached to European devil myths that had been transplanted to South American soil. Nowhere has this confluence of ideas and mythohistoric narratives been more richly explored than in anthropologist Michael Taussig's seminal work, *The Devil and Commodity Fetishism in South America* (1980). Based on ethnographic fieldwork conducted among plantation workers and miners in Colombia and Bolivia, Taussig's book examines the socio-political significance of the devil in the folklore and rituals of the proletarianised workforce, arguing that, 'the fetishization of evil, in the image of the devil, is an image which mediates the conflict between precapitalist and capitalist modes of objectifying the human condition' (1980: xii). In this analysis, as well as symbolising a raw and untrammelled desire for profit and material gain, devil-beliefs serve to channel political dissent towards the structures of an economic system that 'forces men to barter their souls for the destructive powers of commodities' (*ibid*). Within the historical context of socioeconomic changes being wrought on South American workers and their families, the devil, for Taussig, exists as a symbol of alienation: a collective representation 'of a way of life losing its life' (*ibid: 17*). To underscore this further, in his preface to the 30th anniversary edition of *The Devil and Commodity Fetishism in South America*, Taussig reveals how the sugarcane fields in Colombia's Cauca Valley have now been pressed into service of a growing biofuel industry, transforming a once-beautiful valley into a 'boring, barren, rationalized, lifeless place growing sugar for cars' (2010: xiii). From refining oil to refining molasses, the glutinous flow of combustible dark matter continues to take a toll, draining life and sociality in the dogged pursuit of energy.

In a world given over to the delirious clamour of restless hypermobility, the merits of silence and stillness convey something of a contradictory logic that goes against the grain of a culture addicted to speed (Virilio

2006).[5] The idea of retreating to the marginal fringes of the socio-industrial landscape (perhaps lured by Shell's *Springwatch*-esque vision of Stanlow's bucolic bounty) and taking up some sort of psychogeographic residency in the edgeland scrub is to imagine a space whose dimensions overturn or inversely map those of the surrounding territory. A *heterotopia* by the Mersey (Foucault 1986). Or, more obliquely: a mouse to the elephant of Shell/Essar Oil. In the days when Stanlow Abbey drew pilgrims to the less-than-hospitable marshlands of the Mersey Estuary, the temporal power against which the monks' spiritual energies were pitted was the liminal and unpredictable environment in which they dwelt.

Young's description of the Stanlaw (Stanlow) monks in *A Perambulation of the Hundred of Wirral*, paints a vivid picture of some of the forces thrown their way:

So here the good Cistercians dwelt, toiling for the good of men's souls, and endeavouring to leave the world a little better than they found it. Their isolation was complete... but the situation was an ill-chosen one, for the place was liable to floods when the Gowy came tumbling down in fury, and the Mersey rose before the gathering storms. A great eruption of the sea in 1279 is stated by the Annals of St. Werburgh to have done immense damage at Stanlaw... Yet the monks clung tenaciously to the hallowed spot, to which came pious pilgrims, for it held the bones of the illustrious dead. (1909: 69)

Just two years later another major setback befell the Cistercian community at Stanlaw in the form of a 'great fire' that engulfed the surrounding marshes and which 'reduced [the abbey] in a great conflagration'. Once again undeterred, 'the monks [still] clung to the little that remained of their beautiful building' (*ibid*: 70).

The monks who chose to remain at what was left of the abbey stuck it out until the Reformation when they were buffeted by an altogether different torrent of change. Since then the site and ruins have played host to a more mundane history. It was not until the location was rent from the mainland by the Ship Canal, and the ruins brought to heel by the imposing presence of the refinery, that something of its liminal (if not quite sacred) essence was restored, if only on account of the site's now off-limits status. The excretory tide of a contagion that irrigates the soil and waterways that once sustained the modest needs of the monks works its way down to the bones of the illustrious dead, rousing the silent chorus in a wilful disinterment of topographic memory. Wilful, that is, in the sense of paying heed to an intention which recognises that it is within the gift of the alchemist or trickster to muster efficacious energy. 'Magic is possible', as the anthropologist Alfred Gell observed, 'because *intentions cause events to happen in the vicinity of agents*' (1998: 101, emphasis in original). Invocation is the act of the conjurer and diviner: pulling Stanlaw out of the hat of Stanlow.

With these discursions in mind, how might a modern-day pilgrim negotiate the passage to the abbey remains, cognisant of the fact that his or her very presence will qualify as 'matter out of place' (and thus an incursive act) in the eyes of those who have commandeered the territory? And what would such an undertaking accomplish anyway? What conceivable rationale or label could be offered to any curious onlooker puzzled as to the merits of such a folly? Alchemy? Divination? Deep topography? Deep mapping? Urban exploration? Archaeology? Spatial anthropology? All – or none – of the above? These and other questions will doubtless schlep their ponderous way into future dispatches. But for now, it is suffice to imagine a short crossing across the Manchester Ship Canal and a covert trek along a flat and featureless landmass towards Stanlow Island in the shadow of the oil refinery. Here time is spent exploring, note-taking, perhaps contemplating the surrounding land and soundscapes: the blend of natural and industrial noise; the hum and pounding rhythms of the works; the recurrent roar of planes taking off from Liverpool John Lennon Airport on the far side of the Mersey; the screech of wildfowl; the silence of reflection; or the internal mutter of a mind on the brink of slumber or reverie. And, perhaps on top of all that, to spend some time ruminating on the dark petrochemical alchemy which had so troubled the dying Alfonzo, wondering what the reanimated dead of Stanlaw, lurching en masse from Overpool Cemetery to wreak some kind of ghoulish revenge, might actually look like. To ponder the vision of Hellmouth on the Mersey.

5. THIS CONTRADICTORY LOGIC FORMED PART OF THE INVESTIGATIONS THAT LED TO LES ROBERTS'S RHYTHM-ANALYTICAL STUDY OF NEGATIVE SPACE ON THE M53 (MID-WIRRAL MOTORWAY). THIS SITE-SPECIFIC PROJECT INVOLVED A DAY AND A NIGHT MAROONED ON A TRAFFIC ISLAND LOCATED BETWEEN THE NORTH AND SOUTHBOUND LANES OF THE MOTORWAY (SEE ROBERTS 2015; 2018).

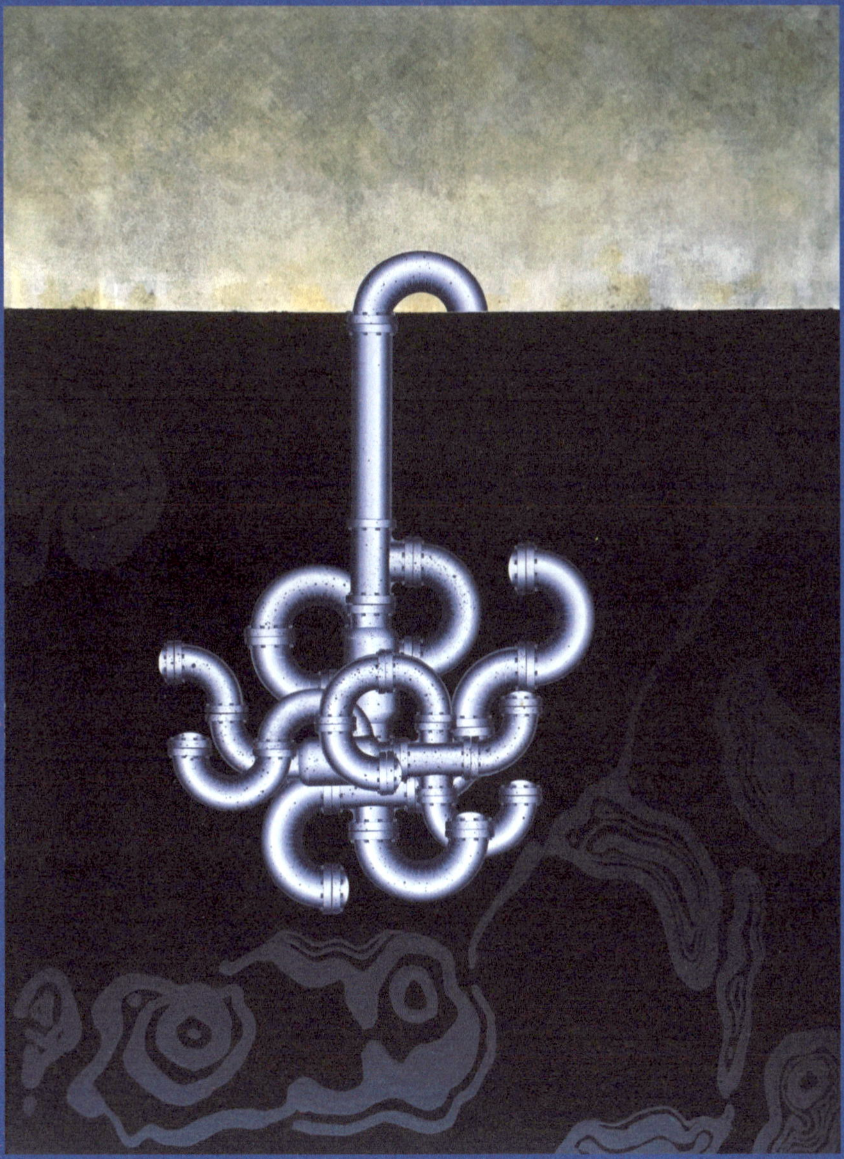

Push under the crust to its sov'reign lair
Collapsed and compressed, expelled of all air
Oozed into the voids, substrated with slime
A morbid life force, enveloping time
That corporate husk remained in your wake
will be repossessed so none will forsake
the sanction to seep round the earth with ease
The death drive delivers where it'll please
So
Cash in your Hydrogen pay off your debts
Cough up the nitrogen cancel all bets
Spent of all oxygen, harbour no grudge
Deposit the carbon your tender's now
sluuuuuuuuuuuuuuuuuuuuuuuuuuuuuuuuudge
A roast for our host the soon to be post-
His gaze set to fixed, gassed, dosed and stoked...

We set you down, to care for us, Stanlow.

AINSWORTH S (2012)
'Stanlow Abbey: A Twenty-First Century Assessment of a Twelfth-Century Cistercian Monastery.'
In SM Varey and GJ White (eds)
Landscape History Discoveries in the North West.
Chester: University of Chester Press.

ARIAS-MALDONADO, M (2015)
'The Anthropocenic turn: Theorizing sustainability in a postnatural age.'
Sustainability 8(1), 10.

AUGÉ, M (1995)
Non-Places: Introduction to an Anthropology of Supermodernity.
London: Verso.

THE ECONOMIST (2003)
'The devil's excrement: Is oil wealth a blessing or a curse?'
The Economist 22 May 2003.
Accessed on 15·6·18 at: economist.com/node/1795921

ENDS (2015)
'Oil firm fined £500k for Cheshire pollution.'
The ENDS Report 29 October 2015.

FOUCAULT M (1986)
'Of other spaces.'
Diacritics 16(1), 22–27.

GELL A (1998)
Art and Agency: An Anthropological Theory.
Oxford: Clarendon Press.

GORDON J (2003)
'Reveling in genre: An interview with China Miéville.'
Science Fiction Studies 30 (3), 355–373.

ROBERTS L (2012)
'The Sands of Dee: Estuarine Excursions in Liminal Space.'
In L Roberts and H Andrews (eds) *Liminal Landscapes: Travel, Experience and Spaces In-between.*
London: Routledge.

ROBERTS L (2015)
'The rhythm of non-places: Marooning the embodied self in depthless space.'
In L Roberts (ed.) *Humanities* 4(4), 569–599.
Special issue on 'deep mapping'.

ROBERTS L (2016)
'Inhabiting the edge: Tricksterism and radical liminality.'
The Double Negative.
Accessed on 15·6·18 at: thedoublenegative.co.uk/2016/02/inhabiting-the-edge-tricksterism-and-radical-liminality

ROBERTS L (2018)
Spatial Anthropology: Excursions in Liminal Space.
London: Rowman & Littlefield.

SINCLAIR I (2002)
London Orbital: A Walk around the M25.
London: Penguin.

SPIELMANN I (1891)
'Exhibition of a skull dredged on the Manchester Ship Canal works.'
The Journal of the Anthropological Institute of Great Britain and Ireland 20, 179–180.

TAUSSIG M (1980)
The Devil and Commodity Fetishism in South America.
Chapel Hill: University of North Carolina Press.

TAUSSIG M (2010)
The Devil and Commodity Fetishism in South America.
30th Anniversary Edition. Chapel Hill: University of North Carolina Press.

TAYLOR PM (1991)
'A pipeline spill into the Mersey Estuary, England.'
International Oil Spill Conference Proceedings 1, 299–303.

THE TELEGRAPH (2015)
'Stanlow oil refinery blast: Firm faces fine after 7,000 gravestones soaked in huge leak.'
The Telegraph 19 Oct 2015.
Accessed on 15·6·18 at: telegraph.co.uk/news/uknews/law-and-order/11940625/Stanlow-oil-refinery-blast-Firm-faces-fine-after-7000-gravestones-soaked-in-huge-leak.html

USEEM J (2003)
'The devil's excrement.'
Fortune 147(20).
Accessed on 15·6·18 at: http://archive.fortune.com/magazines/fortune/fortune_archive/2003/02/03/336434/index.htm

VIRILIO P (2006)
Speed and Politics.
Los Angeles: Semiotext(e).

WRIGHT P (2009)
On Living in an Old Country: The National Past in Contemporary Britain.
Oxford: Oxford University Press.

YOUNG, HAROLD EDGAR. 1909.
A Perambulation of the Hundred of Wirral in the County of Chester.
Liverpool: Henry Young and Sons.

Dry as a Badger and Other Rural Mythologies

Rebecca Chesney
/
Rosemary Shirley

Artist Rebecca Chesney and art historian and curator Rosemary Shirley were brought together through their shared interest in the rural landscape and its place within the popular imagination. Their in-conversation event, *Working the Land: Art, Landscape and the Everton Meadows*, explored how social and political agendas shape perceptions of the British countryside, through reference to everyday things such as litter and weeds. This visual essay, which references an artwork developed by Rebecca during a residency with the Black Mountains-based organisation Peak, is part of a continuing conversation between the authors about our relationship with the natural world.

Myths are stories we are told and stories we tell ourselves. They explain how things have come to be and they keep things the way they are. Roland Barthes said myths turn history into nature, meaning that myths make it seem as if certain beliefs or ways of thinking or behaving are not beliefs or ways of thinking or behaving, but are instead the truth of things. Nature's way. How things have always been and always will be.[1]

The myths we are told and tell ourselves about the countryside are many and varied. Some seem to originate in a kind of long-forgotten folk memory, others have been made up by people who want to sell us things. Peter Conrad in his reworking of Barthes' work *Mythologies* says that today the most powerful myths are brands.[2] Still more mythologies have been constructed to tell us what does and does not belong in the countryside – and, of course, who does and does not belong.

This visual essay is created from photographs that we have collected which map some of the rural mythologies that populate our everyday lives and encounters with the countryside. Each section is named after a colour from Rebecca's piece *Snapshot* (2016), which she made during a residency in the Brecon Beacons. For this work, she created a paint chart featuring 96 colours sourced from the landscape; the names and descriptions of these colours reference the ecology and geology of the landscape together with other issues like affordable housing, tourism, farming and economic and environmental factors. Together they become a portrait of a landscape. The piece also references another powerful rural mythology: our desire to 'bring the outside in', choosing paint colours for our homes named after plants, animals and other features of the landscape.

54 **Hedge**
(or managed and controlled)

Hedges,
boundaries,
right angles,
straight lines,
enclosures.

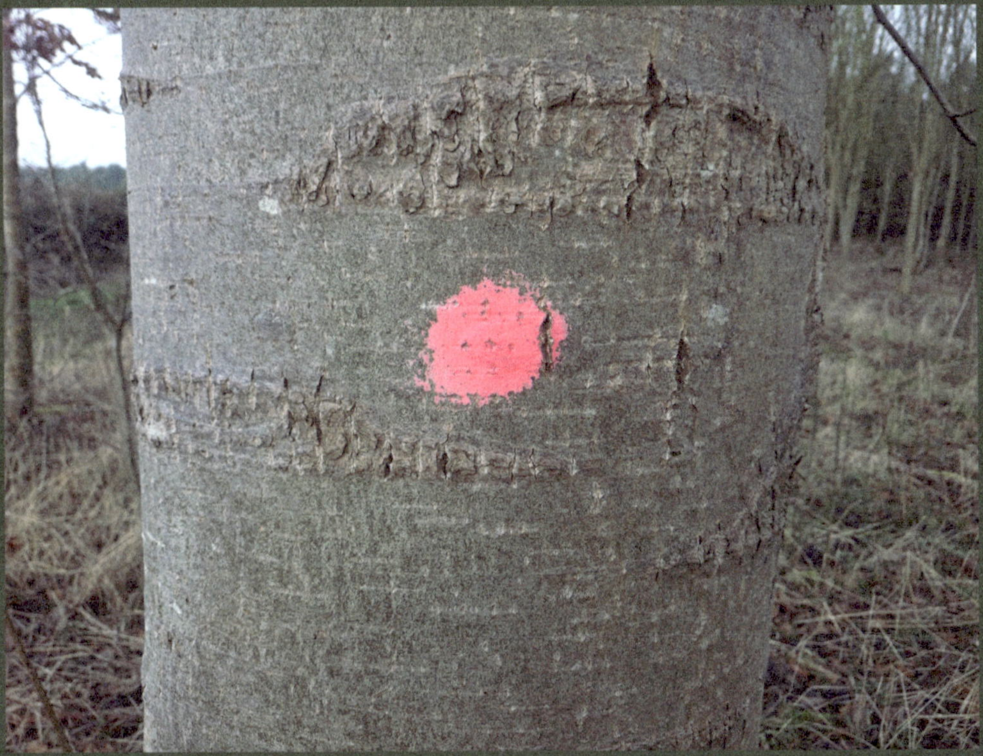

FIG 1

To hedge,

1 — Surround with a hedge.
Enclose, border, bound,
2 — Limit or qualify (something)
by conditions or exceptions.
Hinder, obstruct, impede,
constrain, trap

The pink spot marks the spot.

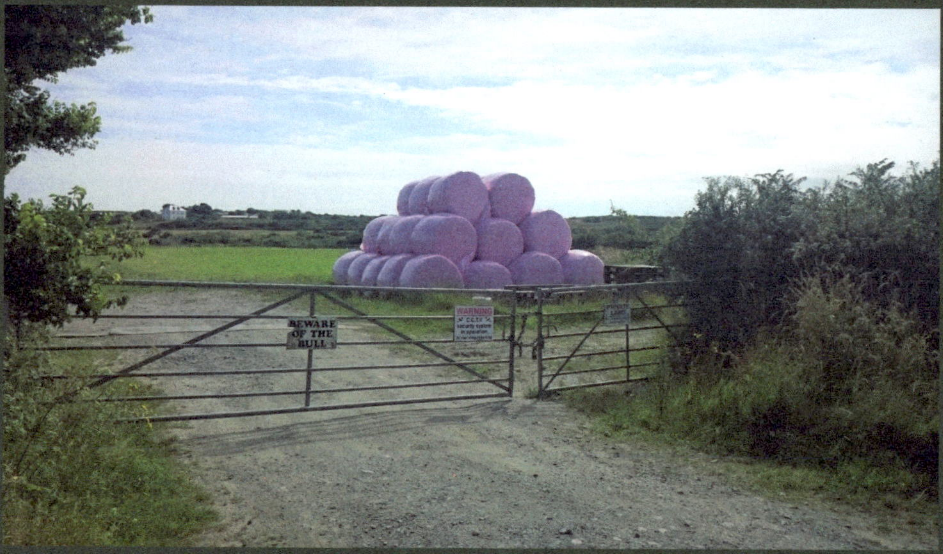

FIG 2

The countryside is wild.
The countryside needs to be managed and controlled.

Two mythologies – one hedges the other.

What appears to be natural is the product of hundreds of years of land management.

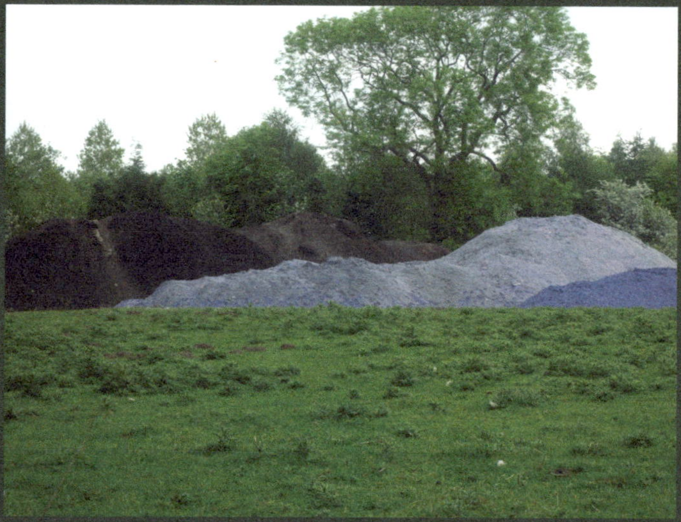

FIG 3

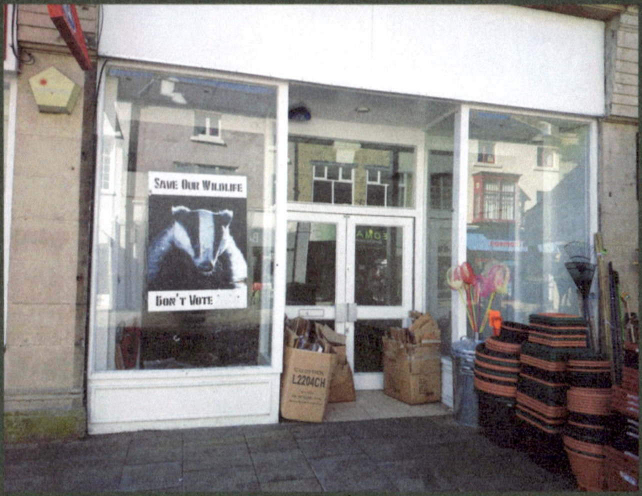
SAVE OUR WILDLIFE
DON'T VOTE

FIG 5

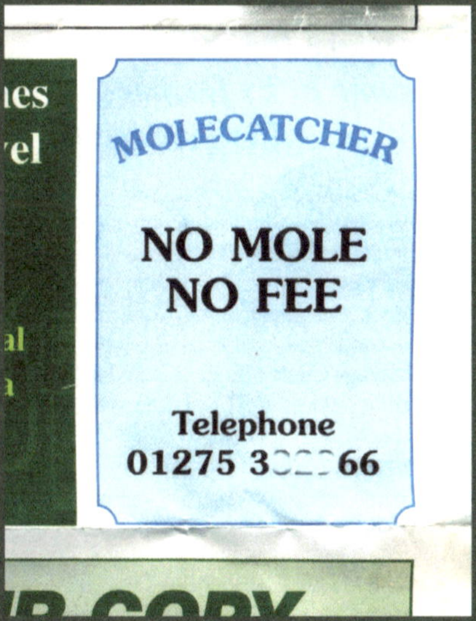
MOLECATCHER
NO MOLE
NO FEE
Telephone

FIG 4

It appears that 'Orderly maintenance of the physicality of the landscape can only be carried out under the leadership of those families and institutions that have accrued so much continuous experience of land management over the hundreds of years in which they have been custodians of the land. In this way the perceived need for physical order leads to reproduction of the social order.'[3]

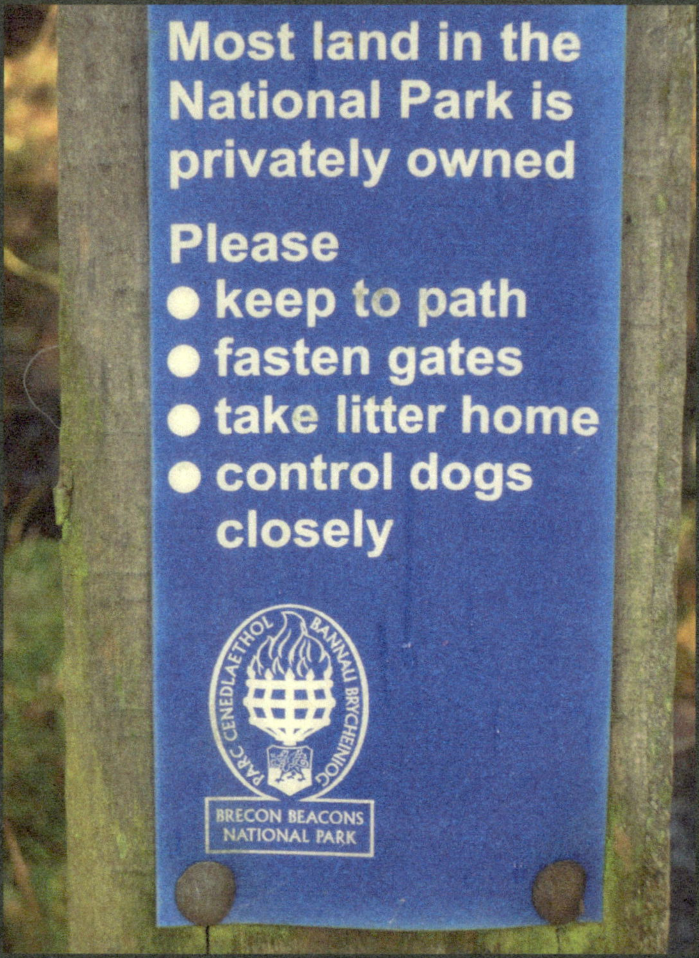

FIG 6

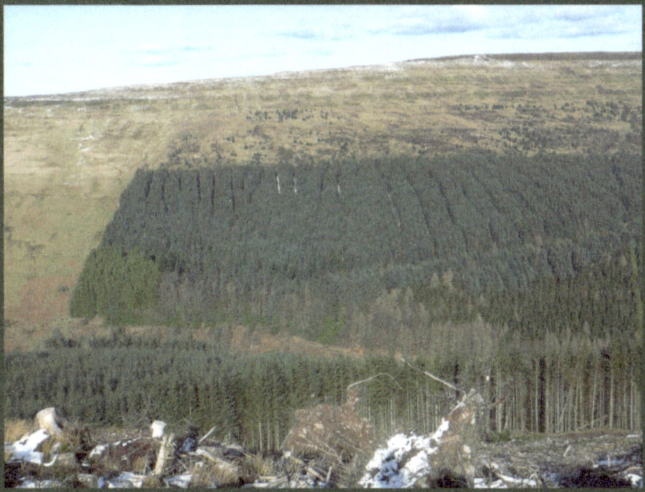

FIG 8

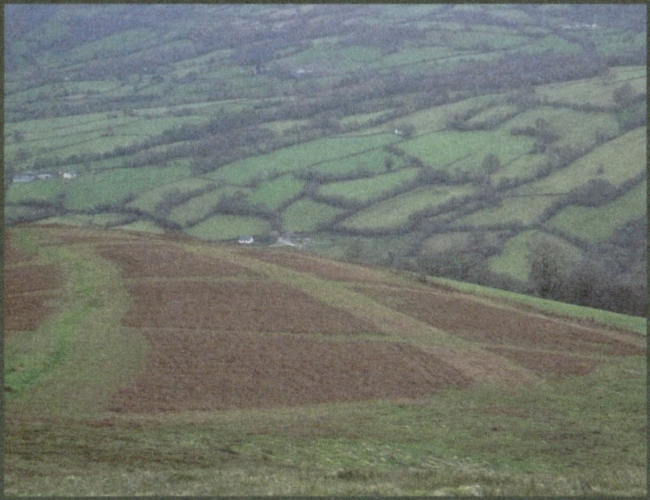

FIG 7

6 Foolhardy (or death and danger)

Nature is out to get us.

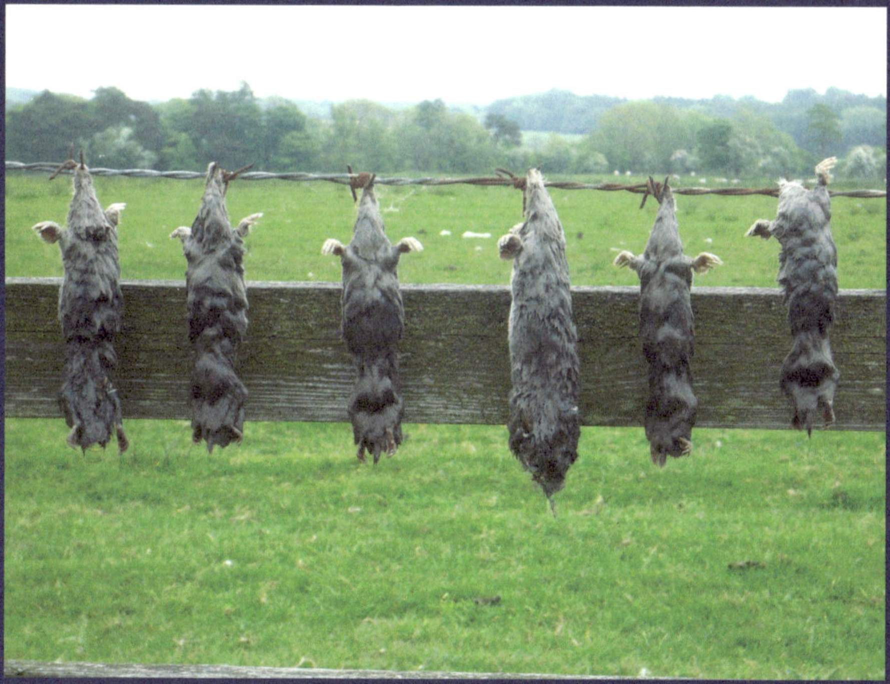

FIG 9

We arm ourselves against it with layers of breathable nylon and stout boots.

We know the dangers of attempting a hike in denim jeans (certain death).

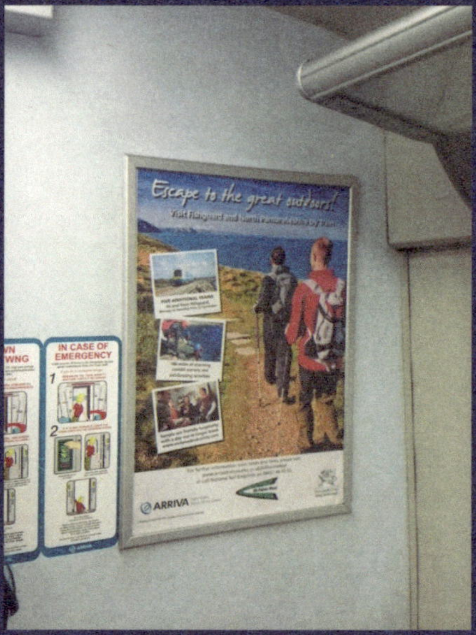

FIG 10

We aim to remain dry as a badger.

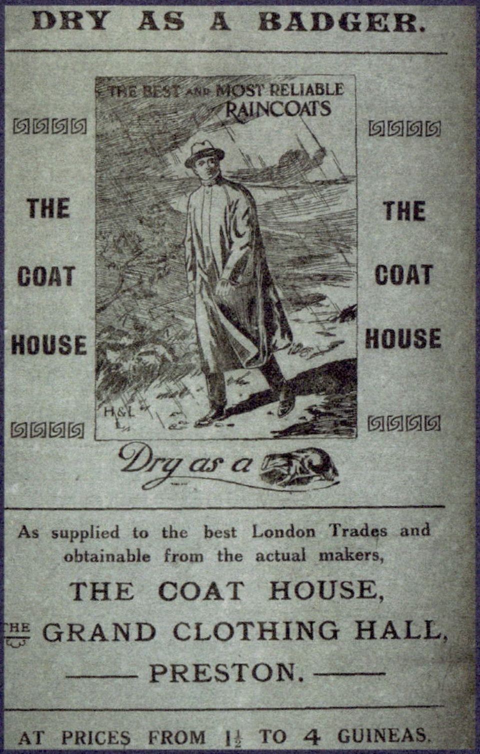

FIG 11

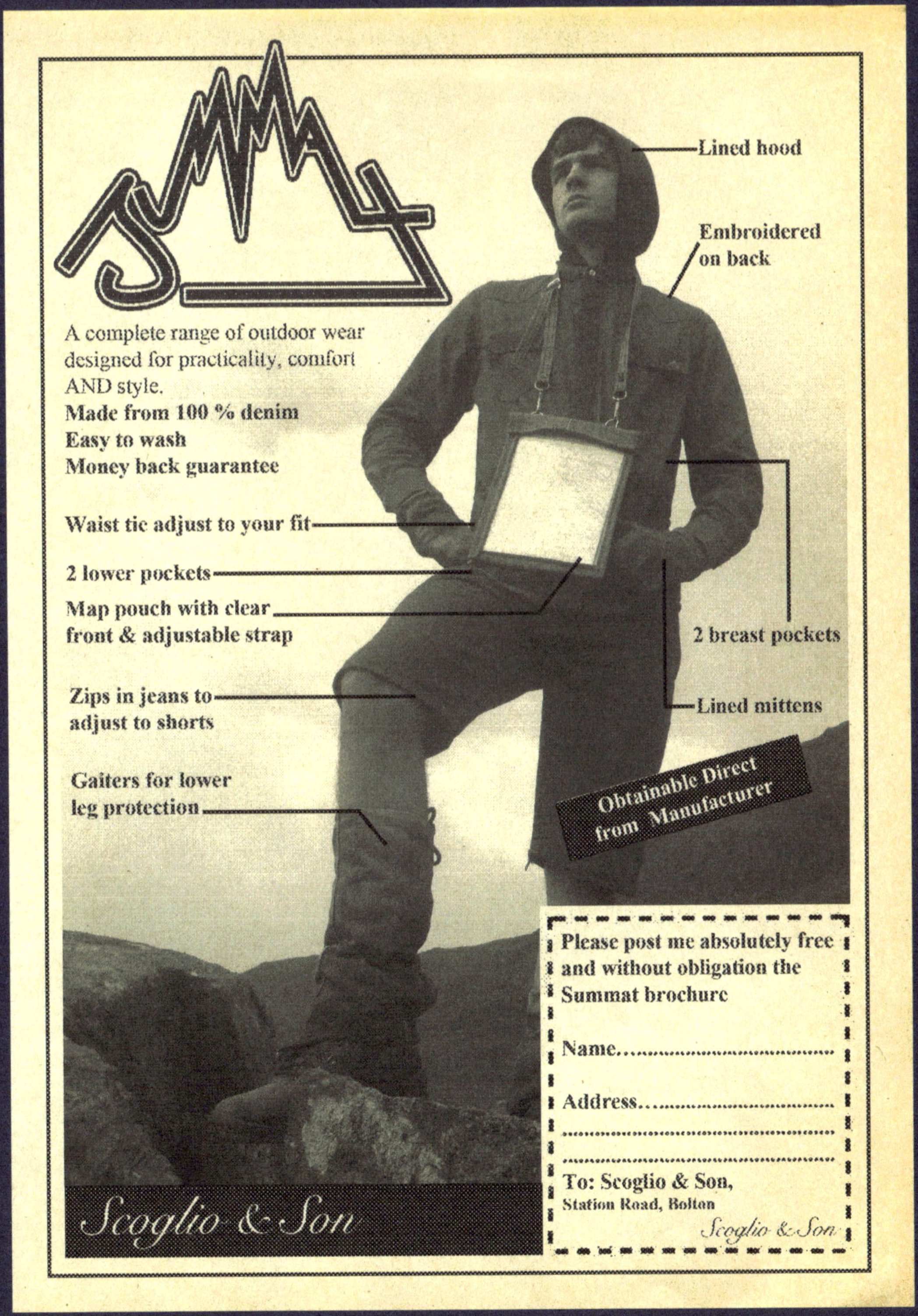

A complete range of outdoor wear designed for practicality, comfort AND style.
Made from 100 % denim
Easy to wash
Money back guarantee
Lined hood
Embroidered on back
Waist tie adjust to your fit
2 lower pockets
Map pouch with clear front & adjustable strap
2 breast pockets
Zips in jeans to adjust to shorts
Lined mittens
Gaiters for lower leg protection
Obtainable Direct from Manufacturer
Please post me absolutely free and without obligation the Summat brochure
Name.
Address.
To: Scoglio & Son,
Station Road, Bolton
Scoglio & Son
Scoglio & Son

FIG 12

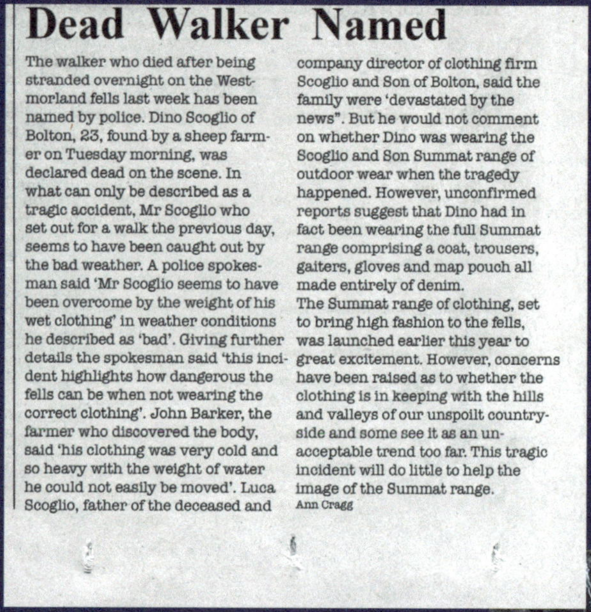

Dead Walker Named

The walker who died after being stranded overnight on the Westmorland fells last week has been named by police. Dino Scoglio of Bolton, 23, found by a sheep farmer on Tuesday morning, was declared dead on the scene. In what can only be described as a tragic accident, Mr Scoglio who set out for a walk the previous day, seems to have been caught out by the bad weather. A police spokesman said 'Mr Scoglio seems to have been overcome by the weight of his wet clothing' in weather conditions he described as 'bad'. Giving further details the spokesman said 'this incident highlights how dangerous the fells can be when not wearing the correct clothing'. John Barker, the farmer who discovered the body, said 'his clothing was very cold and so heavy with the weight of water he could not easily be moved'. Luca Scoglio, father of the deceased and company director of clothing firm Scoglio and Son of Bolton, said the family were 'devastated by the news". But he would not comment on whether Dino was wearing the Scoglio and Son Summat range of outdoor wear when the tragedy happened. However, unconfirmed reports suggest that Dino had in fact been wearing the full Summat range comprising a coat, trousers, gaiters, gloves and map pouch all made entirely of denim.

The Summat range of clothing, set to bring high fashion to the fells, was launched earlier this year to great excitement. However, concerns have been raised as to whether the clothing is in keeping with the hills and valleys of our unspoilt countryside and some see it as an unacceptable trend too far. This tragic incident will do little to help the image of the Summat range.

Ann Cragg

FIG 13

We've seen the films
and watched the TV murders.

We know
that in every wood
there is a body
waiting to be found.

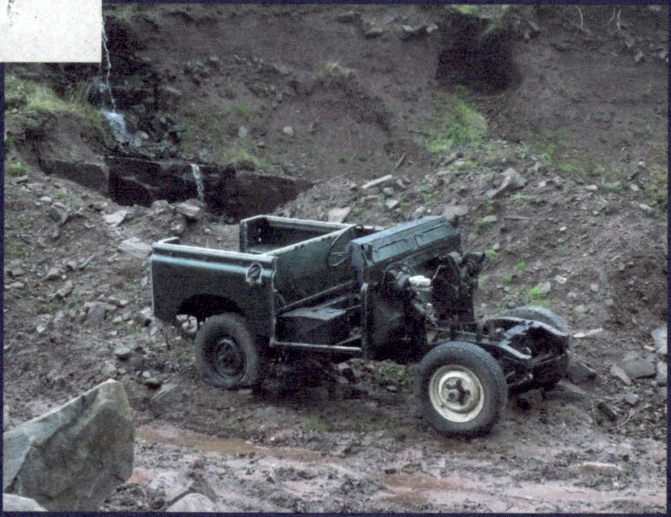

FIG 14

We know
that there is
no mobile signal.

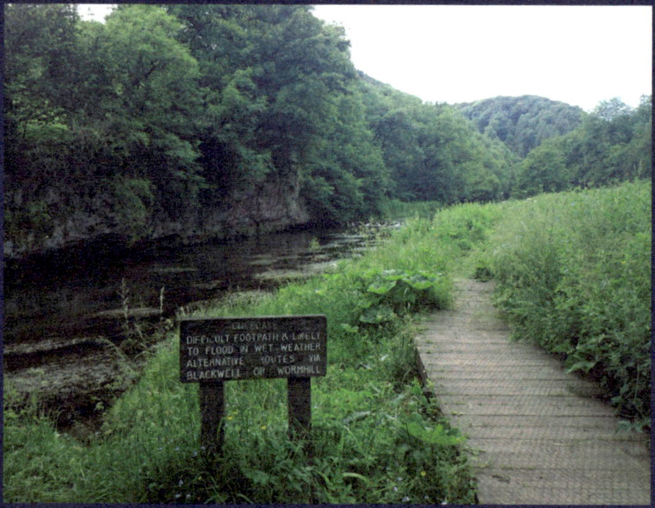

FIG 15

Nature is red
in tooth and claw.

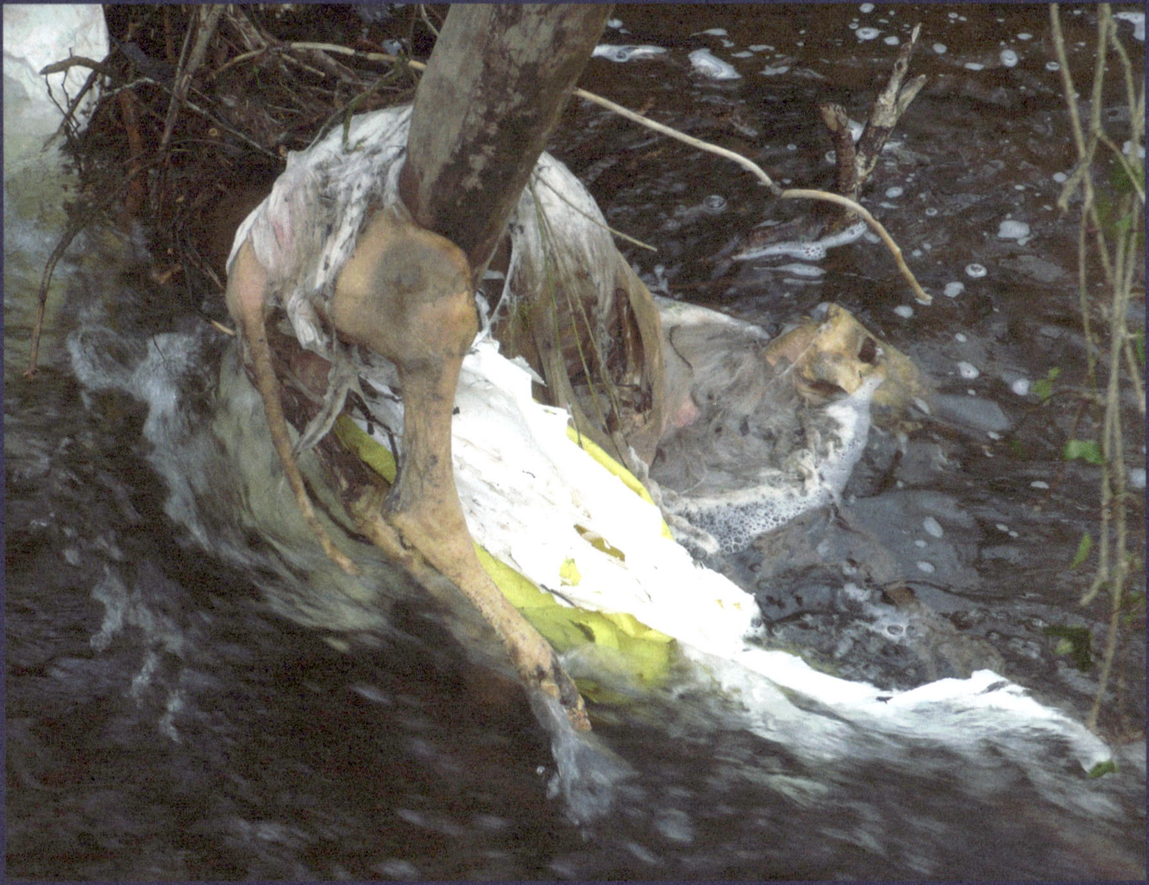

FIG 16

'A sheep wants
nothing better
than to die'.[4]

31 **Cherry Blossom**

(or fresh and clean)

Breathe in deeply. I have some questions.

What is it that you smell?
Can you smell the countryside?

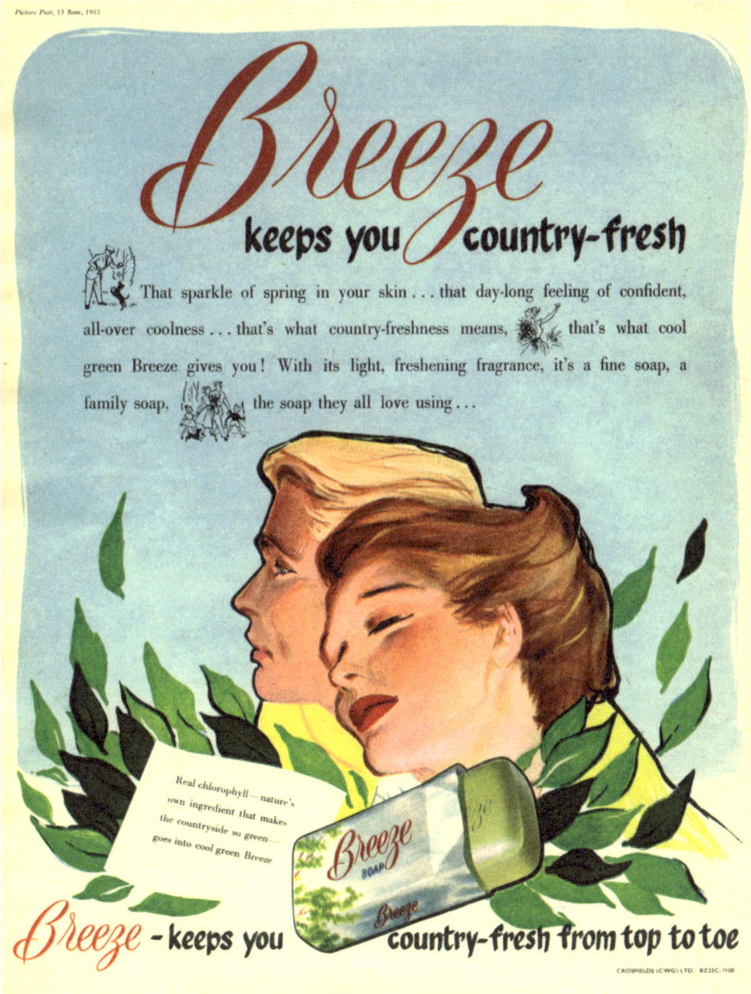

FIG 17

Is it that smell of grass, or manure, or car exhaust, or spring breeze and golden lily, or spring awakening or death?

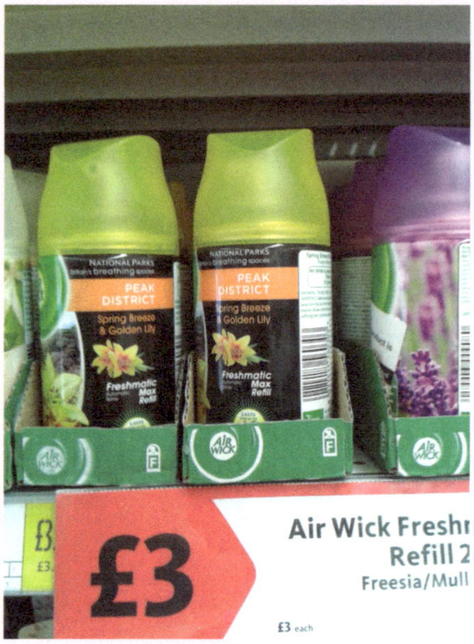

FIG 18

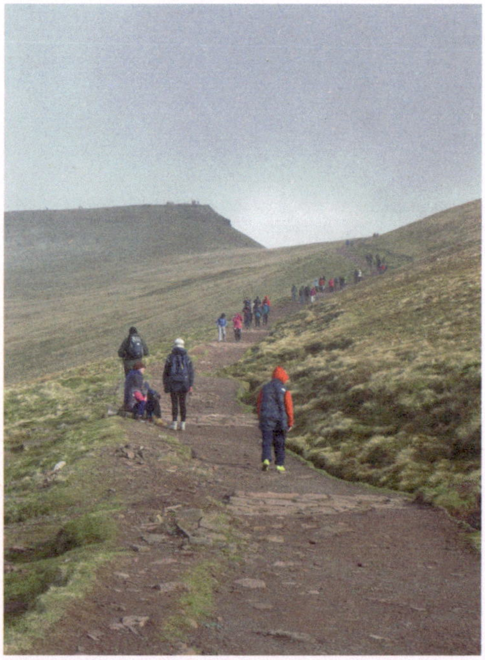

FIG 19

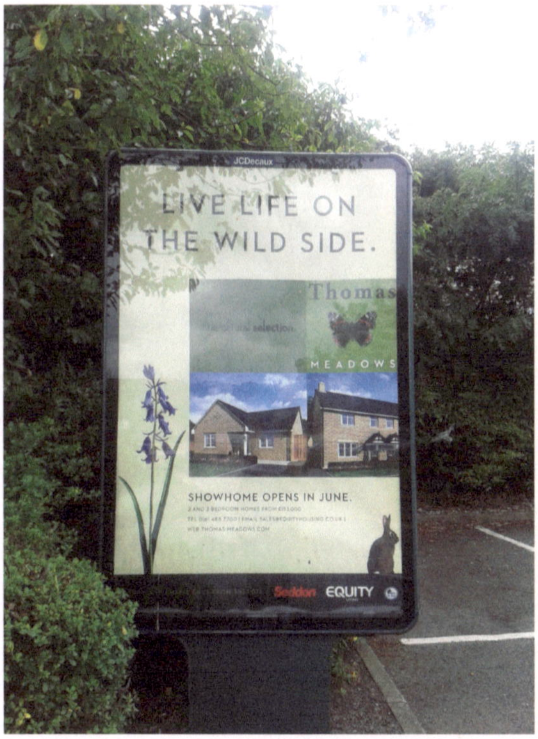

FIG 20

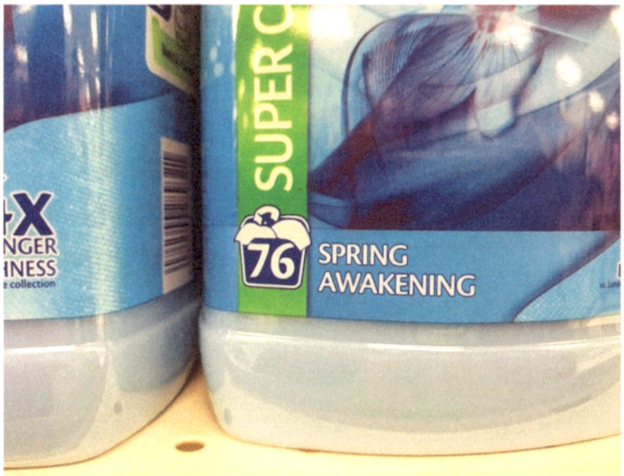

FIG 21

What is country fresh?
And how can I be it?

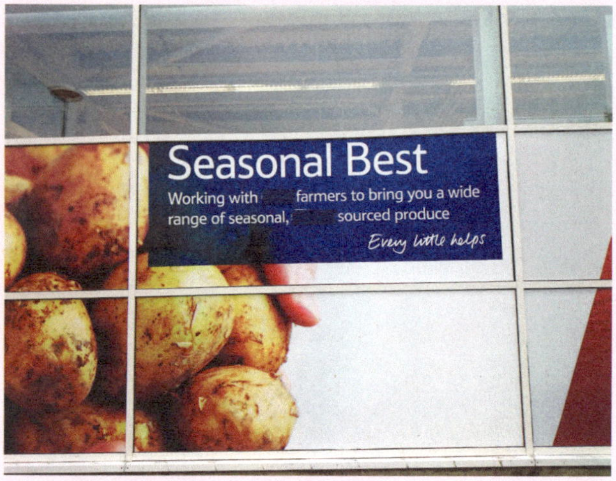

FIG 22

What is seasonal best?
How can I get it?

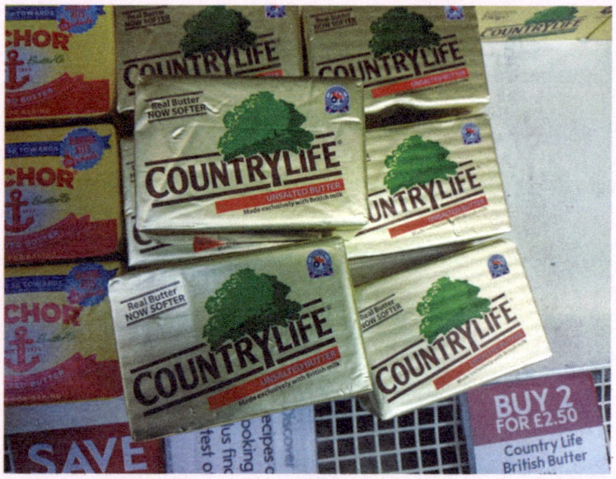

FIG 23

It seems like some vital information
has been redacted.

I'd like to enjoy the countryside without leaving London, is that possible?

How is life in the country made exclusively with British milk?

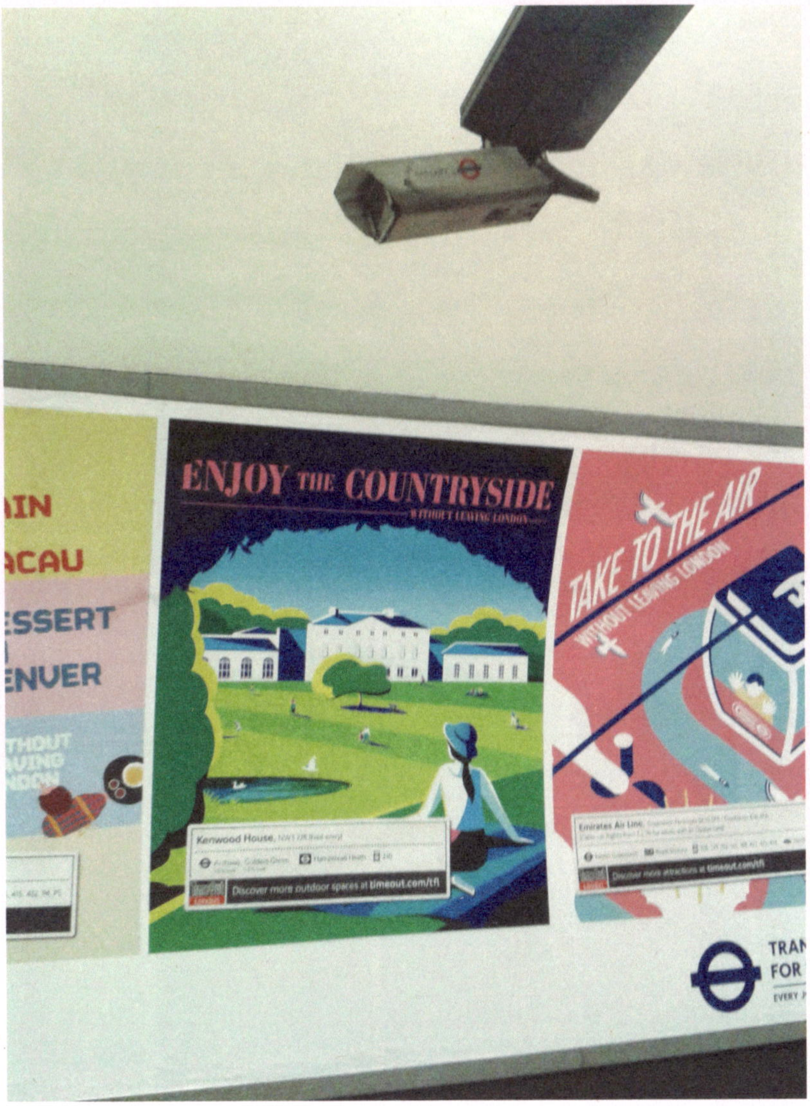

FIG 24

4 Relic

(or figures in the landscape)

The countryside is of the past.
It is a 'vast museumised ruin'.[5]

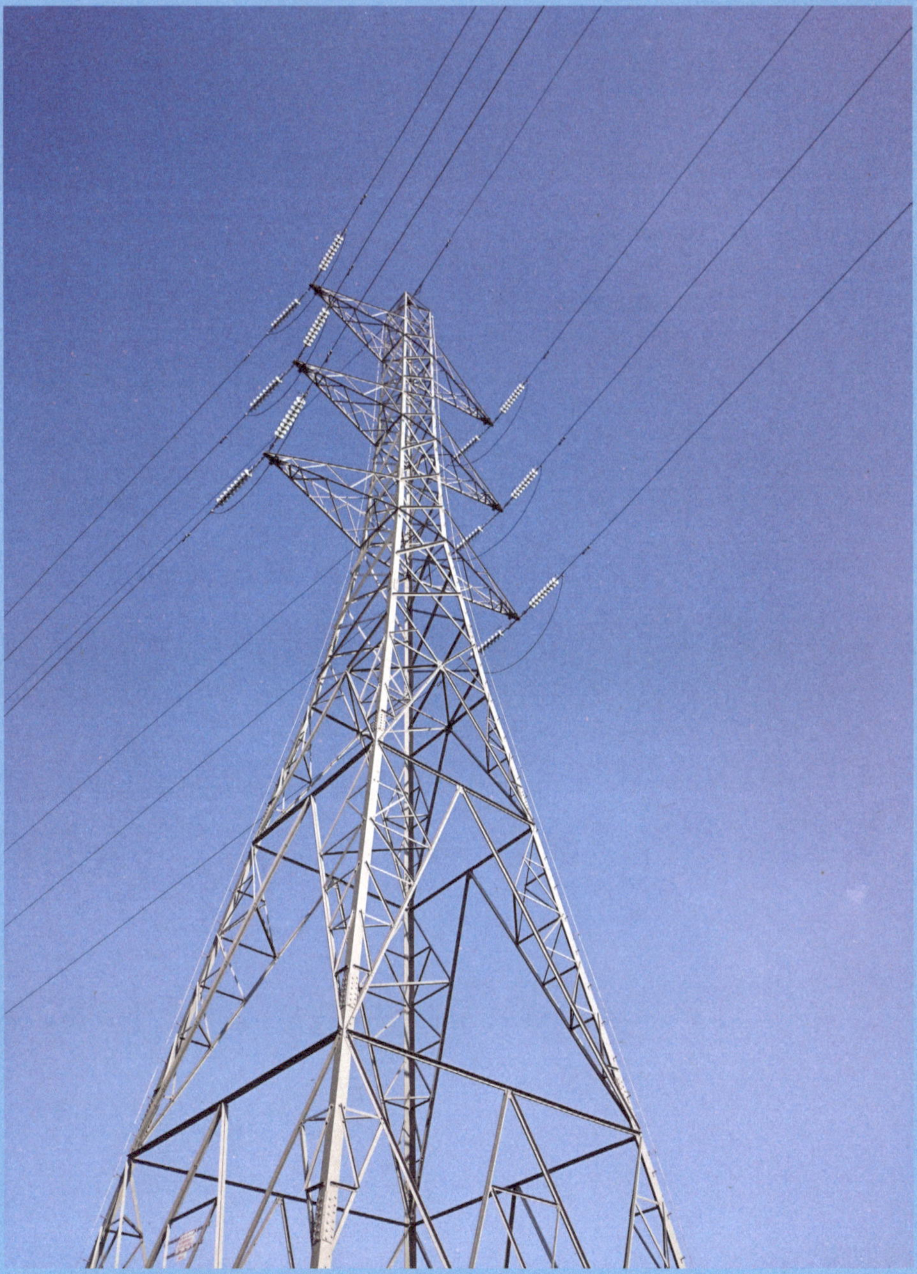

FIG 25

All those uprights and horizontals.
It seems we keep building ruins of the future.

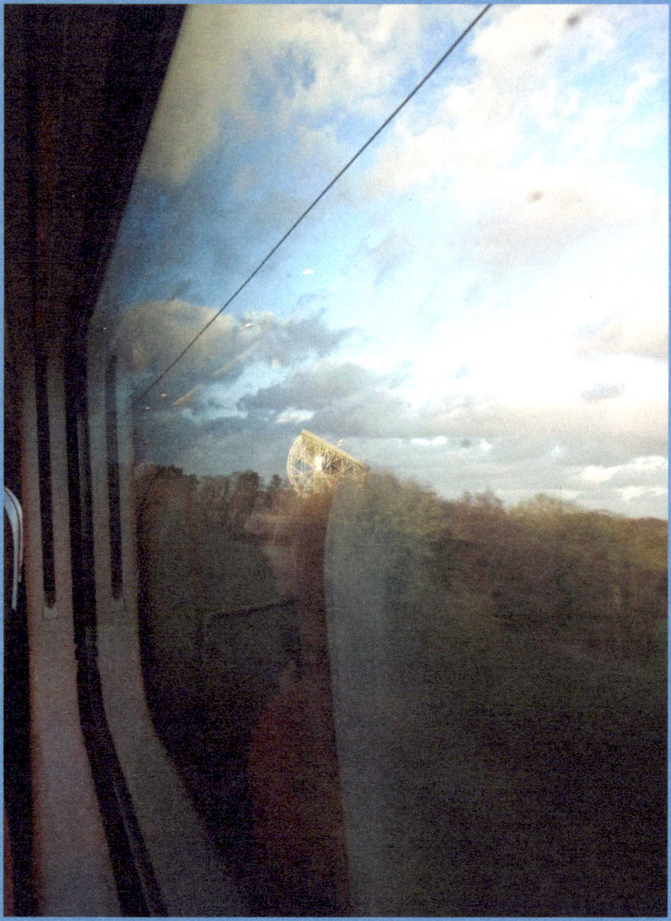

FIG 26

The countryside turns everything old. Even the newest of the new looks like some relic of an ancient civilisation when it sits in a field. Military kit, a giant satellite dish listening to space, spectacular pylons, Victorian viaducts, stacks of plastic-coated bales, a dead tractor, they look as ancient and mysterious as Stonehenge.

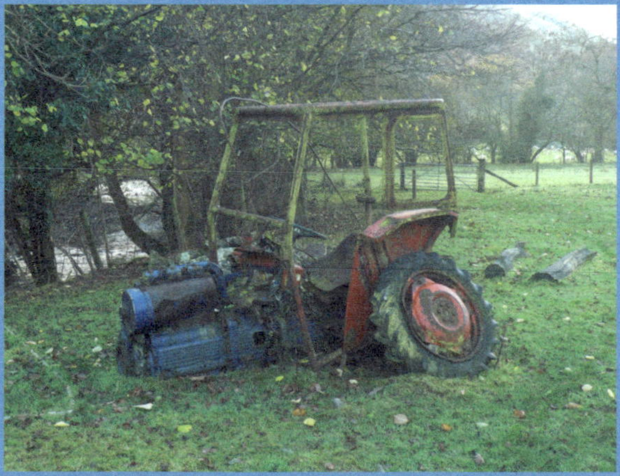

FIG 27

When a barn fell down in a national park it was required that it be preserved in its ruined state rather than repaired.[6]

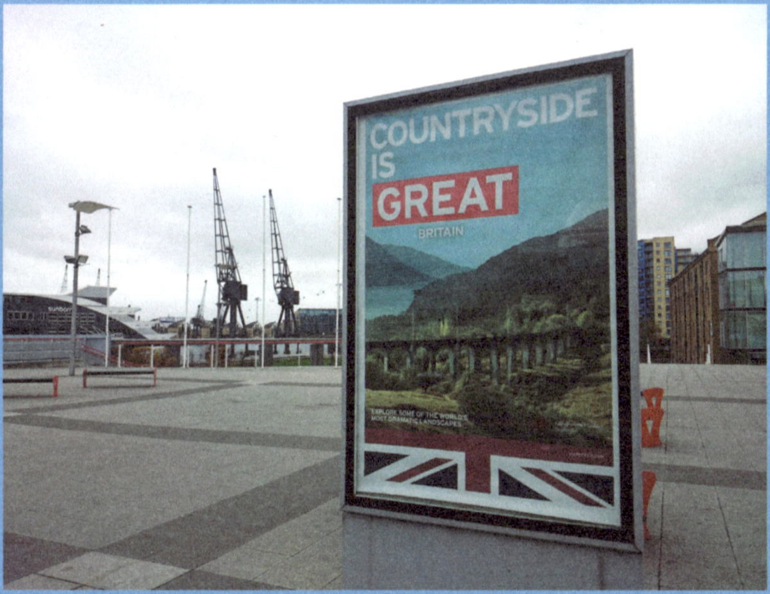

FIG 28

Home of ruins and always on the edge of ruination.

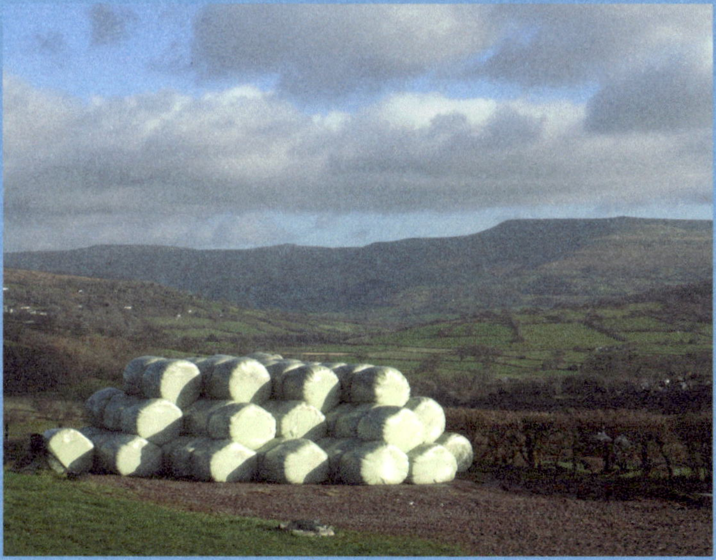

FIG 29

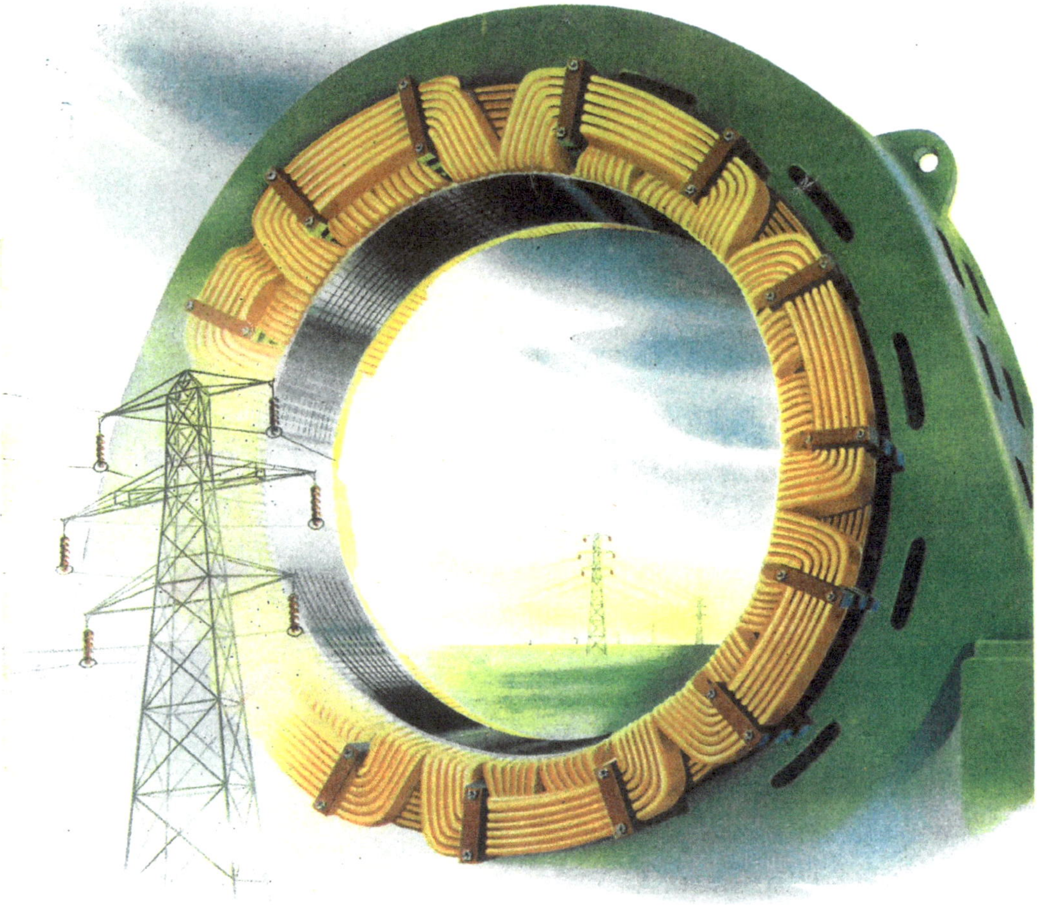

Gateway to civilisation

Heat for home and hospital, light for street and factory, power for train and mine . . . These and a hundred everyday benefits flow consistently from the power of Metrovick alternators. They are indeed a gateway to much that is good in our modern civilisation. In the generation and distribution of power, as in all spheres of electrical engineering, the work of the Metrovick organisation is steadily assisting Progress. Throughout the world, wherever are demanded outstanding skill and craftsmanship in things electrical, will be found the products of Metropolitan-Vickers.

METROPOLITAN-VICKERS ELECTRICAL CO. LTD. TRAFFORD PARK, MANCHESTER, 17

Member of the A.E.I. Group of Companies

METROVICK PROVIDING POWER FOR PROSPERITY

FIG 30

'Pylons spoil the countryside,
that's what everyone says,
[but] by themselves
they are beautiful.'[7]

Pylons offer 'quick perspectives of the future',[8] doorways to another time, looking through them we can see what is yet to come.

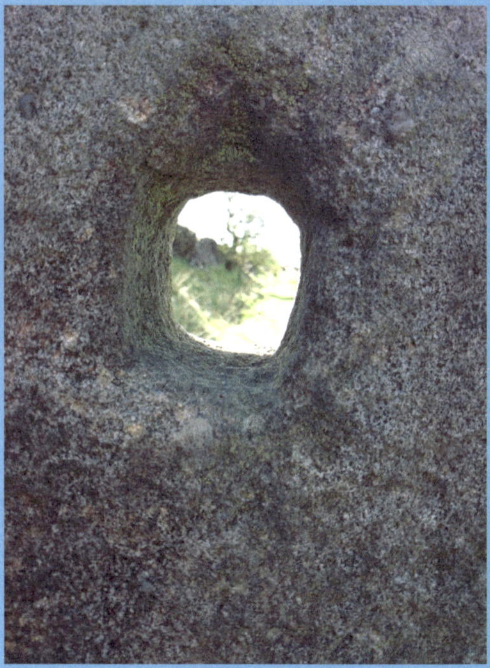

FIG 31

They are nonagenarian
but look simultaneously new and ancient in the landscape.
Like chalk figures
drawn across the land.

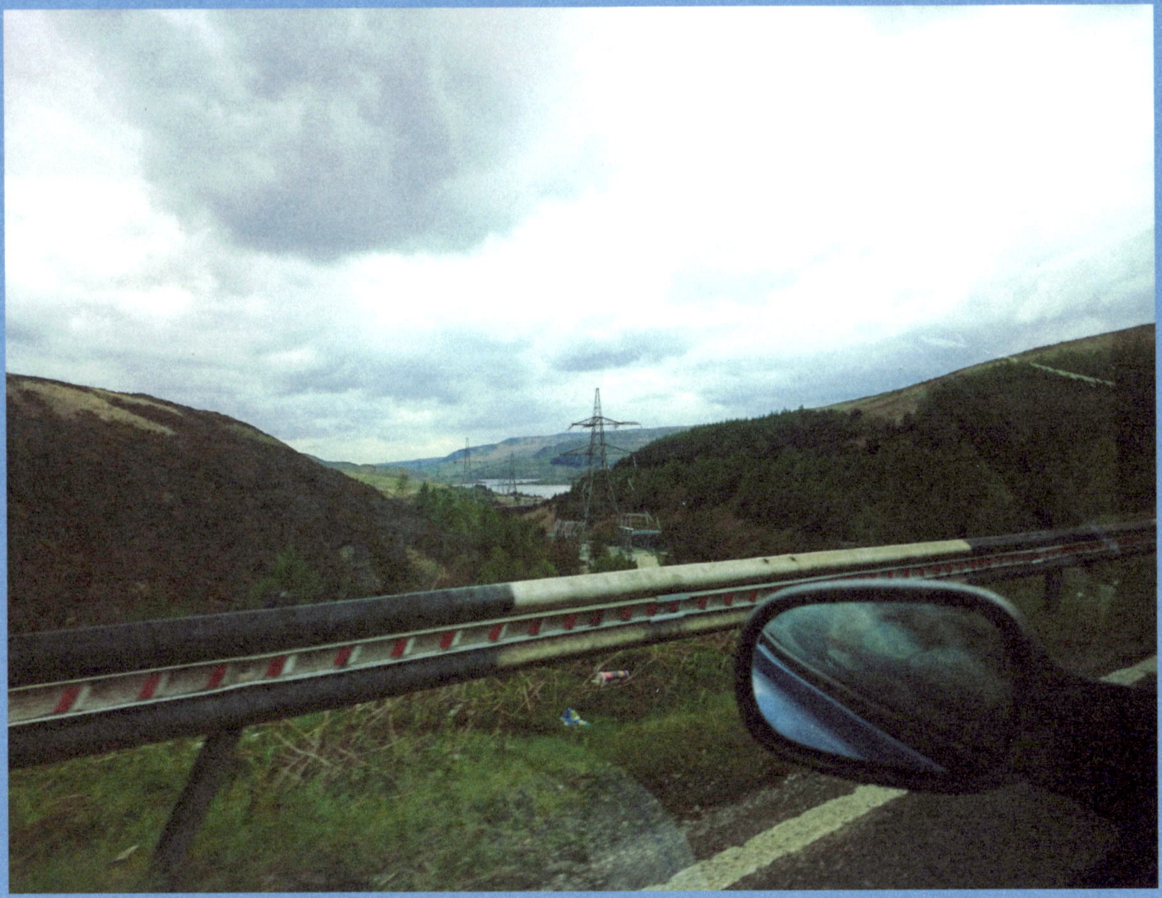

FIG 32

1 BARTHES R (1999 [1957])
Mythologies.
London: Vintage.

2 CONRAD P (2016)
Mythomania: Tales of Our Times, From Apple to Isis.
London and New York: Thames and Hudson.

3 SHIRLEY R (2015)
Rural Modernity, Everyday Life and Visual Culture.
Farnham: Ashgate. p.7.

4 CHESNEY R (2016)
Snapshot.
Quoting from *Addicted to Sheep*, 2016 [Film], BBC.

5 LOWENTHAL D (1994)
'European Landscapes as National Symbols.'
In: D Hooson (ed) *Geography and National Identity.*
Oxford: Blackwell. p.24.

6 NATURAL ENGLAND (2011)
Look After Your Land with Environmental Stewardship.
Accessed on 12·6·18 at:
http://publications.naturalengland.org.uk/file/115013

7 PETIT C (DIRECTOR) (1979)
Radio On [film].
UK: BFI.

8 SPENDER S (1933)
The Pylons [poem].

FIG 1 A TREE MARKED FOR FELLING BY THE FORESTRY COMMISSION, THE NATIONAL FOREST, 2015.
–
ROSEMARY SHIRLEY.

FIG 2 A TRIO OF WARNING SIGNS AND BALES WRAPPED IN PINK PLASTIC, AN INITIATIVE TO RAISE FUNDS FOR BREAST CANCER CHARITIES, CORNWALL, 2016.
–
ROSEMARY SHIRLEY.

FIG 3 SUPPLEMENTS FOR FARM LAND, TROUGH OF BOWLAND, 2016.
–
REBECCA CHESNEY.

FIG 4 MOLECATCHER ADVERT, LOCAL NEWSLETTER IN SOMERSET, 2012.
–
REBECCA CHESNEY.

FIG 5 ANTI BADGER CULL POSTER, 2015.
–
ROSEMARY SHIRLEY.

FIG 6 'MOST LAND IN THE NATIONAL PARK IS PRIVATELY OWNED' SIGN, BRECON BEACONS NATIONAL PARK, 2016.
–
REBECCA CHESNEY.

FIG 7 FARMLAND, WALES, 2016.
–
REBECCA CHESNEY.

FIG 8 FORESTRY COMMISSION LAND, WALES, 2016.
–
REBECCA CHESNEY.

FIG 9 DEAD MOLES HUNG BY THEIR NOSES ON BARBED WIRE, TROUGH OF BOWLAND, 2016.
–
REBECCA CHESNEY.

FIG 10 COMMUNICATING CARRIAGES – THE TRAIN ADVERTISES TWO DIFFERENT FORMS OF ESCAPE, 2016.
–
ROSEMARY SHIRLEY.

FIG 11 DRY AS A BADGER ADVERT. DATE UNKNOWN.

FIG 12 DEATH BY DENIM: SUMMAT ADVERTISEMENT IN RURAL LIFE MAGAZINE, 1973.
–
REBECCA CHESNEY.

FIG 13 DEATH BY DENIM: LAKELAND SUN ARTICLE, 1973.
–
REBECCA CHESNEY.

FIG 14 DERELICT LAND ROVER, 2016.
–
REBECCA CHESNEY.

FIG 15 A DIFFICULT FOOTPATH IN THE PEAK DISTRICT, 2015.
–
ROSEMARY SHIRLEY.

FIG 16 DEAD SHEEP IN A STREAM, 2016.
–
REBECCA CHESNEY.

FIG 17 BREEZE ADVERT, 1952.

FIG 18 IN 2014 THE NATIONAL PARKS WORKED IN PARTNERSHIP WITH AIRWICK TO PRODUCE A SET OF AIR FRESHENERS THEMED AROUND THE UK'S NATIONAL PARKS. THE PEAK DISTRICT FRAGRANCE WAS SPRING BREEZE AND GOLDEN LILY.
–
ROSEMARY SHIRLEY.

FIG 19 PATH TO PEN Y FAN, BRECON BEACONS NATIONAL PARK, 2016.
–
REBECCA CHESNEY.

FIG 20 LIVE LIFE ON THE WILD SIDE: THE NATURAL SELECTION. ADVERT FOR A NEW RURAL HOUSING DEVELOPMENT, 2015.
–
ROSEMARY SHIRLEY.

FIG 21 FABRIC CONDITIONER, 2015.
–
ROSEMARY SHIRLEY.

FIG 22 SUPERMARKET SIGN WITH GAFFER TAPE REDACTIONS, 2015.
–
ROSEMARY SHIRLEY.

FIG 23 COUNTRYLIFE MADE EXCLUSIVELY WITH BRITISH MILK, 2015.
–
ROSEMARY SHIRLEY.

FIG 24 ENJOY THE COUNTRYSIDE WITHOUT LEAVING LONDON, 2015.
–
ROSEMARY SHIRLEY.

FIG 25 QUICK PERSPECTIVES OF THE FUTURE, 2015.
–
ROSEMARY SHIRLEY.

FIG 26 JODRELL BANK SEEN FROM THE TRAIN, 2012.
–
ROSEMARY SHIRLEY.

FIG 27 DERELICT TRACTOR, 2016.
–
REBECCA CHESNEY.

FIG 28 EXCEL CENTRE, LONDON DOCKLANDS, 2015.
–
ROSEMARY SHIRLEY.

FIG 29 BALES OF SILAGE IN THE LANDSCAPE, 2016.
–
REBECCA CHESNEY.

FIG 30 ADVERT FROM THE FESTIVAL OF BRITAIN TOURING PROGRAMME, 1951. LICENSED UNDER THE OPEN GOVERNMENT LICENSE V.2.0.

FIG 31 STONE GATE POST, 2015.
–
ROSEMARY SHIRLEY.

FIG 32 ROADS, RESERVOIRS AND PYLONS, 2015.
–
ROSEMARY SHIRLEY.

The Cul-de-Sac in the Forest: the Supermodernity of Center Parcs

Amelia Crouch
/
David Cooper

This collaborative essay is the product of conversations between artist Amelia Crouch and literary geographer David Cooper about the role of language within experiences of place. Their public event, *Vocal Landscapes: Bodies, Language and Place,* explored the intertextuality of space, place and landscape, through reference to David's research into the Post-Romantic literature of the Lake District and Amelia's use of text as a device for reframing or questioning the meanings of places. This text explores the mediating power of language and the influence of literary and digital culture upon our perceptions of the landscape, through a creative account of a holiday at a Center Parcs resort.

Whether to zoom in or to switch to Street View, clicking the mouse fulfills a two-thousand-year-old dream. (della Dora 2012: 4)

DROP PIN

54° 38' 23.2188" N 2° 39' 9.504" W

Okay, let's zoom in on our centre point. The location where we begin. A table, in a room in a leisure village in a landscape (don't worry, we'll come back to these) where right now nobody is about. Let's be nosey and take a look around. On the table there is a watch and a map. The watch has a large, round face and a well-worn leather strap. Its owner (let's guess) is male and middle aged. A family man; in fact, here with his family. He is not cheap nor flash; he is sturdy and middle-range. The watch is of a type that one might buy in any high-street department store but, through use and affection, becomes a personal item.

The map is even more generic; one of an often-repeated bulk print run. A sheet of A4 paper with a pseudo village spread out on its surface in muted technicolour. It has been folded, rolled and creased – in a back pocket perhaps. But now it's discarded.

Let's think about these items and why they have been left. It's a Thursday which, in our present circumstances, would count as being near the end of mid-week. The inhabitants (here since Monday) have learnt their way around, they have got their bearings and have made the transition from plan-every-moment-must-do-all-the-activities to a facsimile of laid-back holiday time.

◆

The first Center Parcs Village was opened in the Netherlands in 1968. A year – elsewhere in Europe – of turmoil and protest; but, at De Lommerbergen in Limburg, the emphasis was on retreat. The ethos then was on simple living with proximity to nature. Accommodation was basic and comforts were few. By 1987 the concept of the villa in the forest made its way to the UK with a first site established at Sherwood Forest. Over time, four more sites followed and, gradually, the holiday offer shifted towards the promise of a fully immersive leisure experience. Center Parcs' website today invites visitors to: 'enjoy staying in the forest without losing the comfort of modern furnished, stylish interior design' (Center Parcs 2017). According to Robert Pogue Harrison, forests exist in 'the shadow of civilization' (Harrison 1992). The Center Parcs experience, however, involves an ordering of that otherly space; 'award-winning Target Living-design' brings light into the gloom (Center Parcs 2017).

◆

'Here' – where we find ourselves now – is Center Parcs, Whinfell Forest. This Cumbrian Center Parcs came into being in 2001 when Center Parcs plc took over the site, just off the A66, from Bourne Leisure. Bourne, in turn, had, a few years previously, bought the complex from the Rank Group. Rank – a brand name more familiarly associated with the paradigmatic non-place of the motorway service station – was responsible for converting this Eden Valley site into its original leisure guise as the Oasis holiday park in 1997. 'Here', then, is a palimpsest of venture-capital-backed purchases; a piece of paradise which has been shaped by off-site transactions and off-the-peg toponyms.

One might argue that which Center Parcs we're visiting is neither here nor there. Sherwood in Nottinghamshire, Longleat in Wiltshire, Elveden in Suffolk, Woburn in Bedfordshire or Whinfell in Cumbria: holiday in any of the Parcs and the experience will be more or less the same. The geographically scattered sites come under a single website, advertised together, and activities are, on the whole, identical at each. Whinfell Forest is of particular interest, though, for its close proximity (as the Center Parcs website makes clear) to another destination: the 'picturesque' Lake District National Park; a land of 'lakes and streams aplenty' (Center Parcs 2017). Two sites, existing cheek by jowl, offering polarised tourist environments and experiences: the texturality of the wild versus the sanitisation of the secure site; the deep temporality of the uplands versus the shallow history of the commodified; the authentic versus the inauthentic.

But let's not get ahead of ourselves. First, let's look around the immediate locality.

LODGE

> *We attain to dwelling, so it seems, only by means of building. The latter, building, has the former, dwelling, as its goal. Still, not every building is a dwelling.* (Heidegger 1971: 145)

Booking a Center Parcs holiday involves (as its central and most expensive element) choosing your accommodation from a drop-down list of options. Our family – let's call them the Joneses – have plumped for a 'Woodland Lodge'.

Mrs Jones made the booking online. As she clicked through her options, she recalled that, once upon a time in the 1980s (before Whinfell Forest), Center Parcs' accommodations were dubbed 'chalets' and there was less differentiation between standard and luxury types. She wonders, was 'chalet' deemed as too 'Butlins', replaced by the now-favoured term 'Lodge'?

◆

'Lodge' is a noun with contradictory connotations. A gateway cottage, a moorland site for field sports, a porter's room at an Oxbridge college, a local branch of the Freemasons and a beaver's nest. Here it signifies both rustic remoteness and temporariness. The Joneses are lodgers, not residents. They are just passing through.

Michel de Certeau defines 'space' as 'a practiced place' which comes into being through quotidian acts and activities (1984: 117). That is to say, through performing daily habits, regular repeated bodily actions, we become a part of such locations and continually recreate them. But is a weekend, a mid-week break or, at most, a week-long holiday enough? Is place genuinely 'practiced', in de Certeau's terms, in this holiday park in the Eden Valley?

◆

In her own childhood visits to Center Parcs (Sherwood Forest), Mrs Jones took simple pleasure in the unfamiliarity of familiar things. New shapes, sensations and textures. A Pyrex plate (could plates be transparent?!) or a potato peeler of a kind never seen before. She was particularly taken with the inventory. She helped her dad check items off the list – four Pyrex bowls, four Pyrex mugs, eight pillows, one colander... They opened up cupboards, hunted and counted, checking all was present and nothing damaged.

In the 1980s the accommodation was bright red and white; boxy furniture and rough textures. Today all is slick and shiny or soft. As she pulls back her bed covers and slides under crisp, white sheets, she thinks: 'I am like the cutlery, slotting into place.' But where the cutlery, crockery and fixtures stay the same each week, the people continually change.

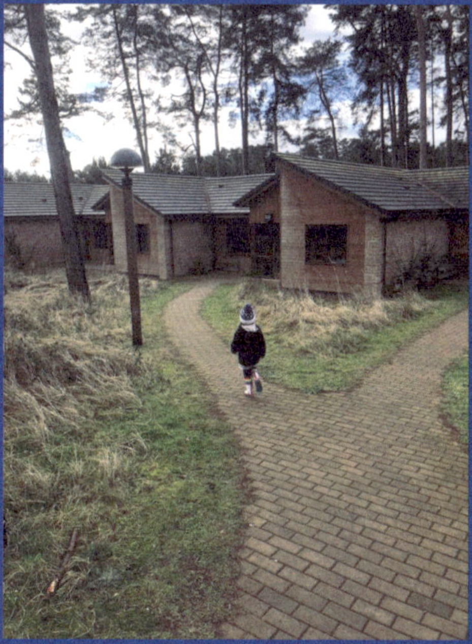

> *All that once was directly lived has become mere representation.* (Debord 1994: 12)

Our Lodge, at the moment, is empty. Let's enjoy the moment of luxury and quiet. The only sound is the ticking of the discarded watch. Sink into the sofa and turn on the flat-screen TV. Play a computer game, watch a film, book the week's activities remotely. The woodland is visible through a large glass, sliding door and mirrored also in the wallpaper of a 'feature wall' indoors. The outside is brought in. We don't have to leave if we don't want to.

Still the ticking is a niggling reminder of time passing, a call to schedule your leisure routine. Hour-by-hour, minute-by-minute. The days in the forest are shaped by the push and pull of technology-aided rest and pre-programmed physical hyperactivity.

◆

The Joneses have gone out, to make the most of the activities on their final day. Their youngest daughter is learning to swim. Imagine (as you relax on the sofa) the sensation of the water on her skin. A hand held to steady little feet on wet tiles and the rub of a towel. Their elder daughter is testing her boundaries on the 'High Ropes Challenge'. Weak knees and rough-rope scuffed hands.

Later tonight they will be back on the sofa – warmed by the glow of the day's achievements and their last ParcMarket-purchased slow-burning log – reviewing the week's activities with a swipe and a click on the iPad. The legacy of the week is a collection of photos and a collection of bruises (seven, at the last count, between them: most likely culprit, 'the rip-roaring Canyon Ride'). The bruises fade, as will the memories, but the photos solidify them in fixed smiles.

Later still, on their return from their holiday, they will encounter a friend – Mrs Smith – who scoffs at these photos (carefully framed and posed). 'I would never go to Center Parcs,' she says, and proclaims her own family holiday – beneath the timeless Pikes in Great Langdale – as somehow more real: 'We climbed a different fell each day and managed to do Crinkle Crags even quicker than last year.'

CUL-DE-SAC

> *...if what is called development is allowed to multiply at the present rate, then by the end of the century Great Britain will consist of isolated oases of preserved monuments in a desert of wire, concrete roads, cosy plots and bungalows. There will be no real distinction between town and country. Both will consist of a limbo of shacks, bogus rusticities, wire and aerodromes, set in some fir-poled fields... Its symptom will be... that the end of Southampton will look like the beginning of Carlisle; the part in between will look like the end of Carlisle or the beginning of Southampton.* (Nairn 1955: 365)

The Lodges are mostly arranged in not-quite cul-de-sacs: a suburban form translated to a sylvan setting. They differ from the strict definition of a cul-de-sac because, instead of dead ends, these short roads loop back on themselves in concession to the unfamiliar visitor (all roads lead back to where you came from or spit you out at a main route).

Though the 'Lodges' are all close to each other, they are carefully positioned and designed to minimise being overlooked. The use of cars on site is strictly policed as 'guests are only permitted to use their cars within the Village for unloading/loading at their accommodation on arrival and departure' (Center Parcs 2017). Lodges, therefore, remain quiet and secluded. Those who come down your road – on foot or on two wheels – are staying there or have mistaken this cul-de-sac for their own.

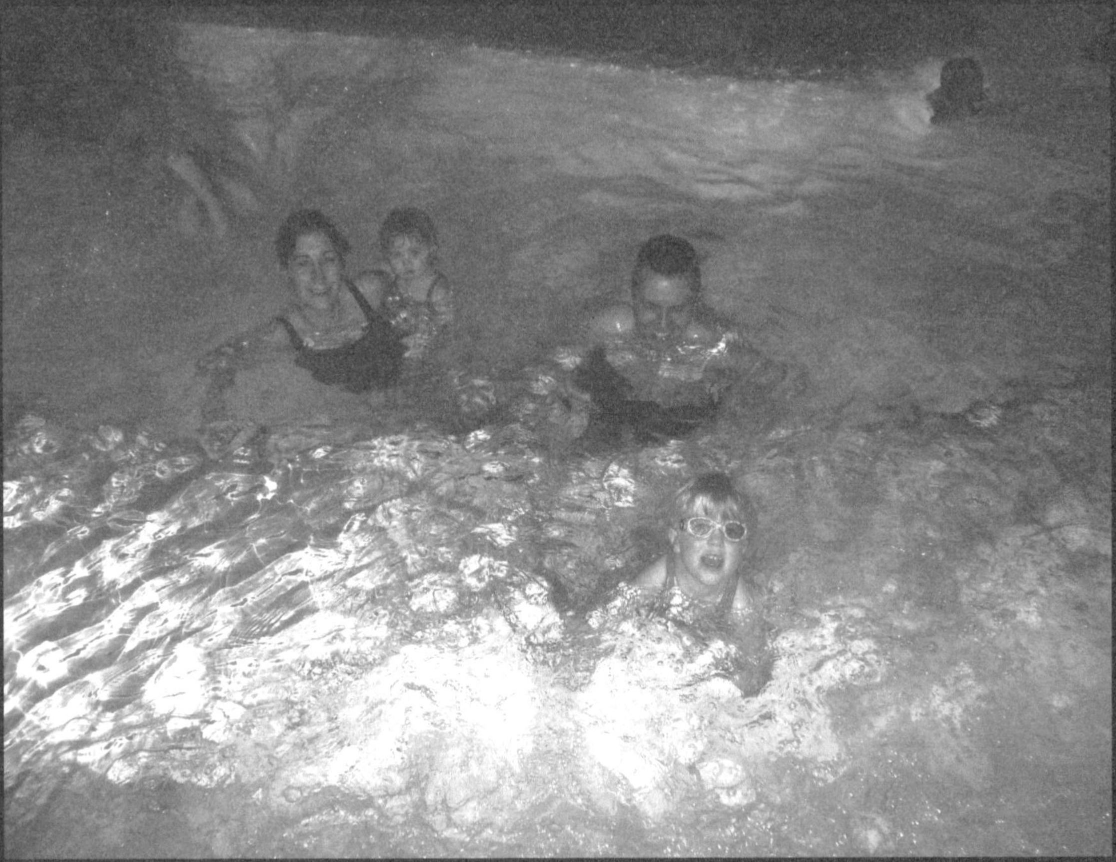

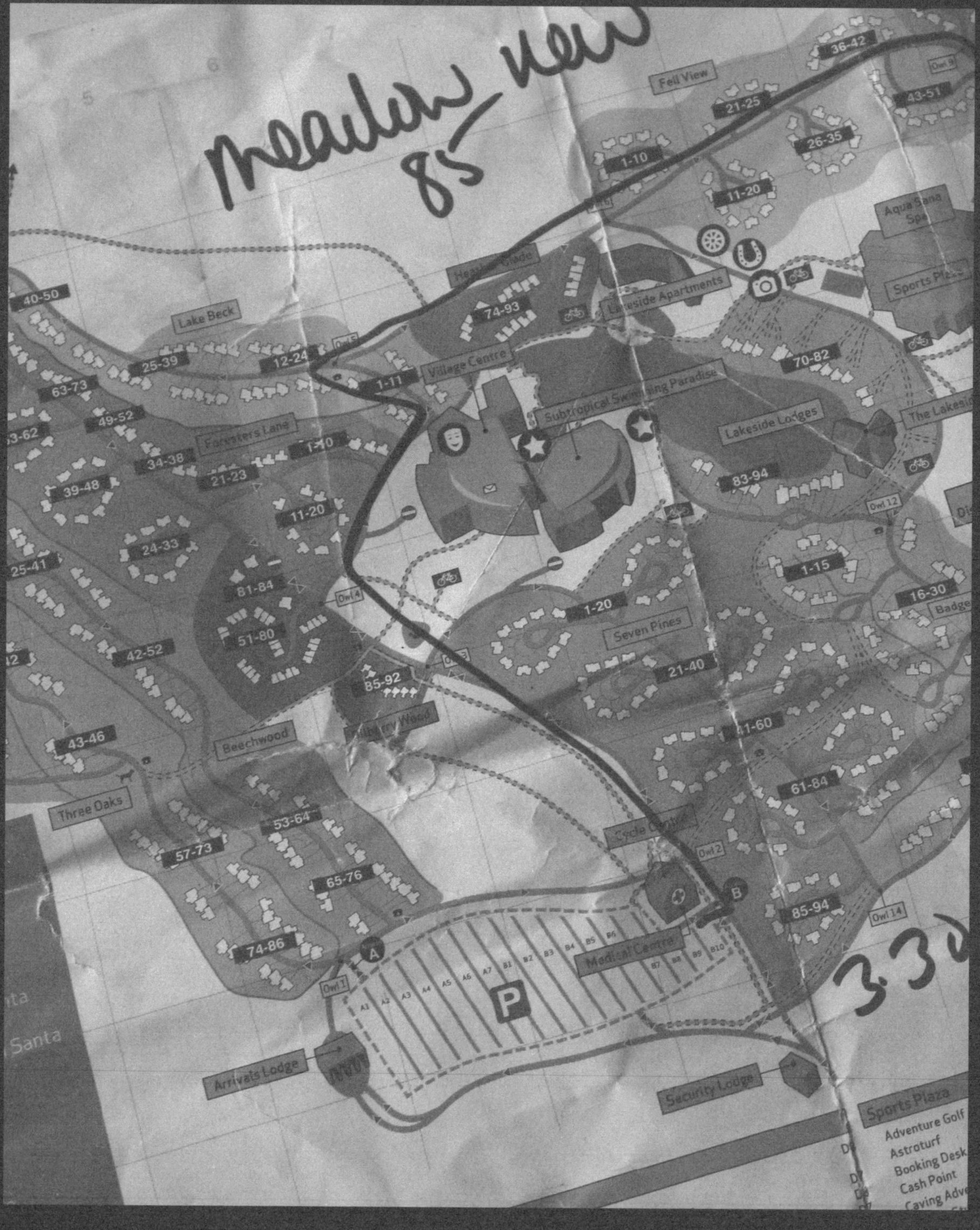
meadow view
85
3.30
Fell View
36-42
21-25
43-51
26-35
1-10
11-20
Aqua Sana Spa
Sports Plaza
Lakeside Apartments
40-50
Lake Beck
74-93
Village Centre
12-24
25-39
1-11
70-82
63-73
49-52
Subtropical Swimming Paradise
Foresters Lane
Lakeside Lodges
The Lakes
1-10
34-38
21-23
83-94
39-48
11-20
24-33
Owl 12
1-15
25-41
81-84
Owl 4
16-30
1-20
Seven Pines
51-80
42-52
21-40
85-92
41-60
43-46
Beechwood
Three Oaks
61-84
53-64
57-73
Owl 2
65-76
B
85-94
Owl 14
74-86
A
Medical Centre
Owl 1
P
Arrivals Lodge
Security Lodge
Sports Plaza
Adventure Golf
Astroturf
Booking Desk
Cash Point

> *The panorama-city is a 'theoretical' (that is, visual) simulacrum, in short a picture, whose condition of possibility is an oblivion and a misunderstanding of practices.*
> (de Certeau 1984: 93)

Each Lodge is modelled on a typical family home with a shared kitchen/dining/living area and accommodation for two, four, six or eight guests. Observational research (look around you and you'll start to see who is here) suggests that extended families (plus grandparents), blended families (permanently or just for the week) and friendship groups are common visitor configurations. The recent addition of lakeside apartments at Whinfell Forest suggests a changing or differentiated market: the list of 'best bits' which prefaces the online Google-powered virtual tour indicates that they are 'ideal for couples'; and the promise of both a 'daily maid service' and 'free wi-fi' might even appeal to the business traveller who has grown tired of the Premier Inn in downtown Penrith. Ultimately, however, the site seems to be primarily designed with families in mind.

◆

Earlier in the week, as they explored the site, Mr Jones commented to his wife on how Center Parcs recalled the garden-city ethos of the early 1900s. He lauded this vision for settled, happy communities and was pleased that he's heard something recently about plans to build 14 new garden villages around the country. 'New communities... new facilities... new jobs,' he delights.

Mrs Jones is more circumspect. She thinks to herself that communities have changed since the early 1900s and that there are those who won't benefit from this post-Brexit utopian vision. She looks around and listens to the voices of other visitors and notices that most are white and (apart from the staff) most accents are English. Is Center Parcs a utopian model of a possible future or a backward-looking nostalgia trip?

She keeps her thoughts to herself for the sake of a happy holiday.

◆

Beyond the cul-de-sac, Center Parcs is organised around a series of 'areas': 'central', 'middle' and 'outer' zones plus a few 'exclusive' enclaves dotted around the park. On the site map these areas are signified by colour-coded rings that fan out from the Village centre: pink and green for 'central' and 'middle'; orange for 'exclusive'; and a dispiriting 'grey' for those 'outer' zones on the periphery of the site. Space is structured yet further as hyper-bucolic sub-areas can be found in each of these zones: Meadow View, Three Oaks, Bilberry Wood or Heather Glade. The nomenclature is a spatial device; a mechanism to help orient your stay. The words are also reassuringly familiar, evoking the generic street-names which furnish the outer reaches of our towns and cities with a hint of the pastoral elsewhere. Seemingly, then, the faux rurality of the suburban has been folded back onto this woodland space.

Here, though, these places *do* have deeper histories, for we are standing in a forest.

Close your eyes and think further back in time... Like the rings of a tree that track back hundreds of years, imagine a time that exceeds us and these current dwellings.

THE VILLAGE

When staying at Whinfell Forest, visitors enter into a contract with Center Parcs plc. Let's read a selection of the 'terms and conditions' one must adhere to 'whilst on the Village'. ('Note: Important information, guidance and updates will be published on the TV (channel 6) in your accommodation and you should check for such information regularly'):

Your behaviour should not be excessive, noisy or disruptive, especially at night.

We may ask you and/or any member of your party to leave immediately if your conduct is considered by us to be inappropriate.

Only non-intrusive photography of your own party and friends is permitted. You may not carry out photography for commercial purposes.

Appropriate clothing and footwear should be worn at all times.

Only one dog is permitted per designated dog villa/lodge.

Please:

Keep to prepared roads, paths and tracks at all times.

Respect the environment, plants and animals.

Treat all property and facilities carefully and appropriately.

You must obey the speed limit on the Village.

Cyclists must give way to pedestrians.

Do not use a scooter, cycle, skateboard or rollerblades in any building or Village Square/Centre.

Do not enter or attempt to use any facility that is closed.

You may only use manufactured slow-burning logs, available in the ParcMarket, in accommodation fireplaces or stoves.

On departure you should leave your accommodation in a clean and tidy condition.

We reserve the right to charge you for any extra cleaning or missing items.

We reserve the right to enter your accommodation at any time for any reasonable purpose.

(CENTER PARCS 2017)

To dwell, in the terms offered by Martin Heidegger, is to be-in-the-world. The Center Parcs website, however, makes it clear that visitors are only ever '*on* the Village'.

> ***The link between individuals and their surroundings in the space of non-place is established through the mediation of words, or even texts.*** (Augé 2008: 76)

Words do things: they control behaviour, they set expectations. One expectation raised by the designation of Center Parcs as a 'Village' is that it will have a centre, and so it does. Here we find a collection of shops (gift shops, recognisable high-street clothing lines and the ParcMarket) plus restaurants and bars, and some of the site's activities – most notably the 'Subtropical Swimming Paradise'.

The words that hail attention in the Village centre are words that seduce, akin to terms like 'Tahiti', 'Marrakesh' or 'cruise' which preoccupy Marc Augé in *Non-Places*: words which, when uttered as prizes in TV game shows, are 'sufficient to give pleasure to viewers who have never won them and never will' (*ibid*: 77). Such words have a kind of specular quality; we might not be in 'paradise' but we can glimpse it, can imagine ourselves there.

Other words are actually images – brand-name logos with visual recognition. Prezzo, Starbucks, Café Rouge – all invite you to picture yourself enjoying a coffee or a pizza, perhaps a glass of wine. Your taste buds are piqued; yet it won't be gourmet, just reassuringly familiar.

Augé writes too of a peculiar quality of words in the 'real non-places of supermodernity'; they are instructions or prohibitions – like our terms and conditions – that are addressed 'simultaneously and indiscriminately to each and any of us' (*ibid*: 81).

BOUNDARY

Hire a bike for the day and you will soon discover that the site is not very big. An area that can seem huge when walking slowly with children shrinks rapidly when pedalling at a moderate speed. Reach the outer edges of the site and you will find a fence to keep out the non-paying, complete with CCTV and warning signs. As this is the end of the road, you turn around and cycle back towards the centre of the Village.

◆

Mr Jones heard a story from a friend of a friend about an improbable guest, forced to visit Center Parcs on a journalistic assignment. After a few drinks at Huck's American Bar and Grill, an unseemly row with his partner ensued. He attempted to walk out of the site in the early pitch-black hours. The Security Officer at the Arrivals Lodge, though, wouldn't let him leave. 'Where do you think you're going to go at this time of night?' With no other choice the guest turned around and made his way back to their Lodge at Moorland View.

For the Joneses, though, any sense of enclosure is of little consequence. They don't notice. They are happy in their constrained site. Or they do notice and don't mind. Mrs Jones thinks something philosophical about how all holidays have their limitations; all life is constrained in some way too.

> ***In the late 20th century, an ancient urban form began to reappear in modern settlements. Fortified and enclave developments have become an increasingly common feature of contemporary suburban building patterns. Older neighbourhoods in some cities are closing off streets to enhance local security and reduce traffic. In general, postmodern cities are becoming more defended, and more defensible, than were industrial cities.***
> (Grant and Mittlestead, 2004: 913)

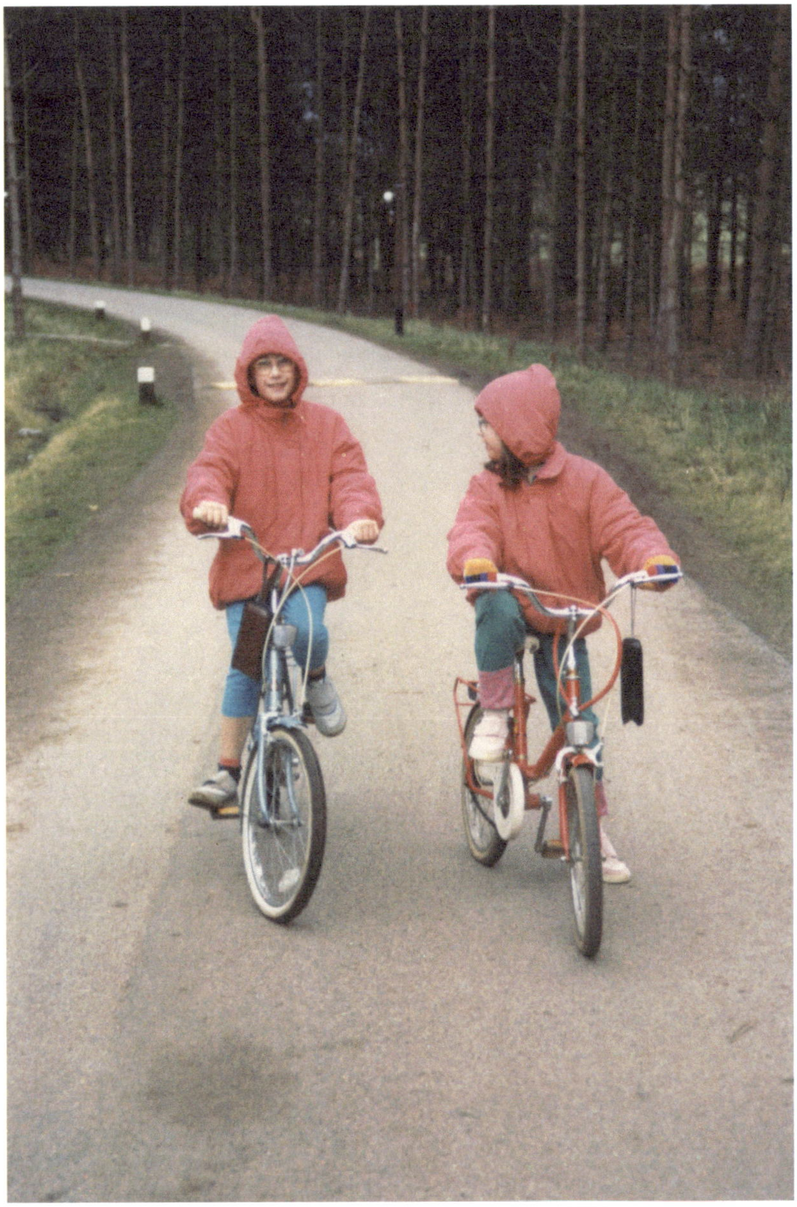

So, we've reached the edge of the site. It's time to change tactics, to try and look at the Village from the outside in. Take the Jones's car and leave by the main exit. As long as you're on wheels, the Security Officer should let you leave.

Drive the long way round: back towards Penrith, across the river at Eamont Bridge, along the straight road to the south of the Parc and then left at Cliburn to head up into Salter Wood. From here we hoped you'd catch a glimpse of the Village but it's carefully concealed deep within the trees. Eventually, though, you spot a gate – padlocked, of course. Pull over and go for a short walk alongside what you'll now make out to be the perimeter fence. A permissive footpath takes you along the north-eastern edge of the site and you are able to look across to the outermost Lodges. Everything is uncomfortably still: it's the middle of the day so you suspect that most visitors have headed out of their Lodges and towards the centre of the Village. Every so often you hear a shout from the Subtropical Swimming Paradise, but there's a disconcerting lack of movement on the other side of the fence.

You look up and realise that the CCTV is focusing on you.

THE FOREST

> *We gather from mythology that their [the forests'] vast and somber wilderness was there before, like a precondition or matrix of civilization, or that... the forests were first.*
> (Harrison 1992: 1)

There has been a forest here, in this corner of the parish of Brougham, for at least 800 years. At one point, Whinfell would have formed part of a great Cumberland forest stretching from the Irish Sea to the Pennines, from the border city of Carlisle to the northern fringes of the Lake District: a dense woodscape of game and poachers, outlaws and myth-makers, which included the great Inglewood Forest. Today, Whinfell Forest is Lowther land[1] and a large part of it is designated by Natural England as Ancient Replanted Woodland.

◆

According to Harrison, forests cast 'a shadow of primeval antiquity', appearing archaic and 'antecedent to the human world' (1992: 1). In myths and literature from the ancient past to the present day, the forest is frequently presented as 'other'. Wilderness cast against civilisation, nature against human culture.

Whinfell itself has made a minor contribution to Cumbria's richly layered literary history. The Forest is mentioned in the diaries of Lady Anne Clifford: the 17th-century High Sheriff of Westmorland. And an oak tree from Whinfell Forest provides the arboreal focus for a sonnet by William Wordsworth: 'Hart's-Horn Tree, Near Penrith' (1835).

The poem recounts the fate of a stag and a greyhound:

> *Both sank and died, the life-veins of the chased*
> *And chaser bursting here with one dire smart.*
> (Wordsworth 1936: 310)

1. PART OF AN EXTENSIVE ESTATE OWNED AND MANAGED BY THE LOWTHER FAMILY: THE LARGEST PRIVATE LANDOWNER IN CUMBRIA.

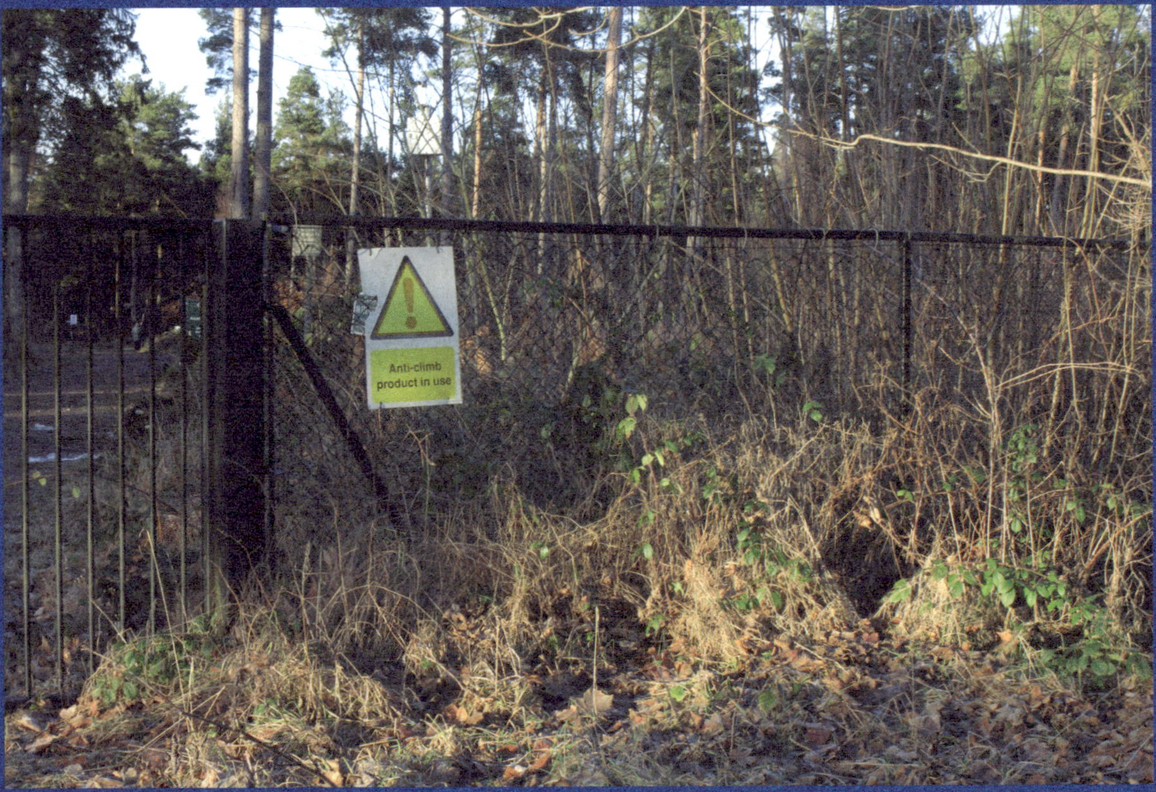
Anti-climb
product in use

As the poet acknowledges in a note, the tree's relevance had earlier been identified by Nicholson and Burn in their *History and Antiquities of Westmoreland and Cumberland* (1777): 'In memory [of their deaths] the stag's horns were nailed upon a tree just by' (Wordsworth 1936: 718).

Wordsworth's late poem – commemorating the 'pitiless' (*ibid*: 310) waste generated in the name of sport – suggests that a tension between the forest as wild nature, economic resource and human playground is longstanding. Even when casting the forest as wilderness, then, we do so, ultimately, to reflect back on ourselves.

◆

These local literary references are lost on the Joneses, but they too know the ambivalent allure of the forest, featured in fairy stories: Hansel and Gretel, Little Red Riding Hood and The Tinderbox.

They had not thought much about the forest before they arrived. Like the feature wall in their Lodge, it was seen – at first – as just a backdrop. But the children love it: the smell, the crunch of fallen bark and leaves trampled as they walk. They learn that the forest is a conservation area dominated by Scots Pine and Norway Spruce; they observe fat, almost tame, animals and try to spot more elusive red squirrels. The elder Jones child claims to have seen a flash of red dashing up a tree, but on the whole the week is dominated by greys. No matter. They understand – implicitly at least – the forest as a place of imagination, of possibilities. They inhabit it only briefly, yet its charm and mystique exceeds their individual lifetimes.

BEACON HILL

54° 40' 30.526'' N 2° 44' 38.039'' W

In *The Practice of Everyday Life*, de Certeau is critical of the 'imaginary totalisations' created by celestial vantage points because they ignore the ground-level activities that cumulatively create place and which carry the potential to resist the hegemonic planning of space (1984: 92). Yet looking down from above can also be useful. High places allow us to develop a greater sense of a whole; they enable us to locate ourselves within wider fields.

So, let's pull back from the forest and enter 'map view', zoom out further and travel slightly to the north-west. It's time to leave the Joneses to enjoy the rest of their stay.

◆

Five miles from Whinfell Forest we find ourselves hovering above the summit of Beacon Hill, a small fell that overlooks the town of Penrith. It's a location of long strategic significance. The tower on the summit was built in 1719 on the site of earlier signal fires that warned of attack from Scotland; and it was last in serious use during a Napoleonic invasion scare at the beginning of the 19th century.

Our primary concern or point of reference in relation to the fell, though, is William Wordsworth. His grandparents, the Cooksons, lived in Penrith, and Beacon Hill – known variously as Fell or Pike – had a prominent place in the poet's imaginative topography. When *we* imagine the Lake District now, Wordsworth – whether we realise it or not – influences the way we see.

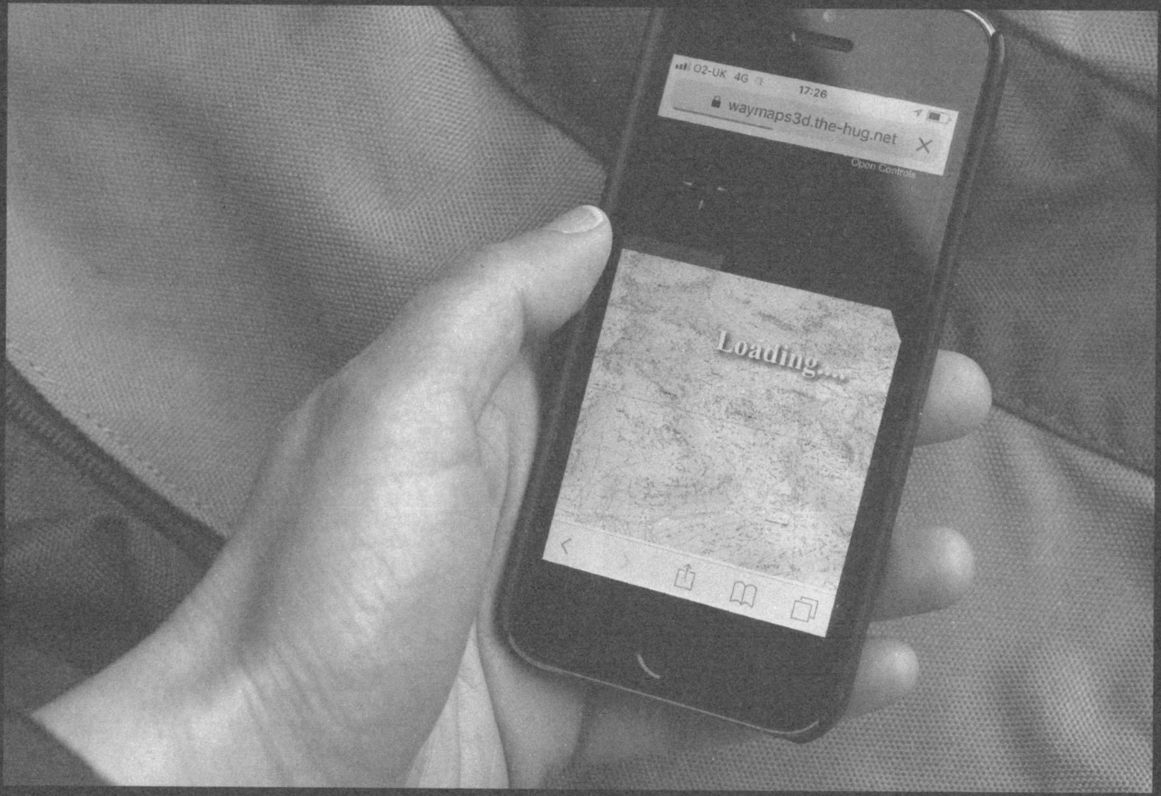
O2-UK 4G
17:26
waymaps3d.the-hug.net
Open Controls
Loading...

Wordsworth grew up in and around the Lake District and returned to the area – to Dove Cottage on the edge of Grasmere – in December 1799. When we read his poems, we experience the Cumbrian landscape – its 'rocks, and stones, and trees' (1936: 149) through his eyes. Yet Wordsworth did more than depict the place. The National Trust – which owns around a quarter of the land in the Lake District – was formed out of the Wordsworth Society at the tail end of the 19th century. When the National Park was established in the 1940s, it was Wordsworth's *Guide to the Lakes* which helped the planners figuratively beat the boundaries. The Lake District is a cultural landscape, a textualised topography in which the well-worn footpaths remind us – if we momentarily avert our gaze from the summit up ahead – that we're following circumscribed routes.

Center Parcs – a forest of signs – appears more culturally over-determined than the wild uplands of the Lake District. Yet the protected, privileged space of the Lake District is similarly constructed through a knotty network of practices and representations.

> *It is widely thought that at particular times in specific spaces, too many people are drawn into the Lake District and that as a result the enjoyment and pleasure of many visitors is reduced. [The] problem, of overcrowding and consequential surveillance and regulation, is particularly acute in the area.* (Urry 1995: 197)

Remember Mrs Smith (friend of Mr and Mrs Jones)? Let's take a brief detour via her family holiday. In Mrs Smith's mind, what the Lake District offers is an authentic experience of nature; an opening up to geological time. To prepare for their walking holiday in the Langdale valley, the Smith family purchased a new rucksack, hiking sticks and OS Explorer OL7 map (Mr Smith knows they have bought this map before but frustratingly cannot find it). All the accoutrements needed to experience the outdoors.

In the event, they did not use the map very much because they also discovered some handy route PDFs from a website called 'Walk Lakes': 'These narrative walks ("turn left at the stile, continue ahead to the stream") make navigation so much easier. You know you're always on the right path.' Their teenaged son teased them for pre-downloading and printing out the routes: 'Surely,' he said 'there's a walking app?' But then his attempts to enliven the walk by chatting to friends on WhatsApp were thwarted by the patchy reception on Crinkle Crags. Instead, he took selfies to upload later using the free wi-fi at the self-styled 'traditional Lakeland inn' near to their campsite.

> *The individual, finally, is decentered in a sense from himself. He has instruments that place him in constant contact with the remotest parts of the outside world. Portable telephones are also cameras, able to capture still or moving images; they are also televisions and computers. The individual can thus live rather oddly in an intellectual, musical or visual environment that is wholly independent of his immediate physical surroundings.*
> (Augé 2008: viii)

We will finish, then, on Beacon Hill. A low summit, a small peak. Come down from the sky, from the digital or imagined realm, and stand with us next to the Beacon. Plant your feet on solid earth. For this piece of writing this liminal location was a starting point.

Let us tell you how it began.

We (the writers David and Amelia) walked out of the town (Penrith) on a cold January afternoon. We walked past the solid, sandstone properties on Wordsworth Street and followed the path up to the top. There we turned our backs on the detritus of the evening before, which littered the foot of the tower, and looked left and found the mid-winter foliage blocked our view.

We looked right and were blocked again.

Wordsworth's poetry is full of disappointments: places unvisited; opportunities missed; epiphanies unfulfilled. We hoped Beacon Fell would provide a vantage point to look both east (to Center Parcs) and west (to the Lake District). We planned to pen a piece of writing here that would allow us to compare both places. But in an anti-climax worthy of the poet, we could see neither, let alone both. We walked up Beacon Hill with a culturally determined sense of what we wanted and needed to see. The trees, though, got in the way. Forced to shift our perspective – we could not write from the point of view of an individual (or duo) standing on this hill – so we stole a method from Georges Perec (1997). Start at a chosen point and zoom out.

◆

Here we are again standing on the Fell, now with you our reader. Still blocked by the trees, we see nothing beyond them, but we know what is behind their branches: to the west the seemingly timeless hills; to the east our holiday 'paradise' nestled in the forest. Both locations are romantic and romanticised, continually created and recreated. Our predetermined, and polarised, senses of these locations no longer hold.

As we can't see through the trees, we focus instead on the twisted branches that prevent the long view and think about entanglements: sylvan suburbs and digitised uplands; over-determined National Parks and commercialised conservation areas.

As we turn around, to take one last look at the Beacon, the sound of a curlew breaks through the white noise of the M6 and we get ready to leave.

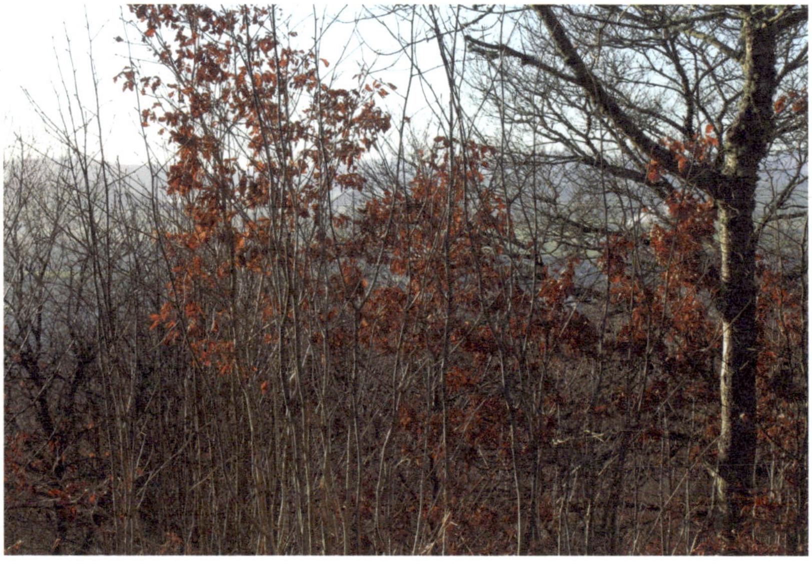

AUGÉ M (2008)
Non-Places: Introduction to an Anthropology of Supermodernity (trans. J Howe).
London: Verso Books.

CENTER PARCS (2017)
Center Parcs.
Accessed on 15·6·18 at: centerparcs.co.uk

DEBORD G (1994)
The Society of the Spectacle (trans. D Nicholson-Smith).
New York: Zone Books.

DE CERTEAU M (1984)
The Practice of Everyday Life (trans. S. Rendall).
Berkeley: University of California Press.

DELLA DORA V (2012)
'A world of "slippy maps": Google Earth, global visions, and topographies of memory.'
Transatlantica 2, 1–28.

GRANT J AND MITTLESTEADT L (2004)
'Types of gated communities.'
Environment and Planning B: Planning and Design 31, 913–30.

HARRISON RP (1992)
Forests: The Shadow of Civilization.
Chicago: University of Chicago Press.

HEIDEGGER M (1971)
'Building Dwelling Thinking.'
In *Poetry, Language, Thought* (trans. A Hofstadter).
New York: Harper & Row. pp.145–61.

NAIRN I (1955)
Outrage.
London: Architectural Press.

PEREC G (1997)
Species of Spaces and Other Writings (trans. J Sturrock).
London: Penguin.

URRY J (1995)
Consuming Places.
London: Routledge.

WORDSWORTH W (1936)
Poetical Works.
Oxford: Oxford University Press.

Ruth Levene / Ian Nesbitt / Bob Johnston

Over eight days in February 2013, artists Ian Nesbitt and Ruth Levene walked the extent of Sheffield's city boundary. They kept a textual and visual diary about the walk, and from this they produced a film and curated an exhibition at Sheffield's Bloc Gallery. Two years later, the arts organisation In Certain Places gave them the opportunity to walk Preston's boundary as part of its programme, The Expanded City. Ruth and Ian conceived of this walk as 'live research'.

The conversation that follows is a reflection on these walks in collaboration with a landscape archaeologist, Bob Johnston. The conversation was held across two events, one in Bloc Gallery and the other in Newcastle upon Tyne as part of Practising Place. This published version retains the themes and broad structure of the events by making the distinction between Connections (the focus in Sheffield) and Disconnections (Newcastle). The conversation explores how Ian, Ruth and Bob's practices, as artists and an archaeologist, forge links between disparate ideas of placemaking, infrastructure, mapping, pilgrimage, history and the precarious countryside.

In a circle

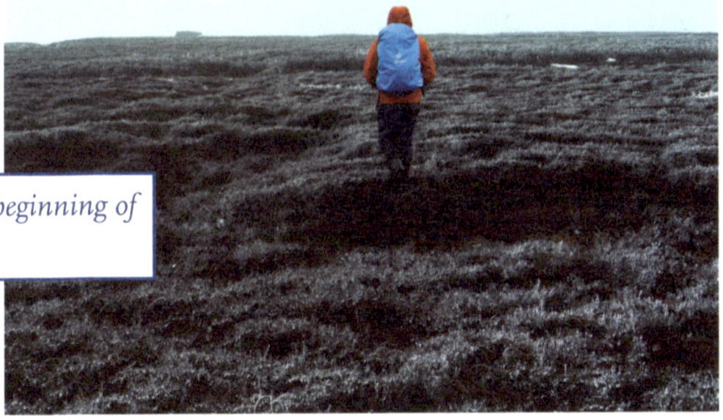

BOB *So, what got you to the beginning of your Sheffield walk?*

IAN We had both recently moved to Sheffield and I think we were at points in our work where we needed to stop and interrogate and consider the next steps. Having known each other's work for some time, it began as a series of impromptu studio conversations about repositioning ourselves as artists in a new city. I had just completed a month-long journey down the St. Michael's ley line which became my film *Taking the Michael*. So, I was rolling around ideas of walking, landscape and pilgrimage but I didn't know where it would take me.

RUTH I was thinking a lot about land use, farming and large-scale physical infrastructure. At the same time, I was also questioning how my role and responsibilities as an artist differed from my role as a citizen. As an artist I had a voice, a privilege to make work about whatever I wanted. It became more and more important to me that the work I made questioned and shone a light on the increasingly urgent issues I experienced around me as a citizen.

I remember spending lots of time in the studio talking and in the end getting quite frustrated that the environment we were in wasn't conducive to doing anything – we were talking in circles. Finally, frustrated, we decided to just go for a walk.

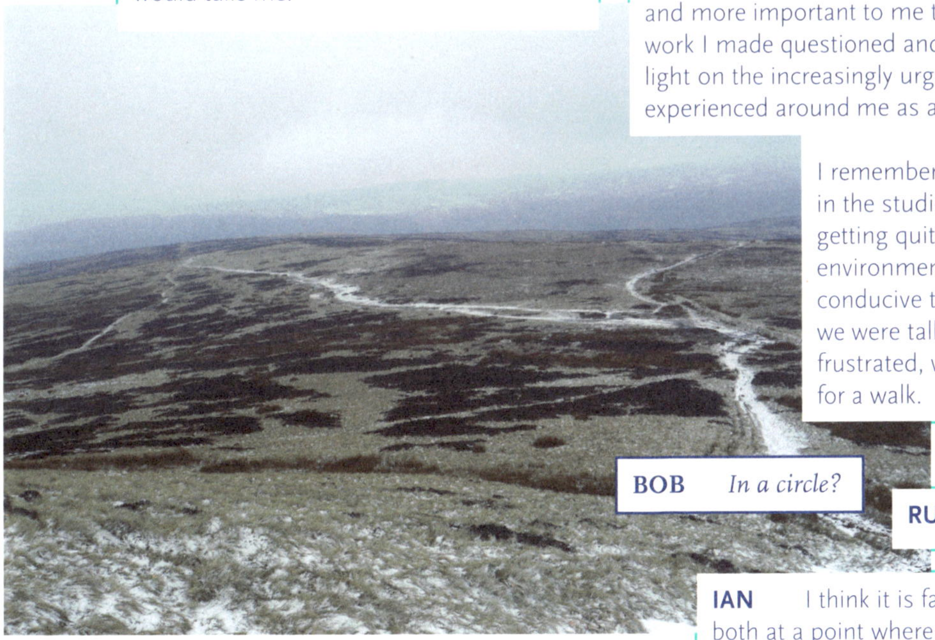

BOB *In a circle?*

RUTH In a circle.

IAN I think it is fair to say we were probably both at a point where we were, for different reasons, dissatisfied with being artists. We set out on this with no goals at all, no funding and no support, just as something to do. It felt like a quite a simple and freeing act.

ALL IMAGES BY RUTH LEVENE AND IAN NESBITT

Connections

RUTH I have used mapping and maps in my practice for many years. I have always been interested in their contradictions, even the obvious idea of transforming three dimensions into two, and the decisions you must make to do that. With The Boundary Walk I was particularly interested in the oddities created by comparing the bureaucratic or administrative map on paper and the human experience of being in the land. We went into the landscape to look for nothing so to speak, there were no paths on the ground to mark the boundary line. There was a ridiculousness and joy in walking this way, for example we would come to a field and there was a clear path, but, oh no, we weren't allowed to follow it. We had to go across the hedge, down a steep bank, into and then follow a stream. It really reinforced the disjunction between the person in the office organising the systems and the experience on the ground. You start to get a quite bizarre and tangible sense of how we order the land. It builds up as a unique story, you form a new relationship with the land because you are walking where you would not normally walk.

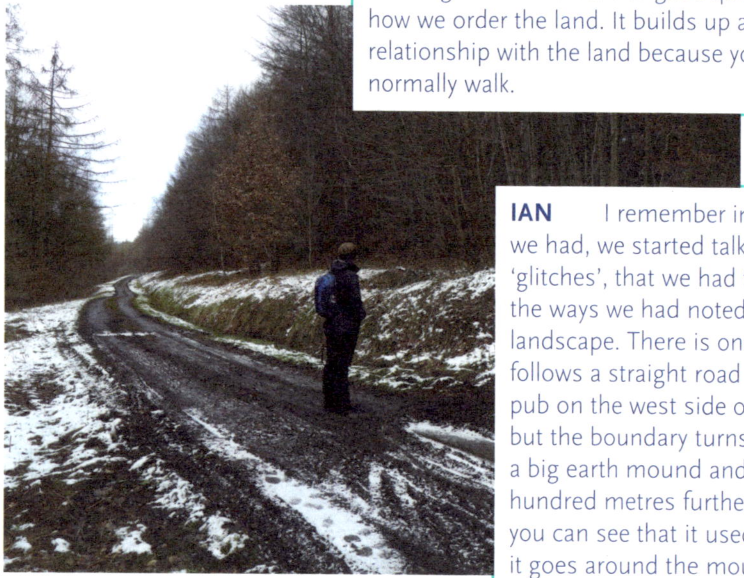

IAN I remember in one of the first conversations we had, we started talking about the oddities, or 'glitches', that we had found in the boundary and the ways we had noted some of these glitches in the landscape. There is one point where the boundary follows a straight road down towards the Fox House pub on the west side of Sheffield. The road carries on but the boundary turns off the road and goes around a big earth mound and rejoins the road a couple of hundred metres further on. There is a vague path and you can see that it used to be a road. You can see that it goes around the mound rather than over the mound because it is flatter and that used to be the line of the road but isn't anymore because they straightened it.

RUTH We didn't think we were actually walking on the road, we just thought we were walking on grass. And then when we looked down and looked more deeply at it, we realised, 'Oh god, this is a road.'

It is like a hole in the landscape, isn't it? Where the boundary hasn't clipped to the new line of the road, which it presumably will eventually.

BOB *It is just these glitches that interest me as a landscape archaeologist. They illustrate how landscapes preserve a history of humans' use of the land. In the case of the glitch at Fox House, I looked at the 1880's ordnance survey map and it depicts just what you thought: the strange wiggle follows the former, now almost invisible, road. One thing you cannot see on the maps and you can see on the ground is that the earlier road curves because the mound in its path was a working quarry, which went out of use before the map was drawn.*

There is another strange wiggle in the boundary close by on the moorland. This is where it diverted around the fields of a long-abandoned farm.

The shapes the boundary takes today are, yes, an administrative product. But they are also a product of the history of the landscape and how it was used, categorised and imagined. There are memories of that history preserved in the line of the present-day boundary. The boundary is constituted by its history.

IAN It is interesting that as an archaeologist you recognise this richer, historical character to the boundary. Our assumption was that it held no meaning for anyone, other than purely administrative. I came to the project thinking about ley lines and pilgrimage routes. Whether you believe that ley lines exist or not, they are established lines in the landscape with certain spiritual connections. When you are travelling on a route like that, you cannot help but feel connected to its history. I think it is natural that if you want to build mythologies about a place then you are going to choose a place that does not already have mythologies. For us, the boundary line did not have a story. It did not have a mythology as such, it was purely bureaucratic. It was purely infrastructure: that's one postcode, that's another, that's one more. For me, part of what we were doing with that first boundary walk was giving stories to the line that we were following.

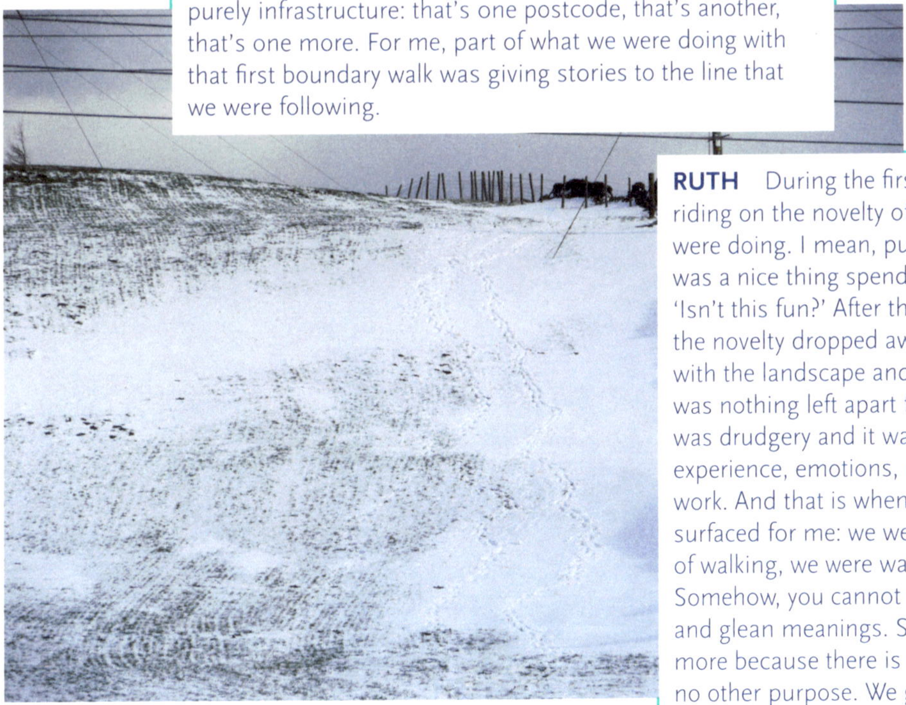

RUTH During the first few days, we were riding on the novelty of the idea of what we were doing. I mean, putting it crudely, it was a nice thing spending the day walking: 'Isn't this fun?' After those first few days, the novelty dropped away and we were left with the landscape and hard work. There was nothing left apart from walking, and it was drudgery and it was just relentless: an experience, emotions, rawness and physical work. And that is when the idea of pilgrimage surfaced for me: we were walking for the sake of walking, we were walking for the journey. Somehow, you cannot then help but create and glean meanings. Stuff starts to mean more because there is nothing else, there is no other purpose. We got really obsessed with the path surface!

BOB *When you could find one.*

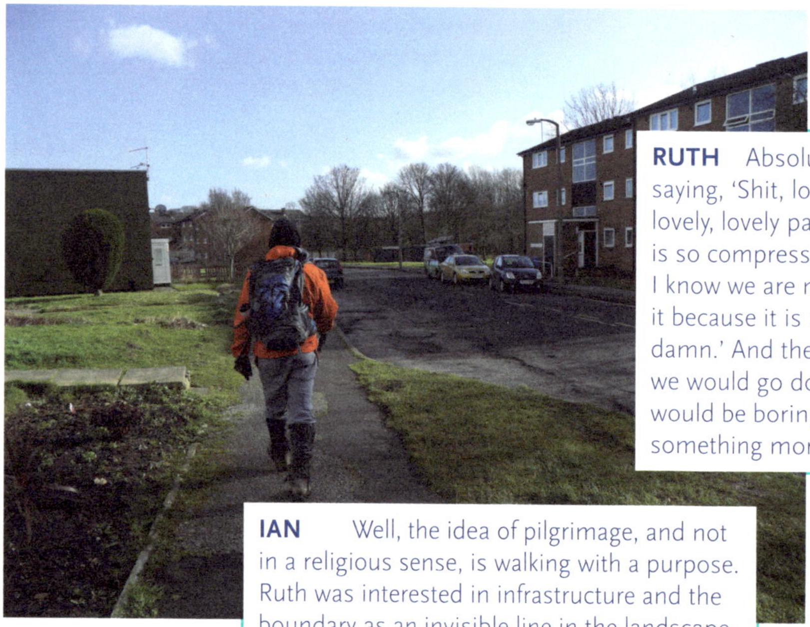

RUTH Absolutely. We were saying, 'Shit, look at that really lovely, lovely path over there. It is so compressed, it is smooth. I know we are not going down it because it is not on our route, damn.' And then later in the walk we would go down one and it would be boring and I wanted something more challenging.

IAN Well, the idea of pilgrimage, and not in a religious sense, is walking with a purpose. Ruth was interested in infrastructure and the boundary as an invisible line in the landscape that did not really mean anything unless you were a person that had to work with that line. And I was there from this other angle, with walking as this central activity. So we always conceived of the walk with the ideas of pilgrimage and infrastructure completely opposing one another: pure bureaucracy on the one hand and antiscience on the other.

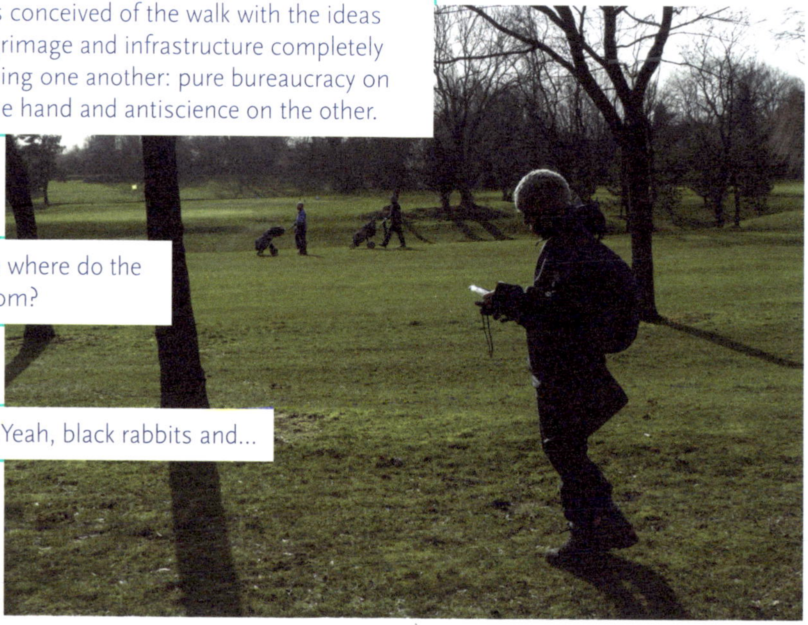

RUTH Antiscience – like where do the wild black rabbits come from?

IAN ...Yeah, black rabbits and...

RUTH The weird shit?

IAN Yeah.

BOB *I am intrigued by the way you use pilgrimage to give meaning to the walk and to the infrastructure of the boundary. From my disciplinary perspective, I recognise quite a strong relationship between the material and the spiritual in pilgrimage. Self-evidently, pilgrimage has spiritual and philosophical dimensions to it, but pilgrimage also creates and relies upon a lot of infrastructure. Pilgrims follow routes and by the act of pilgrimage they make those routes more important – more solid. There are refuges, villages and towns built to serve the pilgrims. There are objects associated with pilgrimage, such as tokens and walking staffs. Pilgrimage can have a huge impact on the character of the landscape and on what pilgrims wear and carry to identify themselves. The more literal connection that I drew with your walks was with the practice of 'beating the bounds'. This is a long tradition of marking a boundary by perambulating around its extent. In England, beating the bounds originates in the pre-Conquest period (the later first millennium AD) and it remained an important religious ceremony until at least the 16th century. The procession was part of the Rogationtide ceremonies, which took place around Ascension Day. A cross was carried around the boundary of the parish, accompanied by the priest and a group of young and old parishioners. Prayers would be said at points along the route and the priest would bless the fields. Even with the Reformation, which took out some of the religious connotations, beating the bounds retained its importance, certainly on a secular level. And it continues to happen in some areas of the country.*

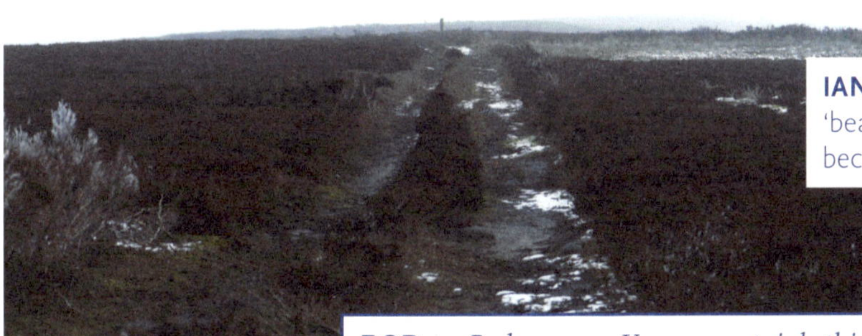

IAN Why did people begin 'beating the bounds'? Was it because of the lack of maps?

BOB *Perhaps, yes. You can certainly think of it as a way to delimit the parish and for the young in a community to learn its extents. A thousand years ago mapping was conceived in a different way to how we understand it now. Boundaries were described in texts as linear narratives, rather than depicted as measured geometric shapes. Anglo-Saxon charters, for example, describe territorial extents as though you are walking along them. The text describes the boundary as the path it follows and the landmarks it meets along the way, such as track junctions or burial mounds. The boundary was conceptualised as a linear narrative and it was then marked and people were reminded of its existence by walking around it once a year. Beating the bounds is very much tied to our sense of region, our sense of place, and how a community forms itself and reminds itself of who it is and where it is in the landscape. I think this takes us back to where you started, relatively new to Sheffield and wanting to know what Sheffield was or is and how you could be a part of Sheffield. It intrigues me that what you then chose to do, without any real reference to that earlier tradition, was to set about walking Sheffield's bounds.*

Disconnections

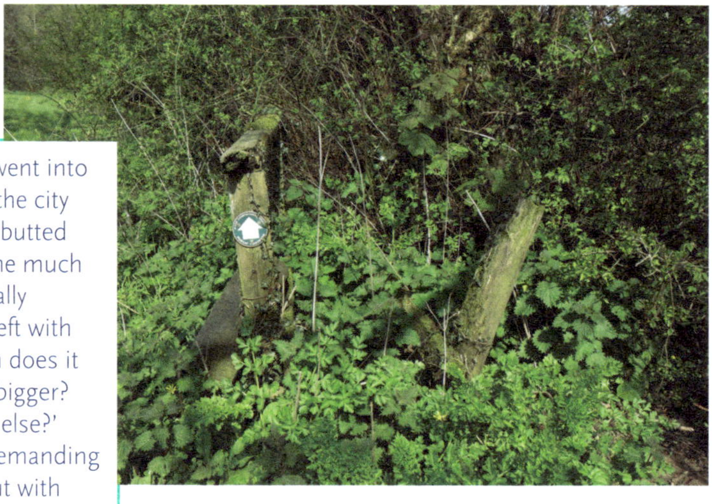

RUTH After the Sheffield boundary walk, we went into the archives and looked at maps showing how the city had expanded and at what points it stopped or butted up against something else. In Preston, it became much more apparent that when the city grows, it literally subsumes a village into itself. And then, I was left with the questions, 'Where does the city stop? When does it stop? When does it stop becoming bigger and bigger? And when does it stop and become something else?' Unlike the sometimes painful, arduous, cold, demanding journey in Sheffield, the Preston walk started out with gentle undulations on hot, sunny days leaving us with a sense that this would be a walk in the park, quite literally at times. This turned out to be far from the case. In fact, by the end and despite the blue skies, it had become a precarious adventure akin to a political act.

IAN The Sheffield and Preston walks were very different for a lot of reasons. For one thing, the whole of the west of Sheffield is enshrined in a National Park. This means that the landscape is going to stay the same to a much greater extent than in Preston, which is a much more precarious, or maybe you could say endangered, landscape. We were working in Preston as part of The Expanded City programme, which is concerned with large swathes of new housing across the northern and north-western sides of the city. It is a big change on the edges of the city and, obviously, to the infrastructure in those areas.

...

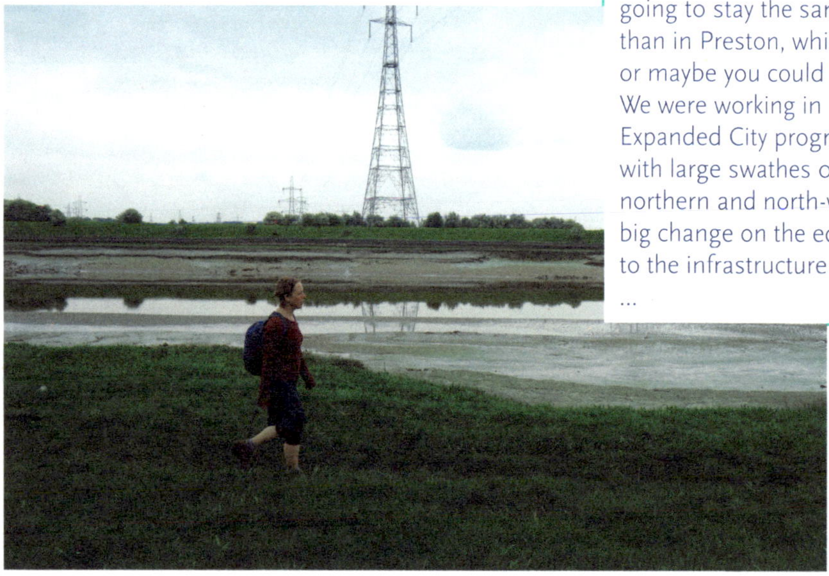

Another big change which happened after we finished the walk is that the proposed fracking sites on the boundary have been approved. Those places, too, are soon going to look very different. Also, on a more day-to-day level, the footpaths we walked in the agricultural land around Preston were very often deliberately or not so deliberately obstructed in ways that we did not come across in Sheffield. Other important differences between Sheffield and Preston were that we were visitors in Preston – it isn't our city – and that we were undertaking a boundary walk for the second time. ...

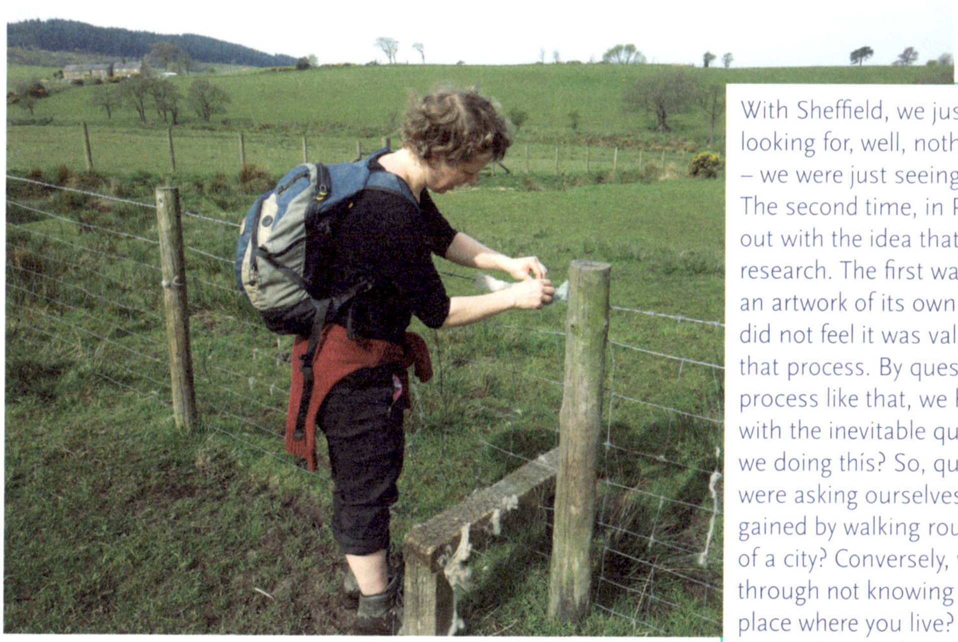

With Sheffield, we just stepped out looking for, well, nothing in particular – we were just seeing what we found. The second time, in Preston, we set out with the idea that it was a piece of research. The first walk had become an artwork of its own right, and we did not feel it was valid to just repeat that process. By questioning our process like that, we had to grapple with the inevitable question – why are we doing this? So, quite quickly, we were asking ourselves what is to be gained by walking round the boundary of a city? Conversely, what do you lose through not knowing the edges of the place where you live? Not being able to stand on the boundary and look out and look in, and walk around it and see the city from every angle. Then we are back to beating the bounds.

BOB *So do the limits of our senses of community and our senses of place lie at the edges of what we can reasonably perambulate? Perhaps, once a city gets too large for us to take it on as a circular walk, it loses some of its meaning for us as individuals.*

IAN Except, in the larger of the two cities, Sheffield, the countryside seems more cherished. In Preston, the landscape feels extremely vulnerable, despite the boundary being shorter.

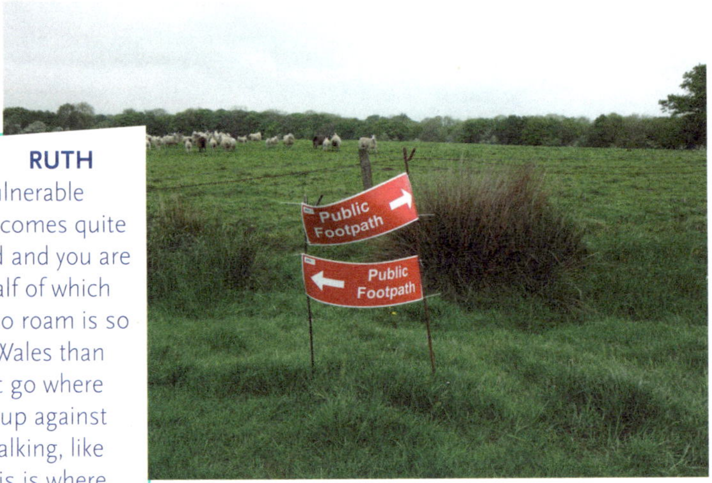

RUTH

It is very apparent how vulnerable this walking infrastructure can be. It becomes quite saddening because there is all this land and you are legally restricted to very small paths, half of which have been closed off to you. The right to roam is so much more restricted in England and Wales than Scotland. I cannot go anywhere, I must go where this path tells me. And then you come up against what I call superhighways for leisure walking, like the Trans Pennine Trail. You are told this is where you 'do leisure', this is the compressed path, this is the nice landscape around you and this is where you park the car and buy your coffee. Don't get me wrong, they make areas much more accessible and encourage walking, which of course is great, but they are also heavily manufactured, managed and to some extent commercialised, almost how I imagine the boundary line would manifest if it were to exist as a real-life path. This conflict is what intrigues me about physical infrastructure: by building a path and creating a route you set in stone (or tarmac) the course and direction people take and at the same time close off so much. I think in Preston that became apparent because so many of the footpaths through the farms were either neglected or, in many cases, actively blocked. We came across barbed wire wrapped around stiles and fences put up next to the stile to block the path. The vulnerability of the footpaths is made more apparent by the fact that footpaths on the original register, that is before 1949, must be re-registered by 1 January 2026 to still exist. If they haven't been walked and re-registered, a huge swathe of footpaths will disappear. And, in one sense, that does not matter if you live in those places and you do not feel like the footpaths can take you anywhere. From another perspective, the paths are living arteries in the land and they are vital for the blood to flow. What happens if you block these arteries? What do you stop seeing?

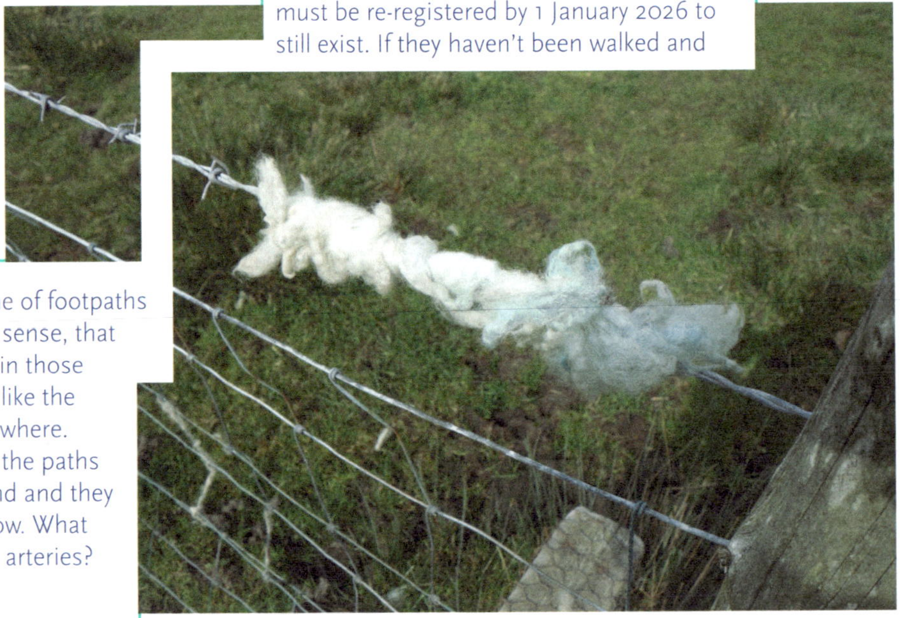

BOB *I grew up in the north of Ireland, where there are almost no public footpaths. It never occurred to me that you would have rights to cross farmland. When I was young, it did not matter because we did not care and we roamed the fields as harmless youngsters. Once I became more conscious of the distinctions between private and public land then I felt inhibited by the lack of rights. I notice the differences between Ireland and England especially acutely now when I return to Ireland to visit family. I am now used to England, where there are many freedoms and routes that you can take through farmland, woods and onto the moors. When I go back home the fields are bounded and inaccessible. It can feel incredibly claustrophobic. And yet, compared with my optimism, your Preston walk revealed a vulnerability. Perhaps this was more visible because you were avoiding established, 'sanitised' routes. You had to drive your own path through. You had to constantly read the map and read the ground to find the line of the boundary. Part of this vulnerability in Preston was the distinction between the rural and the urban that the boundary was holding back. I had initially come to this conversation thinking that you were grappling with an opposition between a culture of creating boundaries by walking along them and a culture of defining boundaries through mapping. In a way, this is more of a tension than an opposition. You are in a space that exposes the tension between the map and the experienced boundary. In the process of inhabiting this in-between space, you better understand the ways in which the map, boundary and landscape are related.*

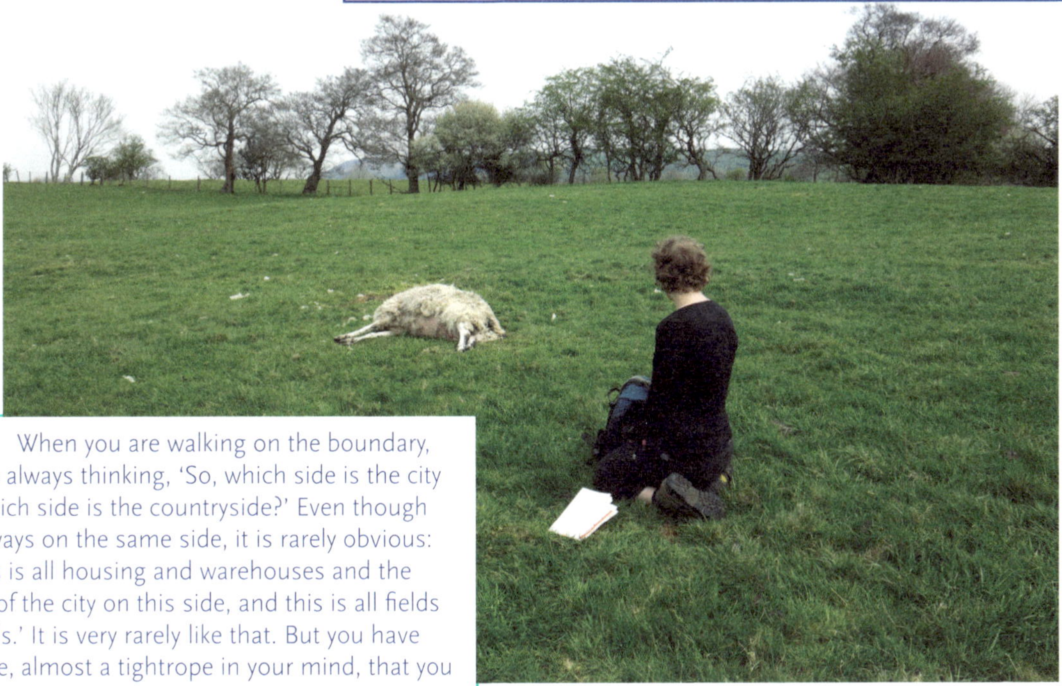

IAN When you are walking on the boundary, you are always thinking, 'So, which side is the city and which side is the countryside?' Even though it is always on the same side, it is rarely obvious: 'So this is all housing and warehouses and the things of the city on this side, and this is all fields and hills.' It is very rarely like that. But you have that line, almost a tightrope in your mind, that you are thinking about and tracing. You cannot help but try and make relationships between the two things. And that goes back to what I was saying about giving the land character, forming a direct relationship with it. In Preston, there is a precarity to the landscape that surrounds it. Its future is changing fast, very much in question and subject to mainly market forces.

…
I am sure it is true of all cities in this country that things are changing very quickly. When the boundary of a city expands, probably the clear majority of people living in that city would not know or care that it was happening, nor why. The landscapes around the city change forever and a handful of people care. The question is who is going to take any stewardship for those places? If you do not have any relationship with those places, how can you be expected to care for them? To what extent should we feel ourselves responsible for that?

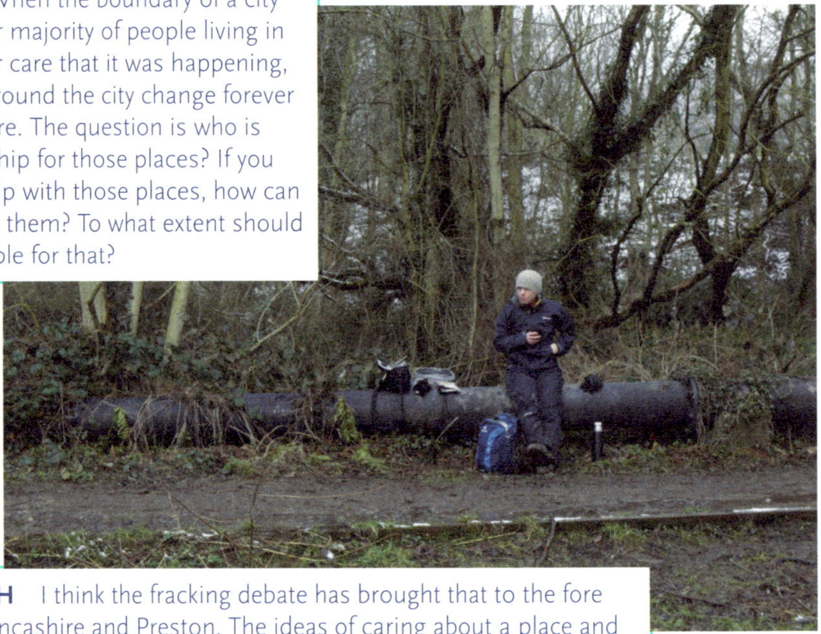

RUTH I think the fracking debate has brought that to the fore in Lancashire and Preston. The ideas of caring about a place and understanding a place are vitally important when so much of our natural resources are commodified in some way. There is a sense that we have a lack of agency, changes are happening very fast, the commodification of resources and landscapes and the disconnection with where our resources come from, whether they be food, energy or water. There is a lack of understanding of these networks, because they are either buried or they are someone else's responsibility. Unless you are a psychogeographer, an artist, a landscape archaeologist, generally we walk either for leisure or we walk to get to the places we need to be. Which means there are swathes of areas which people either do not know about or care about or own. And there is a vulnerability in that, I think.

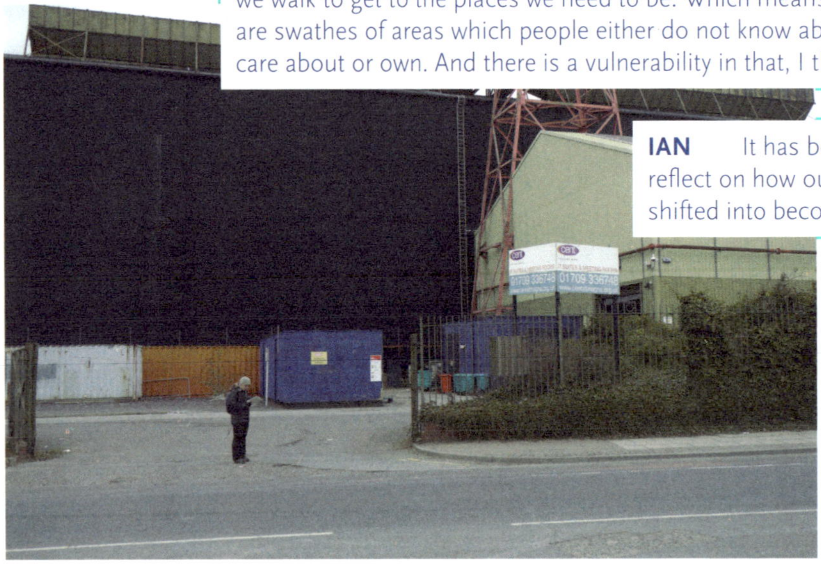

IAN It has been interesting to reflect on how our walking has slowly shifted into becoming quite political.

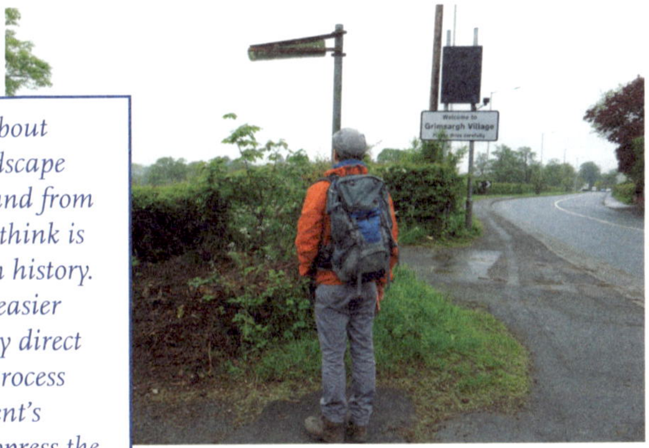

BOB *You talked about commodification of land and about how a lack of engagement with particular parts of the landscape makes it easier to alienate land from people, from society and from ethical concerns. The other process of disconnection that I think is important in this commodification is a disconnection from history. Once you can suppress the history of landscapes, it is also easier to make the case for their exploitation. It happens in a very direct way when archaeology is excluded from the development process and from planning decisions, as some of the UK government's recent planning legislation is now enabling. If you can suppress the historical character of a place, then it is much easier to carve that place up for corporate interests in the present. And many of those interests are much larger than us as individuals. It reminds me, drawing from Ian's observation about the politics of walking, of the mass trespass movement in the 1920s and 30s. Mass trespass was a movement to reclaim access to principally upland moorland in the north of England. The best-known example is the trespass onto Kinder Scout in 1932, where ramblers met near Hayfield, walked up onto the moor and there was a confrontation with the gamekeepers.* …

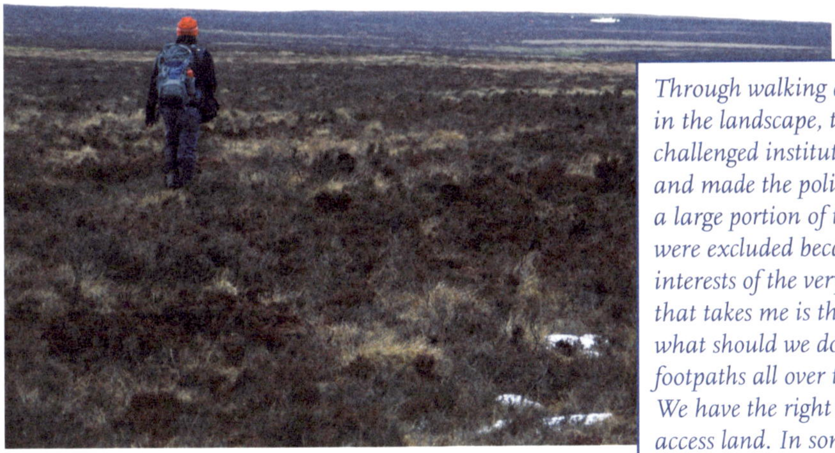

Through walking and being present in the landscape, the ramblers challenged institutionalised interests and made the political point that a large portion of the population were excluded because of the leisure interests of the very few. I guess where that takes me is the question, 'Well, what should we do now?' There are footpaths all over the countryside. We have the right to roam on open-access land. In some senses, we are freer than we have been for centuries. But nonetheless, you have shown that landscapes are still incredibly vulnerable and we have got a tenuous hold on them. From your perspectives as artists and citizens, what should our active response be? What should we be doing to challenge the vulnerabilities you have, rightly, articulated through your walks?

Reconnections

RUTH During the Preston walk there was a fantastic incident with a guy who had a poster outside his door that said, 'Walking paths is what keeps them alive.' Before we had seen the poster, we were walking the footpath that went to the side of his house and he ran out and offered us a cup of tea. He was so excited that someone had walked that path.

BOB *If walking paths is what keeps them alive, then what keeps boundaries alive? Is walking a way of keeping boundaries alive?*

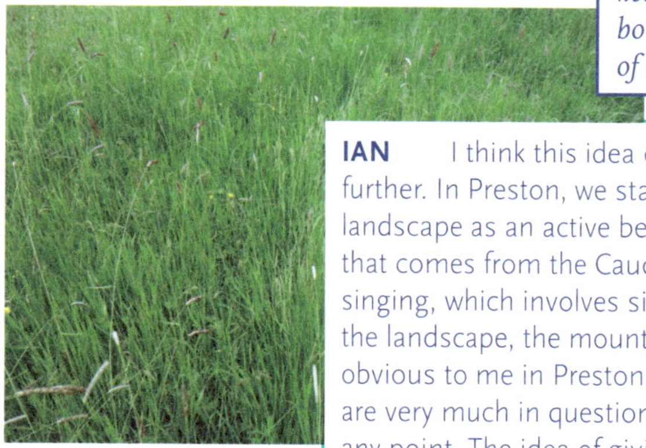

IAN I think this idea of being alive is worth looking at further. In Preston, we started talking about the idea of the landscape as an active being. There is a tradition of singing that comes from the Caucasus Mountains, called noxchi singing, which involves singing flirtatious love songs to the landscape, the mountains and the rivers. What was obvious to me in Preston is that the rights of the landscape are very much in question and could slip away very easily at any point. The idea of giving the land character in this way strikes me as an extraordinary and potent act of collective imagination in response to the kinds of pressures currently being exerted on these places.

RUTH It is interesting to think here about people elsewhere in the world who have a clearly defined sense of sacred land and how that sacred land also fulfils a role as their infrastructure. It might be a bit of land that they never go to but it is where the animals graze, the fish live, or their water comes from, all of which sustain them. It is a very different way of thinking compared with an island like Britain, which has lots of different concerns, needs, commercial interests and stakeholders, all seeing the land in different ways. It is a tricky balance to manage different needs, and with economic pressures and desires often shaping decisions. With economic thinking and market forces at play, something else must give. So who wins? Is it people over nature? Is it natural resources? Is it rich over poor? Is it urban over rural? There is something that just keeps sitting at the back of my mind about sacred land to do with identifying a cohesive and a collective respect. A way of seeing the land as home that will ultimately look after, feed and nurture us. Maybe it is about the sense of stewardship that comes with the idea of the sacred. But if we saw our cities or our areas in a more collective and respectful way, then we would not be quite so vulnerable to all those administrative and market forces.

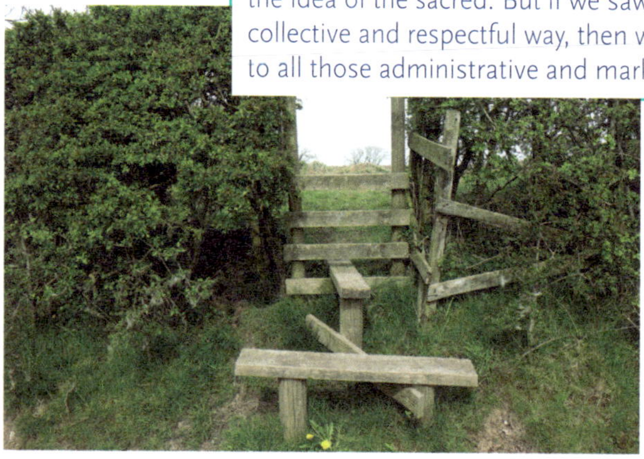

BOB *Do you mean that a continuing engagement with landscape is the means through which you appreciate the complexity of the world and are much better placed perhaps to debate and affect its future?*

RUTH Well, by walking around the cities we felt we were listening to the landscape and allowing the landscape to speak to us by being in it, rather than observing it and compartmentalising it. At walking speed, you have much more time to notice the small things, the incremental changes, the oddities, you are able to get up close and in between, you become much more aware of how the landscape dictates and shapes you and in turn how much we have carved and shaped it.

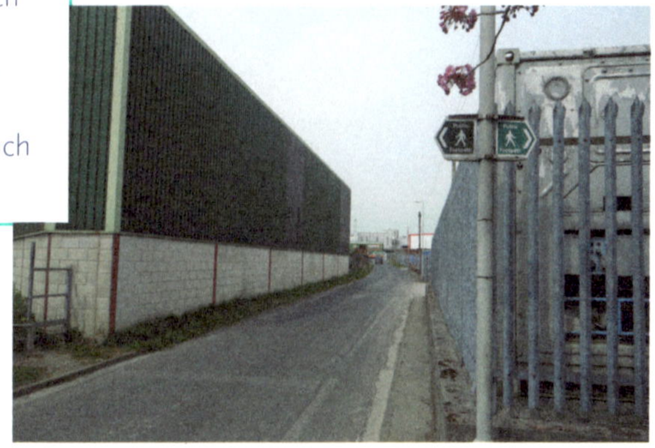

IAN Returning to the idea of pilgrimage, when you say I am going to go between these two points, it is the act and not the destination that is important. When you are walking with a purpose (and this is difficult to explain without getting too cosmic) the landscape opens up to you and your relationship with it becomes blurred. There is a to and fro, you feel more aligned with your surroundings.

RUTH Walking on and off the paths is a good start. Getting the skills, knowledge and confidence to go somewhere that you would not normally go is important. When you come upon a place which you have always known, but you have never come upon in that way, you frame and see it differently. You understand it from a new perspective. And I think that brings a fantastic sense of understanding a place that maybe would not be there before.

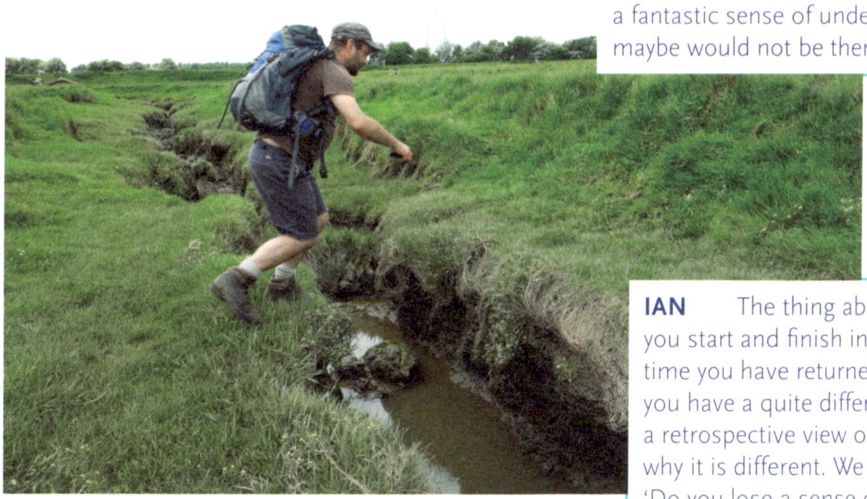

IAN The thing about walking in circles is that you start and finish in the same place. By the time you have returned to your starting point, you have a quite different view of the same place, a retrospective view of what you have done and why it is different. We started with the question, 'Do you lose a sense of your city if you can no longer easily walk the bounds?' Maybe we need to flip that question around and ask what was gained. What sense of a city do you gain when you walk its bounds? Maybe, that is a useful question to ask in terms of what we might be able to do in the future as citizens, as potential stewards of the land, in the ways we have been talking about. Ruth and I certainly came to a whole new set of ideas and ways of looking and understanding just by stepping out there and starting a walk. It is easy to do. It is really easy.

Between Noise and Silence: Listening to the Modern City

Magda Stawarska-Beavan
/
James G Mansell

Artist Magda Stawarska-Beavan and historian James G Mansell's contribution to this book takes the form of a collaborative project, which examines Manchester Central Library from a historical and phenomenological perspective. The project, which is concerned with the politics of urban noise, builds on the themes of their in-conversation event, *Urban Vibrations: Selfhood, Sound and the City*. Dealing with issues of social control, architecture and personal/public space, the project reveals the complex spatial narratives of urban soundscapes and explores how art and historical methods can encourage different forms of 'critical listening'.

The illustrated text is accompanied by a sound artwork by Magda, which is available to listen to at practisingplace.org

MS-B *A few years ago, I took a month-long artist residency in Vienna, where I was living in the city centre with a window facing busy Burgstrasse. I was working on a sound piece, 'Kraków to Venice in 12 hours', compiling field recordings from 12 different cities across Europe. After the residency, I returned to my parent's house on the outskirts of a small town in Poland. Having just stayed in a busy city and having been immersed in my sound work, my parent's house sounded alien and almost too quiet. One evening when I was alone, I decided to capture that silent ambience. As I sat in the room on this summer evening before I switched on my recorder, I started to listen. I heard, not silence, but instead the rhythmic purring of the cat, the distant ticking of the clock above the fireplace that I had never noticed before and, eventually, I felt my own heartbeat. I then tried to shift the focus of listening from close, almost claustrophobic sounds, to the ones further away. As I opened the terrace doors, the cicada sounds flooded in. While listening to the quiet, my mind amplified the subtle sounds around me. I recorded all the elements of that evening, including my heartbeat, in this case using my mother's doctor's stethoscope. From these elements, I created the work 'Inside Outside', in which I explore the process of deep listening and the relationship between the recordist and her acoustic surroundings.*

JGM As a field recordist and artist, Magda Stawarska-Beavan's approach to sound could not be more different to my own. As a historian, I listen to the past by reading written accounts of the encounter between hearers and their auditory environments. Yet when the Practising Place programme invited us to collaborate, we quickly found common ground. Both of us, in our different ways, were seeking to recover something of what Georges Perec (2002) would call the sonic 'infraordinary', the mundane sounds surrounding us every day which, although we might not always notice them, have a role to play in producing and connecting us to place. By paying attention to the undulations of these sonic rhythms and vibrations, both of us were seeking new ways to engage with questions of identity and affect. We were interested in how sounds situate us as certain kinds of selves. When we first met, I had just finished a book called *The Age of Noise in Britain: Hearing Modernity* (Mansell 2017a) which traces reactions to the mechanical sound worlds of the early 20th century. It argues that complaints about everyday noise, spearheaded by organisations such as the Anti-Noise League founded in 1933, indexed a range of anxieties about what it meant to be modern in this period. Attempts to reshape the auditory environment, to provide spaces of auditory refuge in the modern city, were intended to secure the very future of civilisation, such was the urgency attributed to the 'noise problem' at this time.

Magda had also been specialising in recording and presenting urban sounds in works such as 'East {Hyphen} West: Sound Impressions of Istanbul'. But what, we wondered, might there be to hear in a city beyond its strident, complained-about noises? For centuries, towns and cities have been characterised, auditorily, as places of unruly and intrusive sound. Historians and theorists of auditory culture have dedicated voluminous attention to noise in this sense, to the point where it has become difficult to imagine the audible city in any other way. The sonic dimensions of urban identity have also been tied quite tightly to the category of noise: who is said to make it, who deserves respite from it, what does it tell us about power and resistance, and so on. What if we were to set out in search of urban quiet, instead? The noise abatement advocates I had researched certainly promoted it. In his 1916 book *City of Din: A Tirade Against Noise*, Dan McKenzie described concert halls as 'sanctuaries' for the 'philosopher of Quiet', a place where the sensitive soul could rest their noise-jangled nerves (McKenzie 1916: 67). Not silence, but *quiet*. That was the ideal. Does quiet have a history? Can we record it and use it as an artistic resource? These were the questions that we set out to investigate in a shared project. Above all, we wondered: if quiet has been such a highly prized resource in the modern urban environment, what does it sound like, and what role does it play in the politics of identity and place?

Reading about the rapidly changing city soundscape of early 20th century Britain in The Age of Noise in Britain, I started to reflect on the role of the quiet place in the contemporary city. As we learned from the avant-garde composer John Cage (1961), experiencing silence, even in an anechoic chamber, is impossible, but surely within the complexity of the urban matrix we should be able to hear numerous levels and qualities of soundscape. After several conversations, we decided to examine the sound space of Manchester Central Library – both protecting and controlling – and its relationship to the city whose voices it reverberates. Libraries, as 'sanctuaries' of quiet, are unique places, both culturally and acoustically: they soundproof our thoughts from the distraction and the noise outside their walls. But they also coerce us into behaving quietly, amplifying the sounds we make beneath their domed acoustic chambers. However, today's library – embedded with technology – is full of discreet, barely audible sounds, which reveal its inner life. Using audio-visual recording, I began to investigate how the acoustic environment and the architecture of a building can affect our behaviour in a public space.

Magda's planned new work on Manchester Central Library offered me the opportunity to think afresh about the question of quiet. While writing *The Age of Noise in Britain*, I had spent a long time thinking about what noise is and how we define it. I realised that I had barely stopped to consider quiet in the same way. Yet writers on noise such as McKenzie had clearly valued it. He wrote, for example, that 'The world outside the walls of the City is full of pleasant sounds, bringing joy, health, and quiet breathing. And were these all the sounds that this world would contain, how placid would our natures be!' (1916: 24–25). The Anti-Noise League called their quarterly magazine exactly that, *Quiet*. It was what they were promoting, even if they spent most of their time trying to suppress its opposite. Opened on 17 July 1934, Manchester Central Library was the centrepiece of the city's modernist regeneration. Its showpiece, a magnificent domed reading room, provided just the kind of sanctuary from city noise that McKenzie and the Anti-Noise League were calling for. In fact, the League was busy at the time of the library's opening, having just held its inaugural conference at the University of Oxford. The city of Oxford had famously first introduced the 30mph speed limit to combat road noise and encouraged its milk delivery vans to use silenced pneumatic tyres to avoid waking its citizens up early in the morning. The choice of Oxford as a location was no coincidence for other reasons, too: supporters of noise abatement thought of quiet as especially important for thinking people – professionals, leaders of industry and scholars. The 'age of noise' was a threat to such people because it threatened to remove the acoustic conditions necessary for their thought-work. It threatened, in fact, the norms of quiet that, it is evident, had deep roots in 19th century middle-class culture. Quietness was being defended by middle-class activists in the early 20th century city because it had long been carefully crafted and entwined within the bourgeois auditory habitus. It was essential to the temples of middle-class culture founded in the 19th century – the concert hall, the art gallery and the public library – where McKenzie's 'philosopher of Quiet' could find peace but, more importantly, where all kinds of visitors, including those who were not predisposed to seek out respite from noise, could learn, among other things, *the rules of quiet*.

Indeed, public libraries tell us a good deal about the auditory ideals of urban elites as they evolved over the 19th and early 20th centuries. Public libraries were provided in order to extend the quiet culture of the middle classes to the less well off. Kelman (2001) and Joyce (2003) both view them, additionally, as spaces for disciplining bodies. Joyce points out that the Public Libraries Act (1850) made money available not for books, but for buildings, and argues that public libraries such as Manchester's, first opened as the Manchester Municipal Free Library in 1850 (2003: 129), were built by civic leaders who believed that 'the physical environment had a direct impact on perception and behaviour' (*ibid*: 131). Public libraries were to be places where all the citizens of a locality could gather and generate shared understandings of citizenship and public norms of behaviour. They reproduced middle-class ideals of civilized behaviour in the bodies of their working-class visitors. Joyce points out that readers in a library were rendered visible to the gaze of the disciplining librarian, who could regulate behaviour as in a panopticon. Kelman argues, alternatively, that libraries were not so much places of visual discipline, but places where one learned *how to be quiet*. 'Anyone who would like to may enter the library,' he explains, 'but once inside, behaviour is quietly regulated and carefully choreographed' (2001: 25). Not panopticism, Kelman argues, 'but panauralism... The librarian can always hear you' (*ibid*: 38). Indeed, Kelman concludes that 'Controlling noise at the library was a critical feature of its civilizing ideals' (*ibid*).

Public libraries, including in Manchester, had, since the middle of the 19th century, provided spaces for quiet self-improvement. As Kelman has interestingly pointed out, public libraries are the urban epicentres not of silence but of quiet: readers are disciplined there into a culture of silent reading, but the library itself has to make sound in order to function. Were the library 'too silent – no footsteps, no pages turning, no pencils scraping – we could not be certain that the machine was working' (*ibid*). Silence, then, is not a particularly useful category of social analysis in this case, because the word implies an idealised absence of sound that was never in fact in operation in the disciplinary spaces of the modern city. Instead, in concert halls, art galleries and public libraries, visitors learned *how to sound*, how to behave in the auditory habitus of bourgeois urban space. This begs the question to the historian and artist of what quiet does and what quiet means. If noise has been so heavily invested with significance and social power, might it not be worth pausing to ask similar questions of the social functions of quiet as we do of the social functions of noise? Gallagher (2011) has done so in the case of the primary school, a space in which quietness, he argues, is a central affective resource for producing self-governing subjects. Quietness enables auditory surveillance, according to Gallagher, enacted both by the teacher on the pupils and from one pupil to another.

Equipped with binaural microphones and a discrete recorder, I set off to visit Manchester Central Library. I start my walk from Albert Square, in the centre of the city. Walking south along Mount Street, I realise that although I have lived in the north west of England for the last 20 years, I have recorded Manchester very little in the past. On reaching St Peter's Square, I stand outside the library listening and absorbing the vibrant ambience; the sound of a nearby building site, the voice of the Big Issue seller calling the same words like a mantra, punctuated by a tram bell echoed by the façades of the iconic Midland Hotel. Manchester, the birth city of the Industrial Revolution, is, to me, a city that keeps changing as it constantly adapts to the fluctuating socio-political situation. The hum of building machines is almost constant, shifting through various parts of the city centre.

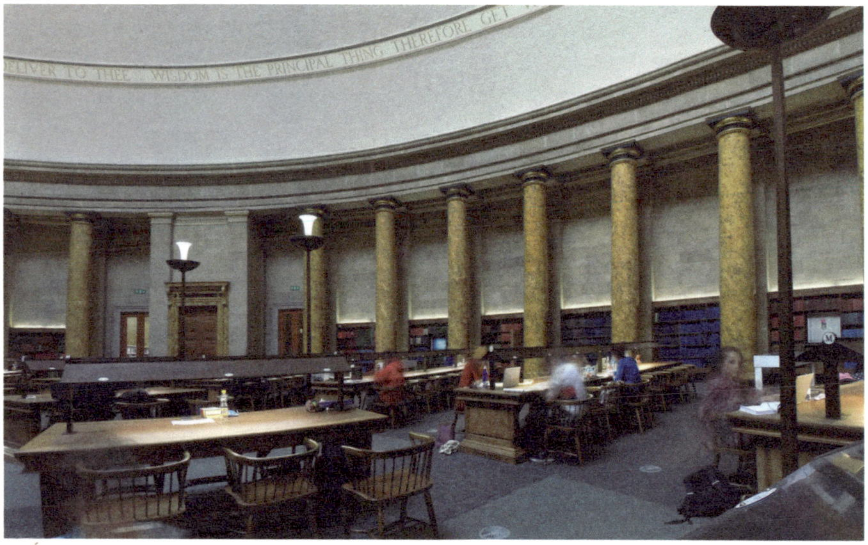

6'5

I approach the columned portico of the library and walk up the steps towards the automatic sliding doors of the main entrance. The whoosh of the doors followed by the hum of the overhead heater creates a sonic threshold between the outside and the inside. The hall is full of people, a visiting school group with their teacher explaining the history of the place. I take a quick look at the main ground floor, where the new café, archive and media pods are placed. It feels like a spot to hang around; people of different generations are talking, browsing, reading. Amid the clutter of coffee cups and milk-frothing machines, nobody particularly keeps their conversation quiet, but instead they seem confident to create sound without fear of disturbing other people. Manchester City Library reopened to the public in 2014, after four years of refurbishment. The ground floor was previously used mainly for storage, with little access granted to the public. The new open-plan design, with its many interactive screens and media pods, is the result of recent investment and seems to appeal to the present demands of the public for spaces to connect with others, both virtually and face-to-face.

I take the main staircase to the first floor, the sound of my heeled shoes echoing against the stone floor. Outside the reading room I pass relaxed readers sitting with their tablets and laptops on comfortable, lounging, grey-felt chairs. Walking past a large window, I can still hear the sound of the trams, traffic and building sites seeping in from outside. As I open the heavy, wooden door of the reading room, I become aware that I have stepped into another acoustic territory.

The reading room, placed in the heart of the building on the first floor, is filled with natural light, making it the perfect environment for the reader. The room is designed on a circular plan, with 28 neoclassical columns supporting a domed ceiling. Painted in gold below the dome is a text, which reads: 'Wisdom is the principal thing; therefore get wisdom: and with all thy getting get understanding.' As I walk towards one of the available reading spaces, the sound of my heels is muffled by the soft, grey carpet, yet still audible in this beautifully echoing chamber. I sit down and, as I open my bag to get my notebook out, I become even more aware of the sound I make. The structure of the domed ceiling creates echoes; the sound reflected by the curved surface travels with a delay and changes direction, making it difficult to tell where it originates. Compared with the ground floor of the building, the room seems quiet. However, it is filled with the amplification of subtle, intimate sounds: a pencil against paper, the turning of a page, shuffles of a chair, sniffling and coughing. As these sounds mix and become displaced from their origin, they create a joint experience that turns the reader, engrossed in the private act of reading, into a performer within the public space of the library.

Refurbishment has not changed the room that much. Symmetrically spaced, long, wooden, period desks radiate from a central mahogany information point, much as they do in an archival photo from 1934 displayed on the ground floor. The architecture of this room, together with the wooden chairs, which make us sit in a very formal way, and the acoustics of the space, encourage us to behave in a certain way. There is no need for anyone to officially control the level of noise, as the readers hear amplified sounds and regulate themselves. Reading in silence is such a private experience; each reader is absorbed in their invisible space, but as the sound of their reading reverberates, it becomes a shared practice.

More than 80 years after it first opened, the main domed reading room of Manchester Central Library still has the desired effect. The acoustics of the room amplify the smallest sounds, making one acutely aware of oneself as a sounding subject. Kelman suggests that this was a deliberate feature of 19th century American libraries, such as the New York Public Library. There, he says, 'It does not matter if one is actively being listened to. Instead, those large white marble halls amplify even the smallest sound and betray one's "uncivil" behavior immediately' (2001: 38). This was part of the 19th century public library's function to actively cultivate its readers as civilised auditory subjects, argues Kelman. This is the kind of power that Foucault (1991) describes in relation to vision as panoptical; the very architecture of a space can inculcate self-regulation, leading to the situation that Joyce (2003) describes as the 'rule of freedom'. The architect who designed Manchester Central Library, E. Vincent Harris, drew his inspiration from American public libraries such as the one described by Kelman, so we can conclude that the domed reading room was intended to shape the auditory behaviour of its readers, even if Harris did not realise it.

In fact, the story is more intriguing than that. When it first opened, visitors immediately commented on the interesting acoustics of the main reading room at Manchester Central Library. The *Manchester Guardian* explained that 'The echo in the Great Hall of the new Central Library is somewhat disconcerting at first. It is a ubiquitous echo, stronger in the centre than under the shallower rim of the dome. At the centre one can even hear the echo of a footfall on the rubber carpet. A cough uttered anywhere, it seems, returns to the utterer' (20 March 1934: 13). Not everyone welcomed these acoustic effects. One newspaper article commented that 'The reading room of the new building was not a bad place in which to work if one did not mind strange noises, draughts, and uncomfortable chairs' (*ibid,* 22 June 1934: 12). Care had been taken in the original design of the reading room to stifle too much reverberation, hence the rubber carpet. The *Manchester Guardian* explained that 'Mr Vincent Harris has domed the ceiling with acoustic tiles, and it was to be expected that the bookcases, other furniture, and people would absorb unwanted sounds' (20 March 1934: 13). This was not to prove sufficient, however. Over the years, readers still complained of what were termed the 'library flutters' (*Guardian*, 29 September 1967: 4), and library management sought out ways to lessen the distracting reverberance.

In 1946, with peacetime normality returning after the Second World War, thoughts turned to how the Manchester Central Library reading room might be quietened. The *Manchester Guardian* reported that:

> *There might have come a time when the echo peculiar to Manchester's Central Library... would have attained as great a fame as the whispering of the gallery under St. Paul's dome. This, we are told, will not happen, for the echo has been traced to its origin and can soon be suppressed. These voices, now thunderous, now sibilant, seemingly from nowhere, might have been kept as a marvel if distractions could be tolerated in libraries. As it is, there are far too many temptations to the wandering mind in most modern libraries without echoes being added.* (10 June 1946: 4)

Only minor adjustments, such as adding silencing tips to chair legs, were ever made in 1946, however. In 1968, renewed efforts were made to control the unruly echo. The *Guardian* reported that the library was still 'probably the only one in the country where a library attendant cannot say "shh" without being "shh'd" back' (7 August 1968: 14). The new answer to the problem, as the same article reported, 'involves spraying the inside of the library's dome with a thick coat of asbestos solution' (it was not uncommon to use asbestos for this purpose in the mid-20th century). Although some concerns were raised about the potential health hazard of this path of action, the treatment went ahead.

What these examples show is the extent to which the acoustic territories which Magda describes are shaped consciously for social purposes. The noticeable change in sonic atmosphere when one enters the reading room of the Manchester Central Library is deliberate. The lengths that the library management went to over the course of the 20th century to perfect the ideal acoustics for the reading room testify to the importance of quiet as an affective resource in the production of a certain kind of public culture. Magda describes and captures in her recordings a palpable sense of auditory togetherness and responsibility in the library reading room. One is aware of oneself as a sounding body in this soundscape, but one is aware, too, of the shared activity of reading and information exchange, which generates a sonic life of its own. In his book, *Acoustic Territories: Sound Culture and Everyday Life* (2010: xix), Brandon Labelle argues that 'Sound conditions and contours subjectivity by lending a dynamic materiality for social negotiation.' The public library is a prime example of the kind of space where sound plays this role. Quiet, in the library, is not disinterested, nor inactive. It is actively produced to generate public behaviour. That is not to say, as Magda points out, that these sounds and social negotiations do not shift over time. Magda's recordings and observations highlight parts of the library now alive with more hubbub than would have been imaginable in 1934. As Mattern (2007: 286) argues, 'today's libraries are not as hostile toward noise as their recent ancestors were' because of shifting notions of participation in heritage and education. As the social field shifts, so too does the auditory atmosphere which holds it in place.

In my work, I often wander around unfamiliar cities, searching for points of connection and trying to find a sense of belonging in otherwise unknown contexts. I record places from a very personal perspective and share my experiences with the audience through the resulting artworks. For this project, I was invited to collaborate with James, whose socio-historical research and analysis of sound provided me with excellent food for thought. After reading his book, I reflected on how our ideas of what quiet means and what noise represents have changed and evolved during the last century with the rapid development of technology and increasing dominance of media. Having worked with James on this project, I appreciate much more that to fully understand the acoustics of Manchester Central Library, alongside the activity of intensive listening, we need to hear the building historically. I tried to imagine and understand through his writing how cities, such as Manchester, sounded and were heard a century ago.

The sound work that has resulted from my exploration of Manchester Central Library, 'Resonating Silence',[1] is a brief exploration of the library's many acoustic territories. The composition begins with sounds recorded outside the building, followed by recordings of the reading room, which is the focal point of the piece. The recordings are accompanied by a series of images incorporating a text by artist, Heather Ross, who had never visited Manchester Central Library but responded to the audio using textual descriptions of what she heard. Her words have been superimposed onto the architectural plans of the building to create a visual impression of its rich acoustic fabric. '6'5' and '10'8', meanwhile, provide visual records of the subtle movements of visitors, which are captured in the sound piece.

'Resonating Silence' evokes the shared yet inherently private soundscape of the library. In making the work, I listened to the reverberated sounds of the readers engrossed in their reading experience and tried to imagine their personal narratives, embodied in the sounds they created, which were layered, reflected and merged almost into one. Ultimately, as James emphasises, sound as an acoustic phenomenon cannot be perceived by listeners without the filter of their knowledge and acquired experience: 'when we hear, we do so as particular kinds of subjects living in particular times and places. How we hear is shaped socially as well as biologically' (Mansell, 2017b). As an artist, I see my work as filtering surrounding soundscapes into personal narratives, which can become points of departure for other personal and subjective experiences.

1. PRACTISINGPLACE.ORG

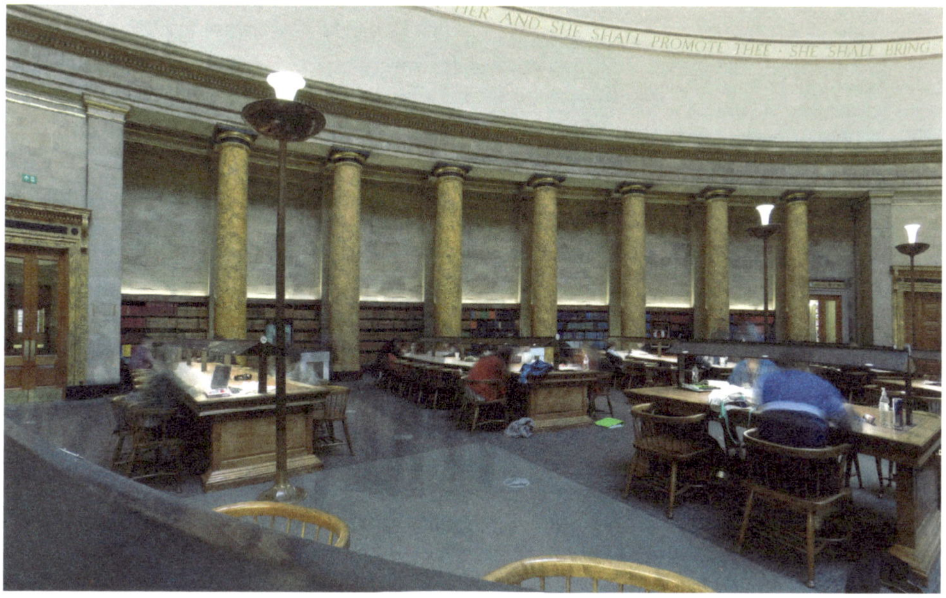

10'8

With her binaural microphones and GoPro camera, Magda can enter into the dynamics of urban sound in quite different ways to those that I usually deal in as a historian. Searching for traces of hearing and listening in the historical record reminds us that our sound environments are social products, shaped over time, but Magda's work as a recordist and artist demonstrates that these sound environments continue to shift and evolve with the changing norms and ideals of public culture and public space. To hear with past hearers we should also listen carefully in our present. Magda's recordings draw us into the intimacy of sound spaces and remind us of the importance of what we hear to who we are. In this shared project, we have attempted to show what might happen if a historian and an artist came together to consider a topic such as urban sound. Listening in two different registers, we have shown that sound is both a deeply personal but also a powerfully social force in our everyday lives.

I claim my usual seat, at the windows in London College of Communication library. They meet and point like an arrow to the almighty blue and cream Goldfinger buildings, just off the roundabout at the Elephant and Castle. Here is the beating heart; my London Symphony... I'll miss you when I leave. And in my ears, the sound of Manchester (or so I'm told), from one city to another, one library to another. My future points north. Information-rich surroundings – a time-based proposition – overlapping events, objects and descriptions – to begin. Then sounds scribbled vertically down the page; a list, a cue sheet of foley – one at a time please... as they enter and exit.

Heather Ross, 2017.

CAGE J (1961)
Silence; Lectures and Writings.
Middletown CT: Wesleyan University Press.

FOUCAULT M (1991)
Discipline and Punish: The Birth of the Prison
(trans. A Sheridan).
London: Penguin.

GALLAGHER M (2011)
'Sound, space and power in a primary school.'
Social and Cultural Geography 12(1), 47–61.

JOYCE P (2003)
The Rule of Freedom: Liberalism and the Modern City.
London: Verso.

KELMAN AY (2001)
'The sound of the civic: Reading noise at the New York Public Library.'
American Studies 42(3), 3–41.

LABELLE B (2010)
Acoustic Territories: Sound Culture and Everyday Life.
New York: Continuum.

MANSELL JG (2017a)
The Age of Noise in Britain: Hearing Modernity.
Urbana: University of Illinois Press.

MANSELL JG (2017b)
'Urban vibrations: Sound, selfhood and the city in the work of Magda Stawarska-Beavan.'
The Double Negative.
Accessed on 15·6·18 at: thedoublenegative.co.uk/2017/02/urban-vibrations-sound-selfhood-and-the-city-in-the-work-of-magda-stawarska-beavan

MATTERN S (2007)
'Resonant texts: Sounds of the American public library.'
The Senses and Society 2(3), 277–302.

MCKENZIE (1916)
City of Din: A Tirade Against Noise.
London: Adlard & Son.

PEREC G (2002)
'Approaches to What?'
In B Highmore (ed) *The Everyday Life Reader.*
London: Routledge.

(Dis)ordering the City: Buildings, Bodies and Urban Space

Emily[1] **Speed**[2]
/
Duncan[3] **Light**[4]

The following creative essay presents artist Emily Speed and human geographer Duncan Light's shared interest in the making and reshaping of urban spaces. Their public event, *(Dis)Ordering the City: Buildings, Bodies and Urban Space*, considered the ways in which urban spaces are performed and how certain practices – such as walking, urban exploration and the creation of 'desire lines' – might be viewed as tactics for 'disordering' the city. This collaborative project further examines the relationship between the implementation of official planning processes as methods of social control and the subsequent subversion of spaces by urban inhabitants.

1. FOOTNOTES AND OTHER INTERVENTIONS BY EMILY SPEED.

2. THE MOVING WALKWAY APPEARS IN MUCH SCIENCE FICTION, INCLUDING 'THE JETSONS' AND FRITZ LANG'S 'METROPOLIS' AND IS A RELATIVELY RECENT ADDITION TO PUBLIC SPACES IN THE UK. THE MOVING SIDEWALK WAS PATENTED BY AN INVENTOR CALLED ALFRED SPEER IN 1871 (HE DESIGNED THEM FOR USE IN NEW YORK AND INTENDED THEM TO HAVE SEATS, VARIABLE SPEEDS AND EVEN SMOKING CARS) AND ONE FIRST APPEARED ALONG THE PIER AT THE CHICAGO COLUMBIAN EXPOSITION IN 1893, SOON FOLLOWED BY ONE AT THE PARIS EXPO IN 1900. MOVING WALKWAYS DID NOT MAKE AN APPEARANCE IN THE UK UNTIL THE FIRST ONE WAS INSTALLED AT LONDON'S BANK UNDERGROUND STATION IN 1960. THE TRAV-O-LATOR, SPEEDWALK OR MOVING WALKWAY IS NOW FOUND IN MANY AIRPORTS, STATIONS AND OTHER PUBLIC BUILDINGS. MY INTEREST WAS PIQUED WHEN FINDING AN OLD COPY OF 'NEW SCIENTIST' THAT CITED RESEARCH BY MANOJ SRINIVASAN, A LOCOMOTION RESEARCHER AT PRINCETON UNIVERSITY (CAMPBELL 2009). HIS MATHEMATICAL MODELS PREDICTED THAT THE MOVING WALKWAY OFTEN HAS THE EFFECT OF SLOWING USERS DOWN BECAUSE PEOPLE TEND TO LOWER THEIR WALKING SPEED AS THEY STEP ON OR THEY OFTEN STAND COMPLETELY STILL FOR A REST. HE SUGGESTS THAT 11 SECONDS OVER 100 METRES SEEMS TO BE THE BEST TIME SAVING WE CAN HOPE FOR. I KNOW I HAVE STEPPED ON ONE MANY TIMES AND TOO OFTEN THE PLEASURE OF STRIDING ALONG AS IF IN REDUCED GRAVITY HAS BEEN ABRUPTLY HALTED BY A LARGE SUITCASE OR A GROUP SPREAD ACROSS THE WHOLE WIDTH OF THE WALKWAY. THE REST OF THE JOURNEY IS SPENT BEING CARRIED ALONG, STANDING STILL, WATCHING WALKERS GO PAST ME AND FILLED WITH REGRET FOR MY CHOICE.

3. MAIN BODY TEXT BY DUNCAN LIGHT.

4. LIGHT HAS BEEN USED IN A MYRIAD OF WAYS TO CONTROL OR GUIDE EXPERIENCES OF ARCHITECTURE AND URBAN SPACE. CIVIC PRIDE SEES SOME SPACES DRENCHED IN LIGHT TO HIGHLIGHT IMPORTANCE AND/OR BEAUTY AND MANY BUILDINGS HAVE LIGHTING PLANNED INTO THEIR DESIGN. LIGHT CAN ALSO BE GOOD MARKETING FOR A PLACE, FOR EXAMPLE, THE TROPICANA HOTEL IN ATLANTIC CITY HAS A DAILY LIGHT SHOW (WITH MUSIC) THAT IS FREE TO THE PUBLIC. OTHER SPACES ARE LIT MORE HARSHLY TO DETER CRIME AND INCREASE THE FEELING OF SAFETY. LIGHT COLOURS THE CITY, ESPECIALLY AT NIGHT, AND STREET LIGHTS NOW VARY FROM ORANGE TO YELLOW TO BRIGHT WHITE TO BLUES, DEPENDING ON WHETHER THE BULBS USE SODIUM, MERCURY, FLUORESCENT LAMPS OR LEDS. RED LIGHT IS A WAY OF COMMUNICATING THE PRESENCE OF THE SEX INDUSTRY, SOMETIMES IN AREAS DESIGNATED BY THE AUTHORITIES AND SOMETIMES ILLEGALLY. BLUE LIGHT IS OFTEN FOUND IN SUPERMARKET TOILETS TO MAKE VEINS DIFFICULT TO SEE AND STOP PEOPLE USING THE SPACE TO INJECT DRUGS. PINK LIGHT IS A MORE RECENT ADDITION, WITH SOME RESIDENTS' ASSOCIATIONS INSTALLING THESE IN PLACES WHERE TEENAGERS GATHER, AS IT HAS THE EFFECT OF MAKING ACNE MORE PRONOUNCED.

Both academics and artists have long been interested in cities. We certainly both are! We have each lived for a long time in cities, in a range of countries. That said, neither of us grew up in cities which, perhaps, increases their fascination for us. One interest we share is the way that space within the city is continually used, shaped, made and remade, by a range of different groups. On one hand, the 'authorities' (such as political elites, planners and urban managers) make and shape urban space in particular ways, striving to create an ordered and orderly city that is intended to encourage particular ways of behaving by the urban populace. And on the other hand, there are myriad ways in which 'ordinary' urban residents respond to the order they encounter and often seek to subvert or sidestep (sometimes consciously, sometimes unconsciously) efforts to create orderly urban spaces. This reminds us of de Certeau's distinction between 'strategies' and 'tactics' (1984). Strategies are top-down initiatives by those in power to impose the 'violence of order' (*ibid*: xiv) upon the city. Conversely, tactics are the responses of the city's residents, undertaken within the context of everyday activities, which have the effect (not always intentionally) of undermining or resisting efforts to impose order on the city. For us, the city is in a fascinating state of flux and tension between attempts to impose order and the ways that urban residents 'disorder' the city through their everyday practices, thereby reclaiming urban space for themselves. In this chapter we explore these issues in more detail.

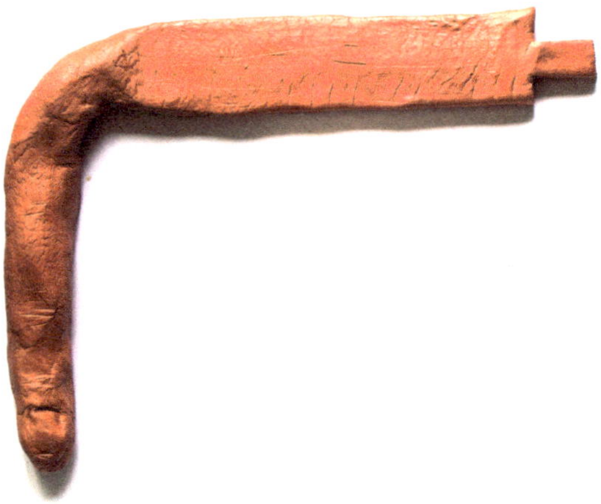

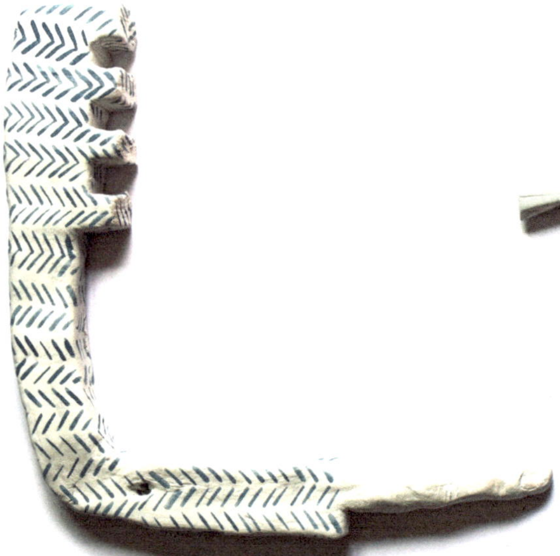

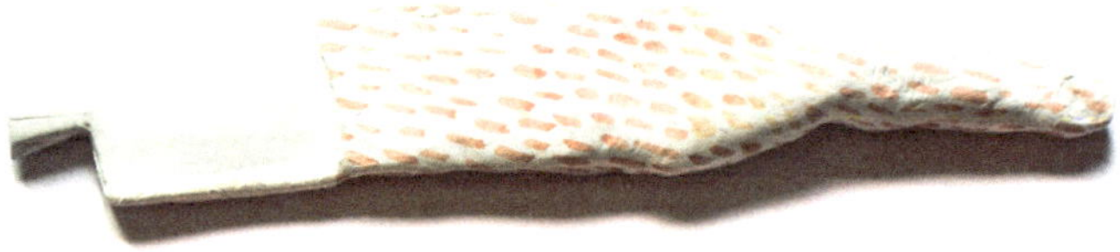

ORDERING PUBLIC SPACE

For as long as there have been cities, elites have sought to impose order upon them. The governance of the city (and the people in it) depends on creating an ordered and orderly public space that can be managed, regulated and controlled. Arranging urban space (particularly public space) is a demonstration of power by those who hold it and a way of making a statement to the urban population. It is also intended to guide the city's residents to behave (and, sometimes, to think) in the ways intended by political elites or urban managers (Huxley 2006). The form and layout of public space in the city is therefore an expression – and exercise – of power.

Imposing order on urban space can take place in a wide variety of ways and at different scales. At one extreme is the effort to lay out the entire city in a regulated and orderly way. The classic example is the gridiron street plan: parallel streets, at regular intervals, intersecting at right angles (Marcuse 1987). Such a layout allows for efficient movement and orientation within the city but, just as importantly, it testifies that somebody has taken control of the city's form. While the gridiron pattern is very ancient, this style of urban planning was perfected by the Romans.[5]

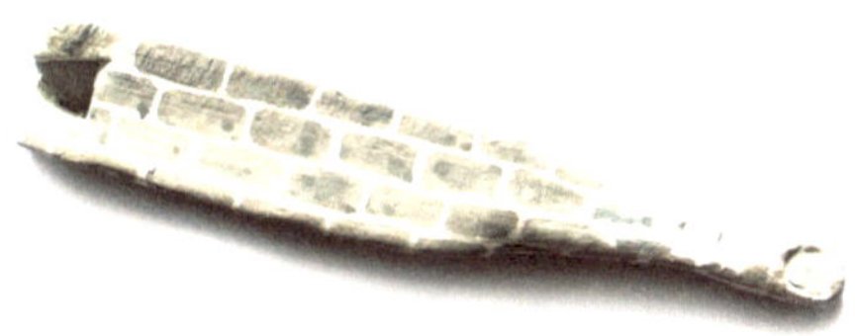

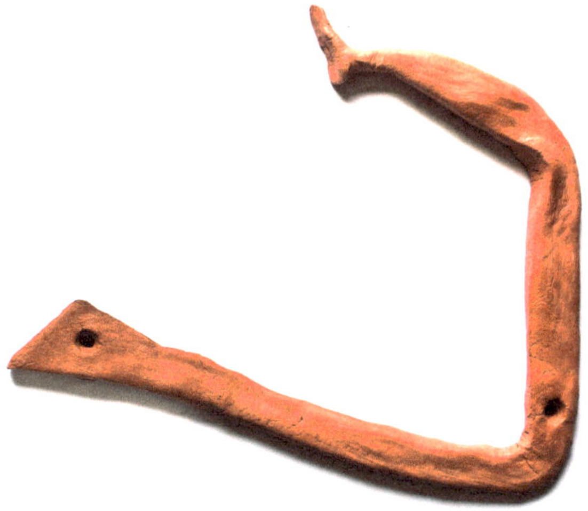

5. ANCIENT ROME USED A SYSTEM OF MEASUREMENTS THAT STARTED WITH THE PES, OR ROMAN FOOT. ALTHOUGH MUCH LARGER THAN AN ACTUAL HUMAN FOOT, MANY OF THE MEASUREMENTS TAKE BODY PARTS FOR THEIR NAME. AT THE ROOT OF ALL THEIR CITIES, ACROSS THEIR VAST EMPIRE, WAS THE HUMBLE FOOT.

It fell out of favour following the collapse of the Roman Empire but was subsequently revived in the medieval era and was widely adopted in Europe following the Renaissance (Valletta in Malta being one of the earliest examples). In the era of colonialism, the gridiron street plan was adopted in colonised territories as an overt way of imposing European values upon local populations (see Lefebvre 1991). The era of modernist urban planning in the 20th century saw the gridiron plan taken up with renewed enthusiasm. Modernism was a movement with an overtly utopian mission to create a better society: it sought to transform society through transforming urban space (Harvey 1987). Modernist planners worked to create rational, orderly and efficient cities which, they believed, would produce happy and contented people. In practice, this meant uniform design, large open spaces, plentiful green space and the dominance of the straight line for roads and walkways (Harvey 1989).[6]

The starkest illustrations of modernist urban planning were the model cities proposed by the Swiss architect Le Corbusier, which were characterised by massive apartment blocks situated in large urban parks. The geometric 'purity' of the gridiron plan had a particular appeal to modernist planners and became the standard form of the planned modernist city. A good example from the UK is Milton Keynes (although here the grid plan is implemented in a more fluid and flexible way).

Another tenet of modernist planning was urban zoning. The ordered city was one in which different areas of the city would be allocated to different purposes (such as housing, business, industry, retail, leisure). Zoning was implemented through city-level plans which were intended to regulate which activities could take place in particular areas. However, plans were often based on the assumption that people would travel around the city by car, meaning that there was poor provision for pedestrians or cyclists.

6. WHERE A STRICT PATH IS CREATED OR BARRIER IS ERECTED, USERS WILL OFTEN FIND A QUICKER WAY AROUND OR MORE DIRECT ROUTE THAT CAN RESULT IN NEW, VISIBLY WORN PATHS OR DESIRE LINES (OR GOAT-LEGS, AS I GREW UP KNOWING THEM) OVER PATCHES OF GRASS AND OTHER SURFACES.

SOME PLANNERS HAVE WAITED FOR SNOWFALL FOR DESIRE PATHS TO BECOME VISIBLE BEFORE PUTTING IN WALKWAYS. WHEN VIEWING GOOGLE MAPS, BOTH VIRGINIA TECH AND MICHIGAN STATE UNIVERSITY CAN BE SEEN TO HAVE ELABORATELY PATTERNED CAMPUSES MADE WHERE DESIRE LINES THAT HAVE FORMED OVER TIME HAVE BEEN MADE INTO PROPER PATHS.

At a smaller scale, city authorities seek to impose order on the city in other ways. One of the best examples is the boulevard: a long, wide, rectilinear axis, often with a focal point (such as a monumental building) at one end. The modern boulevard has its origins in Baron Haussmann's efforts to reshape Paris in the 1850s and 1860s. Mediaeval Paris was, by today's standards, a very disordered city: irregular in form (characterised by a dense network of narrow streets), densely populated, crowded and unhealthy. Movement around the city was difficult, but what was of more concern to the city's authorities was that the city was difficult to control, since local residents could easily throw up barricades[7] across the streets to deny access to the police or army. Haussmann was granted near absolute power to reshape Paris by the autocratic Napoleon III (Cavalcanti 1997). His solution was to tear down much of the old city and replace it with a 90-mile network of wide boulevards, along with parks and squares. He began with major boulevards running north–south and west–east, and then connected these with still more boulevards. The new road network allowed for the easy circulation of people and vehicles, but more importantly they allowed the army to move quickly around the city to quell unrest. The creation of a more orderly city allowed, in turn, urban space to be more effectively governed and controlled by increasing the state's reach into the everyday lives of the population (O'Neill 2009). By reconfiguring Paris so dramatically, Haussmann effectively 'bludgeoned the city into modernity' (Harvey 2006: 3).

[7] ONE OR MORE OF THESE IN A LINE

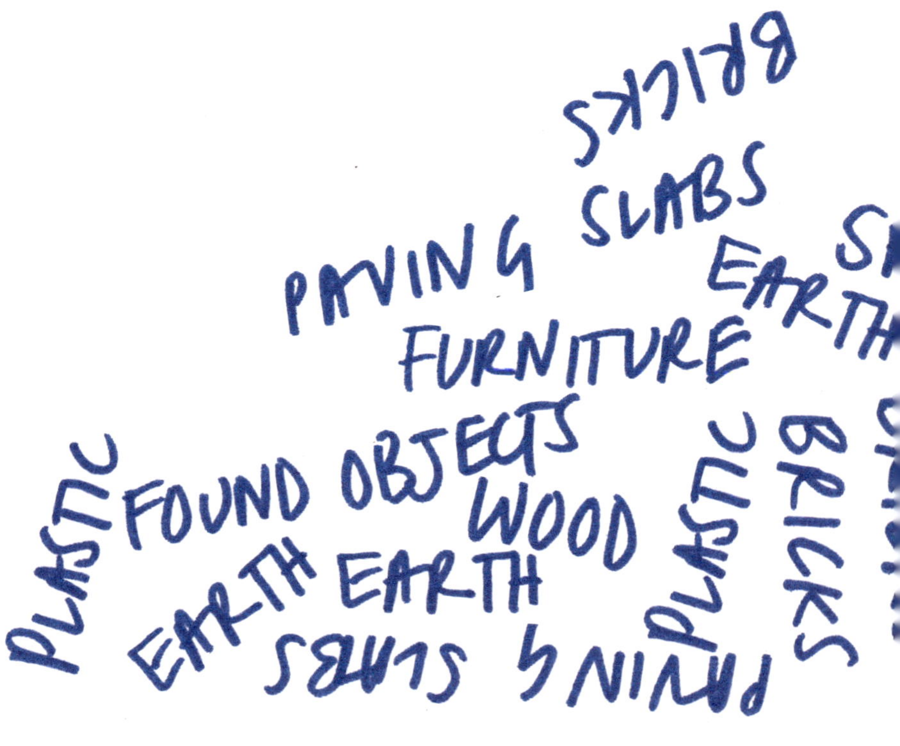

Haussmann had demonstrated how the boulevard could be used as a demonstration of state power, and the use of boulevards for this purpose continued in the 20th century. Indeed, vast boulevards appear to have a particular appeal to autocratic regimes or rulers: they featured prominently in Stalin's reconstruction of Moscow, Speer's plans for Nazi Berlin, and Mussolini's plans for Rome (Cavalcanti 1997). One of the starkest examples can be seen in Nicolae Ceausescu's plans to remodel Bucharest in the 1980s. An earthquake in 1977 which damaged parts of the historic centre gave Ceausescu the opportunity to radically modernise the capital so that it better reflected the ideals of the communist state. Around one-fifth of the historic city was demolished, to be replaced by a vast new 'civic centre'. The centrepiece of the new city was a vast boulevard (reportedly intended to be longer and wider than the Avenue des Champs-Élysées in Paris) which runs from nowhere in particular to a vast building known as 'House of the Republic'. This monumental structure (which covers an area of more than six hectares) was intended to house all the political and governmental institutions of the state. This extreme example of an autocratic attempt to completely reshape urban space was intended to create an urban landscape which humbled and intimidated the individual citizen. As O'Neill (2009: 93) argues, 'Ceausescu turned city spaces into technologies of political control through the production of a new, monumental urban form'. [8]

OR PILE ACROSS
A STREET OR
OTHER AREA:

VEHICLES
RTH BRICKS
BAGS SANDBAGS WOOD VEHICLES
OOD
METAL FENCING
BRICKS
BODIES BODIES SECTIONS
(WITH SHIELDS)
SANDBAGS WOOD VEHICLES

At a much smaller scale, there are other ways of imposing order on urban space. One is the allocation of names to streets within the city, something that is a key element of contemporary urban governance. Naming streets is an administrative act which enables each part of the city to be clearly identified and differentiated. It also allows the city authorities to identify, tax and police their populations and to provide them with services and post (Rose-Redwood *et al.* 2010). Therefore, street names, along with the numbering of houses along those streets (Rose-Redwood 2008), are a means of ensuring that urban space is coherent, ordered and rational.[9] A good example of this is a project by the World Bank to encourage city authorities in Africa to name their streets (and number the buildings along them) as a first step towards the improving urban management and the provision of services for the populace (Farvacque-Vitkovic *et al.* 2005).

However, the project to create an ordered and orderly city goes beyond issues of physical form and layout. Political elites and city managers also go to considerable lengths to organise the meanings attached to (and expressed in) urban space. Here the priority is to ensure that urban space reflects the values, ideology and agenda of the ruling political order. In this context, urban space can be arranged to communicate a message, both to the populace and to visitors from other countries.[10] At one level this includes setting out a clearly recognisable city centre that is visibly 'the locus of decision, wealth, power and information' (Lefebvre 1991: 375). This is achieved through the construction of monumental political, administrative and civic buildings and expansive urban squares and plazas. The symbolic importance of the centre is especially important in the capital city, itself frequently intended to be a statement of state power (van der Wusten 2000).

8. CAN WE THINK FOR A MOMENT, THEN, ABOUT THE CITY AS A KIND OF PALIMPSEST? ONE WITH ERASED STRUCTURES, NEW STRUCTURES, HYBRID FLOOR PLANS. I'D LIKE TO PROPOSE ROME AS THE ULTIMATE PALIMPSEST: NUMEROUS BUILDINGS ERASED, FORGOTTEN, VENERATED, RESTORED, REBUILT AND REPLACED ON TOP OF THE LAST. THIS CITY IS A MULTILAYERED SITE WHERE THE PAST IS INESCAPABLE AND INSISTS ON RUPTURING THE PRESENT CONTINUOUSLY AND VIOLENTLY. I WANT TO POSIT THAT THE CITY CAN NEVER BE WIPED THOROUGHLY CLEAN OR CREATED ANEW BECAUSE THOSE PAST LAYERS WILL STILL BE PRESENT SOMEHOW: PHYSICALLY (IN FRAGMENTS) OR THROUGH INDIVIDUAL AND COLLECTIVE MEMORY, ORAL HISTORIES AND PHOTOGRAPHIC EVIDENCE.

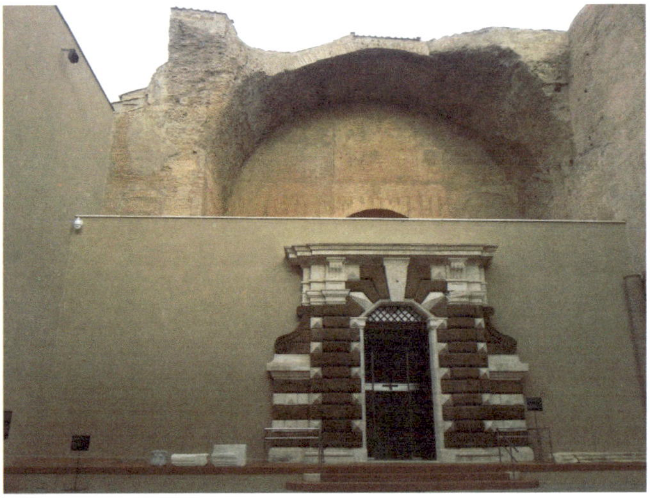

At another level, the meanings attached to urban space can be ordered through placing statues and monuments at key locations within the city. Such statues are intended to freeze particular values onto the urban landscape and signify space in particular ways (Verdery 1999). Placing such symbols in urban space is intended to saturate the consciousness of urban dwellers, providing a constant reminder of the values of the ruling political order. Furthermore, many statues and monuments are commemorative in nature and, as such, they are intended to order public memory by shaping what (and who) are remembered: [11] they are a key element of the ruling regime's effort to establish and promote an 'official' version of history. It is not only statues and monuments that perform this role: street names have a similar function. Streets need not have names since a number will do just as well (as the example of New York clearly illustrates). However, it is common practice to allocate names to streets and many of these are commemorative in nature. Once again they seek to direct what is remembered. In short, spaces contain – and communicate – messages (Lefebvre 1991) to the populace. The placing of symbols in the urban environment is a careful attempt to impose a form of symbolic order on public space.

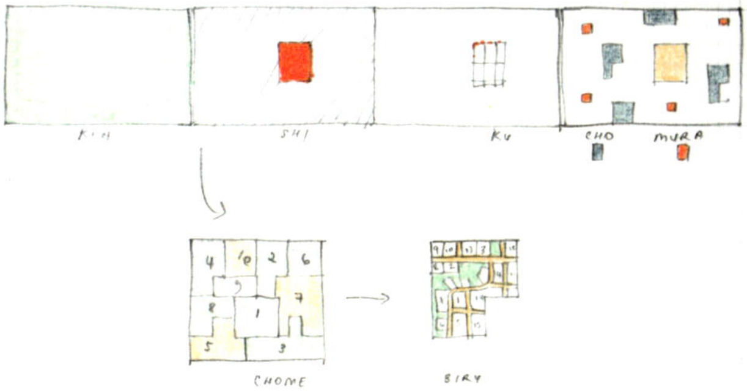

9. UPON ARRIVING IN A JAPANESE TOWN OR CITY, YOU MIGHT JUMP IN A TAXI TO GET TO YOUR HOTEL OR OTHER VENUE. WHEN I ARRIVED IN OTAGAWA (NEAR NAGOYA) SOME YEARS AGO, I FOUND THAT MY TAXI DRIVER WAS NOT ABLE TO FIND THE ADDRESS I WANTED. WE DROVE ALONG, STOPPING TO ASK PEDESTRIANS IF THEY KNEW IT AND, MORE IMPORTANTLY, WHAT BETTER-KNOWN LANDMARKS MIGHT BE NEXT TO IT. SIMILAR TO THE WAY IN WHICH BOOKS ARE APPROACHED FROM THE OPPOSITE SIDE (READING FROM THE BACK AND FROM RIGHT TO LEFT), THE ADDRESS SYSTEM IN JAPAN IS FORMULATED IN A KIND OF REVERSAL TO THE WESTERN ADDRESS SYSTEM (AND KYOTO AND SAPPORO HAVE THEIR OWN UNIQUE APPROACHES). IT IS LIKE AN EVER-DECREASING FRACTAL LANDSCAPE WITH THE LARGEST AREA WRITTEN FIRST, AND THE NEXT LARGEST, UNTIL YOU GET DOWN TO THE INDIVIDUAL BUILDING. THE BLOCK IS THE THING THAT IS NAMED, OR NUMBERED ACTUALLY, SO THAT THE STREETS BECOME NEGATIVE SPACE AROUND THEM. BUILDINGS ARE OFTEN NUMBERED IN THE ORDER THAT THEY WERE BUILT, SO YOU MAY FIND NUMBER ONE NEXT TO NUMBER EIGHT. TO ADD TO THE COMPLEXITY, BUSINESSES THAT WOULD ALMOST ALWAYS INHABIT THE GROUND FLOOR IN THE UK, SUCH AS A RESTAURANT OR BAR, CAN BE ON ANY FLOOR, SO YOU ALWAYS NEED TO REMEMBER TO LOOK UP AS WELL AS ALONG.

10. ALTHOUGH THERE'S NO CERTAINTY THAT THE POPULACE WILL TAKE ANY NOTICE OF THESE MESSAGES.

11. NB MOST STATUES ARE OF MEN. OFFICIAL HISTORY IS SELECTIVE AND GENDERED.

The symbolic importance attached to statues,[12] monuments and street names makes them vulnerable to political change (Azaryahu 1996). In particular, a change in political order is usually accompanied by a rapid reconfiguring of the urban landscape to remove commemorative symbols that are inappropriate and replace them with new symbols which better reflect the ideology and agenda of the new regime. As Lefebvre (1991) argues, each society produces its 'own' space, and a political revolution that fails to produce a new space cannot be said to have succeeded. As such, reshaping urban space is a key component of revolutionary political change.

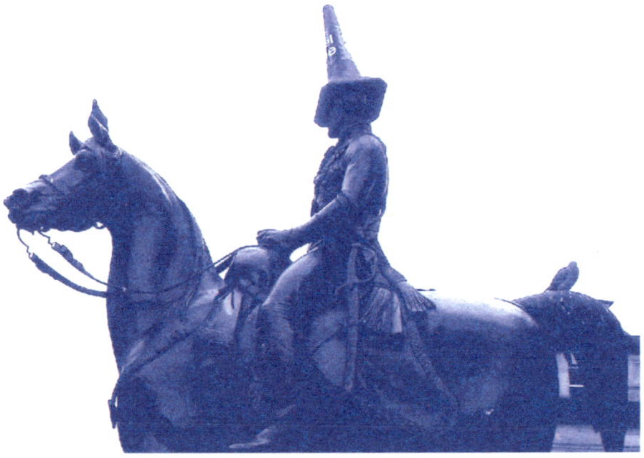

12. STATUES ARE OFTEN TO BE SEEN WITH TRAFFIC CONES UPON THEIR HEADS (ALSO CLOTHING, GARLANDS, BEER BOTTLE IN HAND WHEN THE FORM ALLOWS AND SO ON, IN ENDLESS CREATIVE WAYS) AND THE EQUESTRIAN STATUE DEPICTING THE DUKE OF WELLINGTON IN GLASGOW IS A SPECIAL EXAMPLE OF WHERE INTERVENTIONS BY INDIVIDUALS HAVE BECOME ACCEPTED INTO THE ORDER OF THE CITY. IN 2013 THERE WERE PLANS FROM THE CITY TO RAISE THE STATUE'S PLINTH TO STOP THE CONSTANT VANDALISM (CONE ON HEAD) AND OVER 100,000 PEOPLE SIGNED A PETITION AGAINST IT, ARGUING THAT THE CONE WAS A TRADITION THAT HAD BECOME PART OF GLASGOW'S HERITAGE.

Nowhere illustrates this better than the former communist states of East-Central Europe and the Soviet Union. These countries experienced two dramatic changes of political order in the 20th century: the takeover of power by Communist Parties (in 1917 in the Soviet Union, and after World War II in East-Central Europe) and the collapse of those regimes (mostly in 1989 in East-Central Europe and in 1991 in the Soviet Union). Communist regimes were intent on creating a new society and one of the first parts of this process was a dramatic remaking of urban space in order to 'de-commemorate' the former order and its political values. In practice this meant that statues were toppled, monuments were demolished and streets were renamed. In the following decades Communist Party regimes endeavoured to produce a new space that reflected the ruling ideology and values. However, with the collapse of those regimes, the urban landscape was now discordant with new aspirations for democracy and a market economy. Hence communist-era statues were pulled down, often to be replaced by new statues (re)commemorating events and people from the pre-communist era (and sometimes by the re-erection of statues that had earlier been pulled down by communist regimes). Streets carrying inappropriate names were renamed (and, in many cases, their pre-communist names were reinstated). New uses were found for monumental public buildings associated with the communist regimes (Czepczynski 2008). In many cases such buildings are turned into the base for a democratic parliament, or end up as a stock exchange or department store.[13] In this way, a new form of order is imposed on the urban landscape.

13. IN HIS BOOK, SPECIES OF SPACES AND OTHER PLACES, GEORGES PEREC WRITES IN THE CHAPTER TITLED 'SPACE, (CONTINUATION AND END)':

> I WOULD LIKE THERE TO EXIST PLACES THAT ARE STABLE, UNMOVING, INTANGIBLE, UNTOUCHED AND ALMOST UNTOUCHABLE, UNCHANGING, DEEP-ROOTED; PLACES THAT MIGHT BE POINTS OF REFERENCE, OF DEPARTURE, OF ORIGIN. (2008: 91)

BUT A SPACE WITH INHABITANTS CAN NEVER STOP MOVING AND CHANGING. EVEN A SPACE WITHOUT HUMAN INHABITANTS IS AT THE MERCY OF SMALLER GUESTS AND PLANT GROWTH. THERE ARE ALSO SPACES AND BUILDINGS THAT ARE TOO PROBLEMATIC TO BRING BACK TO ORDER OR TO CONVERT, EITHER FOR WHAT IT IS THEY REPRESENT OR HAVE REPRESENTED IN THE PAST, OR BECAUSE OF AN EVENT THAT OCCURRED ON THAT SITE. IF YOU VISIT THE PRUITT-IGOE PUBLIC HOUSING COMPLEX IN ST LOUIS, FOR EXAMPLE, YOU MUST LOOK CAREFULLY TO FIND IT; THE WOODLAND AREA THERE HOUSES RICH FLORA AND FAUNA AND THE TREES ARE TALL – THEY'VE HAD OVER 40 YEARS TO GROW AFTER ALL. ARTIST JUAN WILLIAM CHÁVEZ EVEN CREATED A BEE SANCTUARY ON THE SITE IN RECENT YEARS. THE ODD LAMPPOST OR STORM DRAIN GIVES IT AWAY, AS DO THE PATCHES OF TARMAC UNDER THE TREES' ROOTS, WHERE ROADS USED TO BE. PRUITT-IGOE IS A PLACE WITH A COMPLEX HISTORY BUT WITHIN TWO DECADES OF ITS BUILDING, IT BECAME DANGEROUS AND UNINHABITABLE AND THE AUTHORITIES DECIDED IT SHOULD BE DEMOLISHED. THIS PLACE COULD NOT BE BROUGHT BACK TO ORDER AND THERE HAS BEEN NO OFFICIAL USE SINCE, ALTHOUGH PROPOSALS WERE RECENTLY MADE TO MAKE THE SITE INTO COMMERCIAL PROPERTY, 45 YEARS AFTER DEMOLITION TOOK PLACE.

AZARYAHU M (1996)
'The power of commemorative street names.'
Environment and Planning D 14(3), 311–330.

CAMPBELL M (2009)
'Airport travelators actually slow passengers down.'
New Scientist.
Accessed on 15·6·18 at: newscientist.com/article/mg20327174-900-airport-travelators-actually-slow-passengers-down

CAVALCANTI M (1997)
'Urban reconstruction and autocratic regimes: Ceausescu's Bucharest in its historic context.'
Planning Perspectives 12(1), 71–109.

CZEPCZYNSKI M (2008)
Cultural Landscapes of Post-Socialist Cities.
Aldershot: Ashgate.

DE CERTEAU M (1984)
The Practice of Everyday Life.
Berkeley: University of California Press.

FARVACQUE-VITKOVIC C, GODIN L, LEROUX H, VERDET F AND CHAVEZ R (2005)
Street Addressing and the Management of Cities.
Washington DC: World Bank.

HARVEY D (1987)
'Flexible accumulation through urbanization: Reflections on 'post-modernism' in the American city.'
Antipode 19(3), 260–286.

HARVEY D (1989)
The Condition of Postmodernity: An Enquiry into the Origins of Cultural Change.
Oxford: Blackwell.

HARVEY D (2006)
Paris: Capital of Modernity.
Abingdon: Routledge.

HUXLEY M (2006)
'Spatial rationalities: Order, environment, evolution and government.'
Social and Cultural Geography 7(5), 771–787.

LEFEBVRE H (1991)
The Production of Space.
Blackwell, Oxford.

MARCUSE P (1987)
'The grid as city plan: New York city and laissez-faire planning in the nineteenth century.'
Planning Perspectives 2(3), 287–310.

O'NEILL B (2009)
'The political agency of cityscapes: Spatializing governance in Ceausescu's Bucharest.'
Journal of Social Anthropology 9(1), 92–109.

PEREC G (2008)
Species of Spaces and Other Places.
London: Penguin.

ROSE-REDWOOD R (2008)
'Indexing the great ledger of the community: Urban house numbering, city directories, and the production of spatial legibility.'
Journal of Historical Geography 34(2), 286–310.

ROSE-REDWOOD RS, ALDERMAN D AND AZARYAHU M (2010)
'Geographies of toponymic inscription: New directions in critical place-name studies.'
Progress in Human Geography 34(4), 453–70.

VAN DER WUSTEN H (2000)
'Dictators and their capital cities: Moscow and Berlin in the 1930s.'
Geojournal 54(2), 339–344.

VERDERY K (1999)
The Political Lives of Dead Bodies: Reburial and Postsocialist Change.
New York: Columbia University Press.

The Seaside Resort: Nostalgia and Restoration

Jenny Steele
/
David Jarratt

This essay forms part of an ongoing conversation between artist Jenny Steele and tourism researcher David Jarratt about the specificities of seaside places. Their in-conversation event, *Nostalgic Landscapes: Responses to the British Seaside*, discussed the significance of seaside resorts within the creation of individual and collective identities and the importance of reminiscence to their enduring appeal. Further discussions, including *Miami to Morecombe: This Building for Hope* – a public symposium organised by Jenny at The Midland Hotel, Morecambe, to which David contributed – have informed the following text, which explores the role of modernist architecture within the seaside's sense of place.

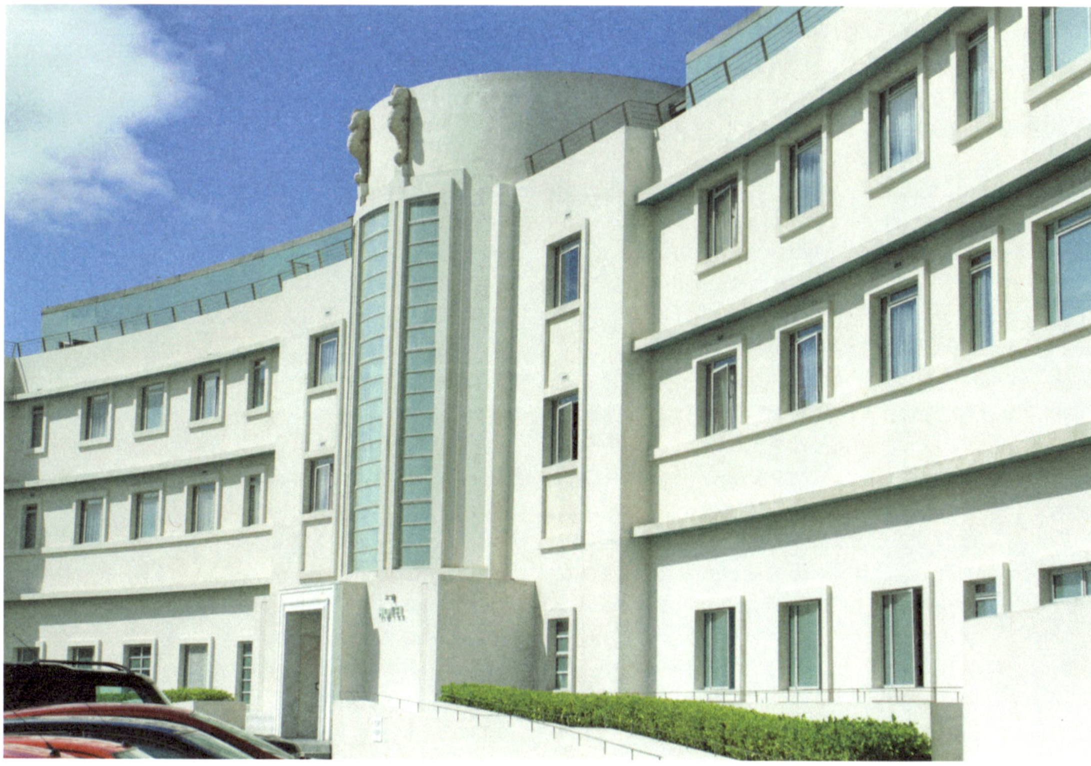

FIG 1

The Story Of The Seaside And Seaside Moderne

DJ The British shoreline has proven a blank canvas, onto which several meanings have been drawn over time. In recent years, the narrative of seaside resorts has tended towards one of decline. However, this perception of seaside towns as failing and irrelevant to modern life is one which both Jenny and I have challenged through our work.

Seaside resorts vary in terms of scale, history, clientele and the extent to which visitor numbers have ebbed and flowed over the years. Some have arguably become ex-resorts through a severe decline in numbers and infrastructure. Yet, despite negative media coverage, image problems and some very real challenges regarding the poverty of residents, traditional seaside resorts do continue to attract visitors. Blackpool, on the north-west coast, is the most obvious example. On the one hand, it is a place of deprivation, as evidenced by its many Houses of Multiple Occupancy (house sharing where the property is rented by at least three people who are not from one family or 'household') and high levels of substance abuse, but, on the other, it continues to thrive as a visitor destination, attracting around 8.6 million day visits per annum and making it the most visited seaside resort in Britain (Visit Britain 2017).

Around 20 miles up the coast, the town of Morecambe faced similar social and reputational challenges and a remarkable decline in visitor numbers. Yet it has managed to survive as a depleted resort and has seen regeneration in recent years. On the other side of Morecambe Bay lies Grange-over-Sands, which has not seen a significant drop in visitors, reputation or affluence since Victorian times. The forces behind the changes are not as simple as the rise of overseas package holidays since the 1960s, although this was a factor along with economic restructuring more generally. Essentially, the seaside fell out of fashion. A growing variety of UK holidays and leisure pastimes competed with the seaside – going for a drive in the country, camping, staying in and watching television and later, the city break. Not only did the leisure boom mean more competition, but the seaside resort slipped down the leisure spaces hierarchy (Urry 1997). Some resorts became retirement centres and/or places of residence for the urban poor due to a glut of accommodation once the spiral of decline set in. Nevertheless, this loss of prestige has not necessarily meant an end to tourism in such places. For example, many people still take their second or third annual holiday at the seaside, for a few days, rather than making it their primary break of the year as was still common in the 1960s, 1970s and even the early 1980s.

It is remarkable that the cotton mills have closed, the age of railway has given way to the age of the car and we now aspire to visit city centres rather than to escape their once polluted environments, yet these seaside towns of the industrial revolution survive. One reason for their continuation is that people have developed a relationship with these places – the resorts are now a tradition and part of Britain's heritage and popular culture. Part of their appeal is that the seashore remains relatively unchanged. It is a rich, multisensory environment which allows us to reconnect with the natural world, relax and recover; just as it did in its early role as a competitor to inland spas. Moreover, these environments, with their connotations of fun and reverie, can evoke happy memories of past holidays and facilitate nostalgia (Shields 1991; Jarratt and Gammon 2016). Since Victorian times the British seaside has been associated with childhood, not only through beach games, family entertainment and funfairs, but also through a long tradition of children's literature that encompasses these places (Walton 2000). However, this nostalgia is not just for our own personal memories (of childhood) but also for a collective or social nostalgia for the past more generally. These themes of sensoriality, restoration, stability and nostalgia inform the traditional seaside resort's sense of place, or *genus loci*, which I refer to as 'seasideness' – a term which I developed during my research in the Lancashire seaside town of Morecambe (Jarratt 2015).

✦

JS *The notion of seasideness and the idea of the seaside as a place of recuperation and recovery is embodied by coastal 'Seaside Moderne' architecture, which is the focus of my current practice. Constructed during the mid-war leisure boom, Seaside Moderne, or 'Nautical Moderne', was inspired by the nautical, long, sweeping curves of ocean liners, creating interiors of wide, open spaces with views out to sea. Influenced by the International Modernist style, it fought against the more decorative aspects of Art Deco, displaying mid-war austerity. The architecture symbolised resilience: no matter what devastation the country had suffered, it could overcome it and rebuild.*

After the trauma of World War I, in the UK and many Western countries there was a social emphasis on health and wellbeing. In 1930s Britain, workers nationally were given an annual holiday for the first time, also powered by efficient rail networks. Many new 'palaces of fun' were built in existing popular seaside resorts, such as Blackpool and Morecambe, to house the even greater influx of holidaymakers. Buildings for exercise, such as the Stonehaven Open Air Pool in Aberdeenshire, were financed by local councils. As were pavilions, such as the Rothesay Pavilion on the Isle of Bute and Largs Pavilion, also both in Scotland, which provided space for tourist entertainment, as well as for local people's recreational needs. Pleasure buildings, like The Midland Hotel, Morecambe and Blackpool Casino, were constructed by private companies, in this case London, Midland and Scottish Railway Company and Blackpool Pleasure Beach Holdings respectively, taking advantage of this new national obsession with recreation, following the death and devastation of World War I.

The ocean liners referenced by Seaside Moderne buildings signified the height of opulence at the time. They carried people across the oceans to new colonial lands where better lives were promised. Similar to the ship's design, the interiors of Seaside Moderne buildings were dominated by opulent features – exotic wood panelling, modern textiles and terrazzo flooring. These grand environments, which differed greatly from the usual surroundings of factory and office workers, created a stage set where people were encouraged to relax and enjoy themselves.

Most significantly, these buildings stood out visually from the previous Victorian and Edwardian architecture lining the coast, which usually consisted of tall, stone buildings with bay windows and decorative detailing. This modern architecture embodied an attitude of collective resilience, optimism and reassurance of social and economic recovery, which can also be seen in the widespread construction of municipal architecture such as town halls in the 1930s (East et al. 2012). Whatever atrocities we had experienced, we could build mighty architecture to overcome it, with hope for a better future.[1]

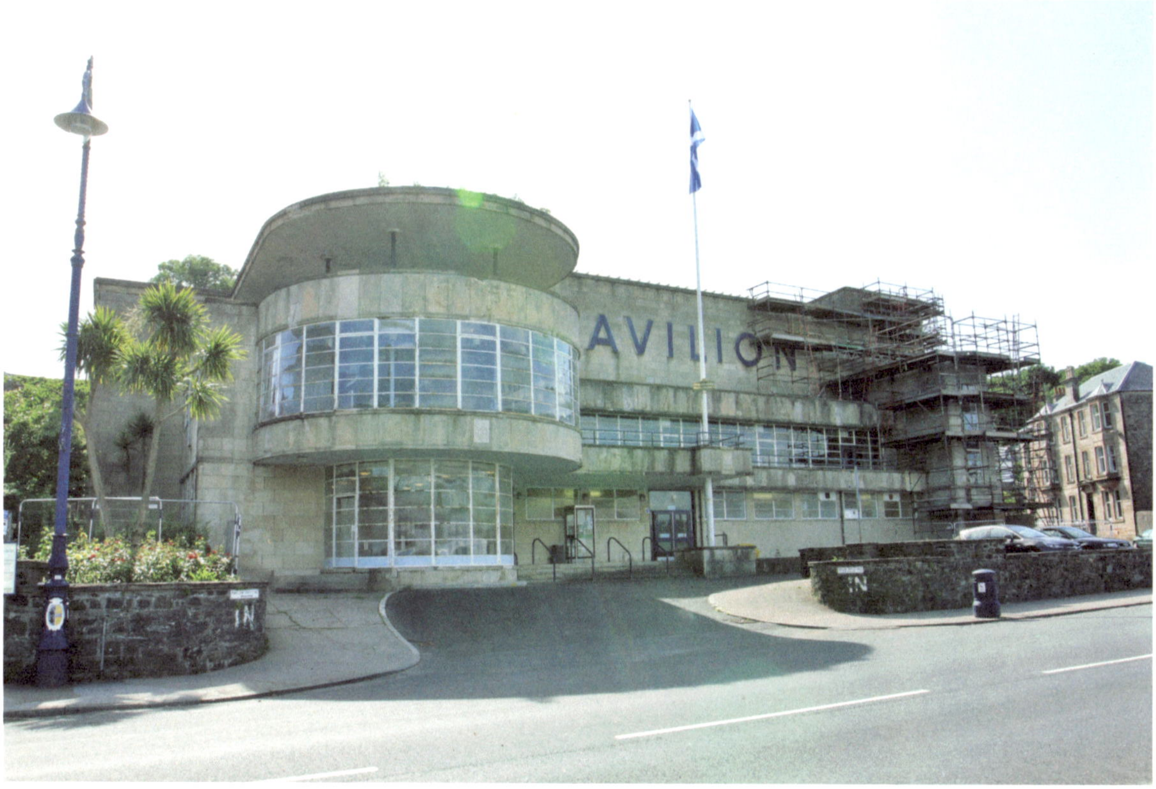

FIG 2

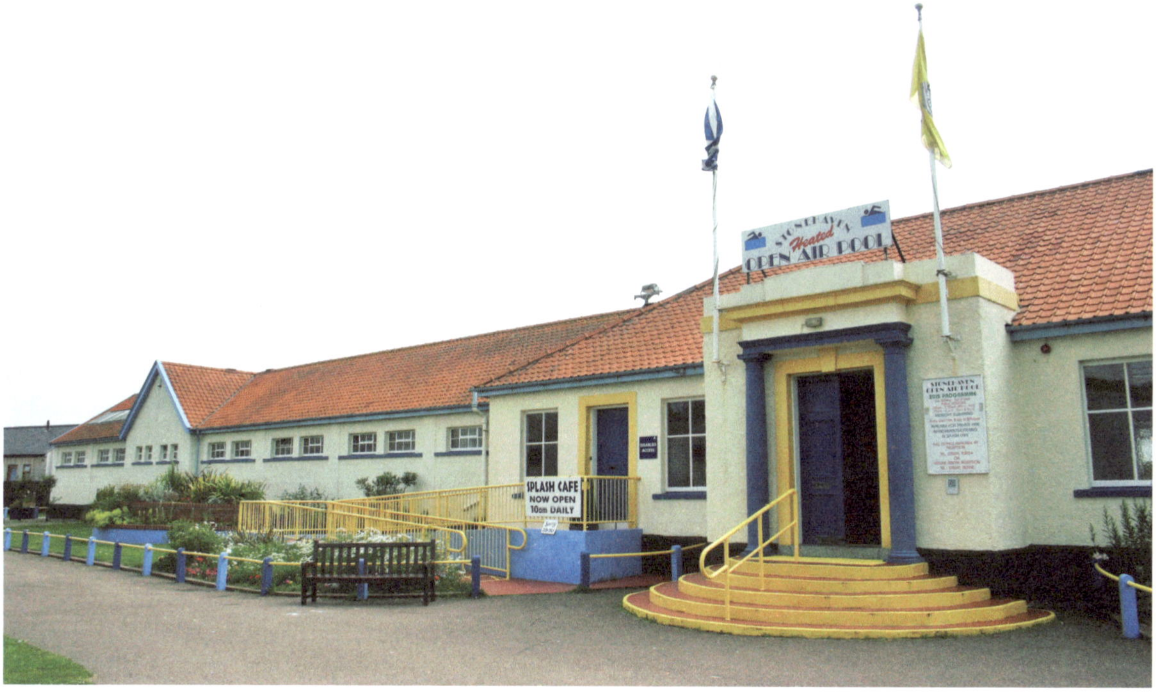

FIG 3

1. THIS OPTIMISM WAS SEVERED BY WORLD WAR II, WHEN PLEASURE ARCHITECTURE TOOK ON NEW UTILITARIAN WAR ROLES. MORECAMBE'S THE MIDLAND HOTEL BECAME A HOSPITAL, STONEHAVEN OPEN AIR POOL WAS A TRAINING POOL AND NEW BRIGHTON PALACE IN NEW BRIGHTON ON THE WIRRAL, AN AMMUNITION FACTORY.

Seasideness — sense of place at the seaside

Seasideness is the specific sense of place which people experience at the seaside. Edward Relph (1976), one of earliest human geographers to pay close attention to the notion of place, identified three key aspects of it: the physical characteristics of the environment, the meaning of place (memories and associations) and the activities afforded by the place, including social interactions. Over the years, these three dimensions have been refined by scholars but still underpin contemporary definitions of place (Patterson and Williams 2005). Sense of place is when place identity is significant enough to be felt or experienced; it is the subjective and emotional attachment people have to place (Cresswell 2015). I have previously defined it as:

> The fluid and multi-faceted way in which we know notable or memorable places through sensing, experiencing, and remembering a geographical location and its features. It is therefore a combination of our interaction with a physical environment and the meanings that we (as individuals and a society) bestow upon it, at the time or subsequently. (Jarratt *et al.* 2018)

My work on the seaside-specific sense of place, or seasideness, has revealed several emergent themes, foremost amongst these are nostalgia and wellness/restoration. Both are central to the visitor experience and were considered reasons to visit the seaside by the people I spoke to during my research, which took the form of a case study and was largely based around interviews with older visitors to the traditional resort of Morecambe. These interviews revealed that seasideness was strongly felt by the interviewees, who described the shoreline as a place to relax, reconnect and reminisce. In addition to the shoreline, beach and promenade, the other physical features which were consistently mentioned were seaside buildings, from modest traditional cafés to grand hotels. This combination of seashore and distinctive architecture provided a fittingly distinctive backdrop to the activities, experiences and memories, which can be described as seasideness.

The historian Fred Gray talks about how our 'complex memories and feelings about the seaside', such as 'sunburnt childhood holidays on a beach littered... with deckchairs and windbreaks or sun loungers and parasols... fumbled first sexual encounters under a pier... a family stroll along a promenade or boardwalk or a cliff-top park... or old people sitting in a seafront shelter watching the world go by' are all 'framed and conditioned by seaside architecture' (2006: 7). As well as the natural environment, therefore, architecture and built heritage play an important role in facilitating such seasideness.

✦

The restorative role of architecture, and specifically Seaside Moderne, as a backdrop or framing devise for the enhanced feelings of wellness and enjoyment encapsulated by seasideness is a central focus of my artwork. I am interested in how the seaside location frames our experience outdoors, whilst the architectural interior envelopes us in a space specifically designed to facilitate enjoyment, release and recuperation.

Restoration is a theme which relates to seaside architecture in more ways than one. For example, some of David's interviewees describe their time at the seaside in the following terms:

> *... And to be able to look at something that is unchanging, and for all intents and purposes will always be like that... has a calming effect, you know, to see that something won't change. Mankind's changing so much.*
>
> *... It takes your mind completely away from all our sort of manmade hustle and bustle. It takes you right back to nature really doesn't it?*
> *(Jarratt 2015: 158)*

Despite the deterioration of many seaside towns, the sense of continuity and mental wellbeing provided by proximity to a 'blue space' (White et al. 2013), alongside personal connections to these places, keeps people returning. In our society we are increasingly overwhelmed by digital visual stimuli, on top of life's inevitable pressures and challenges. We require a release and I believe that the seaside continues to provide a restorative environment for us.

The mentally restorative effects we experience when spending time at the seaside are mirrored by the progression from degeneration to restoration which has taken place in many seaside towns. Each building I explored in my 2015 project in northern Britain, 'Looking Back Moving Forward', and in my recent research into Miami South Beach Seaside Moderne, had its own narrative

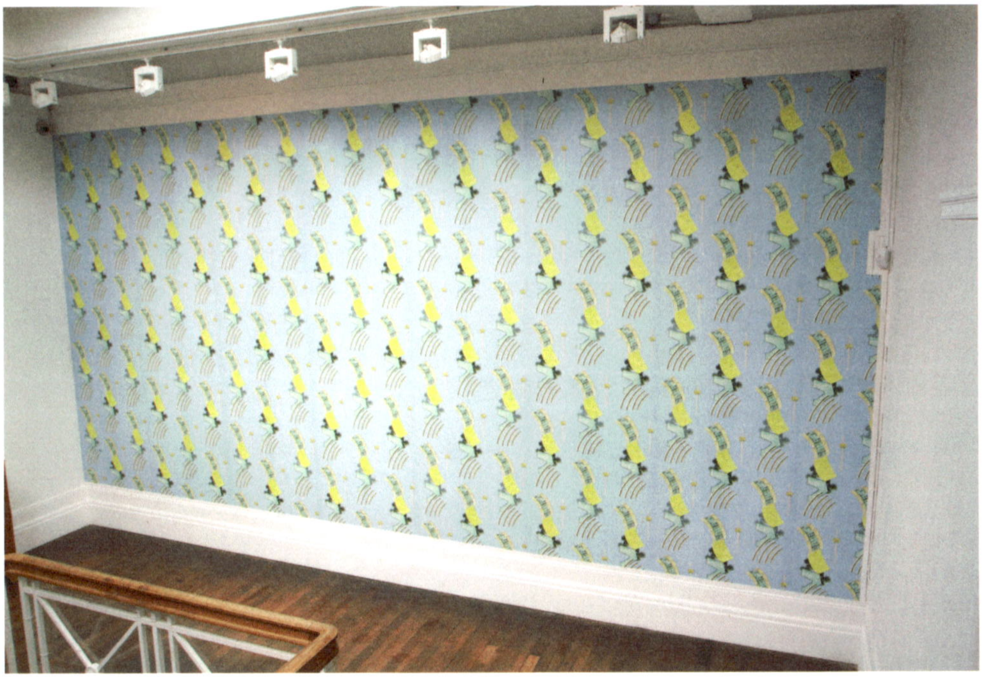

FIG 4

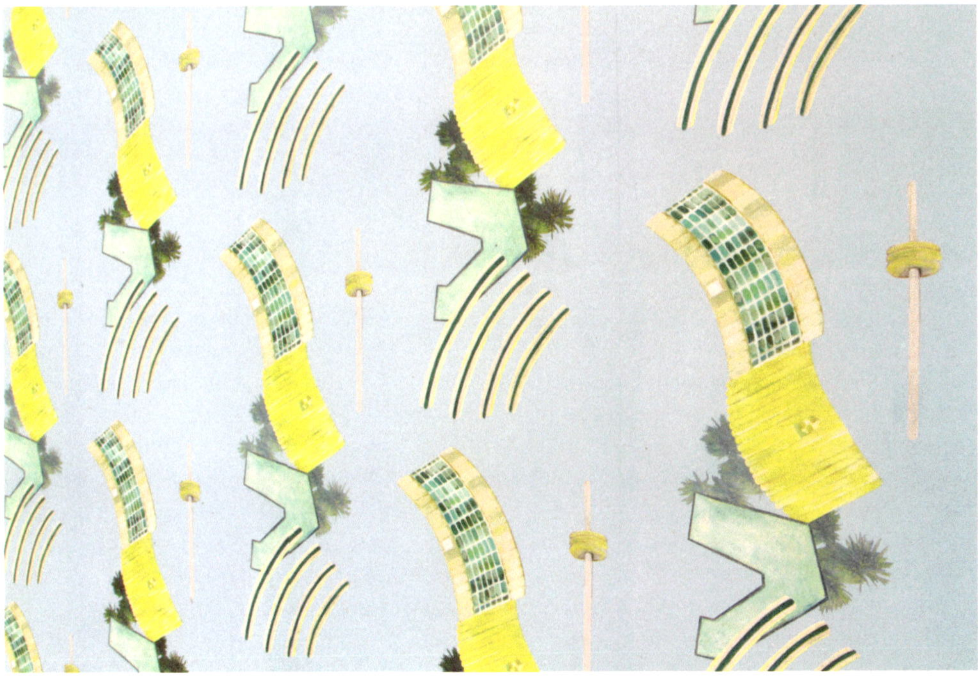

FIG 4A

of decline and, in most cases, revival. The Midland Hotel in Morecambe was renovated in 2008 by developers Urban Splash, and has since thrived as a hotel and events venue, bringing more interest and activity to the town, such as Vintage by the Sea festival, organised by Deco Publique. In Miami, numerous hotels on Ocean Drive and Collins Avenue in Miami Beach, such as the McAlpin and the Breakwater, were renovated in the 1990s, contributing to the area's overall success as a thriving all-year resort.

In recent years, the restoration of 1930s architecture has been used as a catalyst for revitalising seaside economies. Examples such as the restoration of Morecambe's The Midland and De La Warr Pavilion in Bexhill on the south coast have proved successful in generating a steady increase in interest. The Rothesay Pavilion on the Isle of Bute hopes to emulate this with a redevelopment due to open in 2019. What I find interesting is that such refurbishments consciously use nostalgia as a hook to bring in visitors. But unlike the personal nostalgia which seaside resorts seem to evoke through memories of childhood holidays, this is a type of collective nostalgia for past eras which are outside of our direct experience.

✦

Nostalgia for the seaside

Fundamentally, nostalgia is an idealised and selective representation of the past. Christina Goulding (1999) distinguishes between nostalgia for real personal memories and simulated nostalgia, that is, vicarious nostalgia evoked from narratives, images and objects; this allows nostalgia for a period that one has not experienced directly. All nostalgia reflects dissatisfaction with the present, acts as a counterpoint to modernity and can be a reaction to an uncertain or limited future (Dann 1994; Harvey 2000). The need for nostalgia to idealise the past at the expense of the present, or future, sets it apart from reminiscence, which has no such requirement. Nostalgia is often dismissed as pessimistic, looked down upon as a misrepresentation, considered as a loss of faith or even described in terms of a disease (Hewison 1987). Yet, nostalgia can be considered in more balanced terms as an emotional state that allows for ambivalences within it and tolerates the existence of different human realities - it is a melancholic delight; people do not want to be cured of their past (Bishop 1995). Svetlana Boym (2001: xiv) defines nostalgia as:

> A yearning for a different time – the time of our childhood, the slower rhythms of our dreams. In a broader sense, nostalgia is rebellion against the modern idea of time, the time of history and progress.

Identity and continuity lie at the heart of nostalgia, which can also be described as the relationship between personal and collective memory (Boym 2001; Bishop 1995). Not only can it solidify identity, but it can also sustain a sense of meaning and invigorate social connectedness (Routledge *et al.* 2011). As a self-focused emotional process, it gives the opportunity to form a meaningful narrative from memories. This is significant because, for many of us, our past lies at the centre of our sense of identity. David Lowenthal (2011) stresses the importance to wellbeing of identification with the earlier stages of one's own life. For many, this identification with the past is achieved through attachment to certain places which hold memories or meaning. The fact that nostalgia is often shared is significant; it strengthens feelings of attachment, security, perceptions of social support and empathy with others. Fond and selective recollections of past vacations, when people came together, can ward off negative feelings towards the present and future (Fairley and Gammon 2005). In short, nostalgia is melancholic, but the overall experience is positive and can lift our mood (see Routledge *et al.* 2011).

My research has specifically considered seaside nostalgia as experienced by older visitors to Morecambe. For the respondents in this study, nostalgia was strongly felt and a significant part of the seaside experience. Respondents became emotional when recounting memories of family holidays that clearly meant a great deal to them. However, a feeling of loss was tempered by a feeling of continuity; interviewees took comfort in the fact that they now played the role of parent or grandparent in trips to the beach. One of seaside nostalgia's functions is to support these narratives, which dwell on the past but influence the present and will inform the future. Through this work, the three main functions of seaside nostalgia were identified as: a reconnection to childhood memories, to support (family) narratives and to find reassurance/stability through the ability to escape our everyday perception of time and to reconnect to the past or a different perception of time (Jarratt and Gammon, 2016).

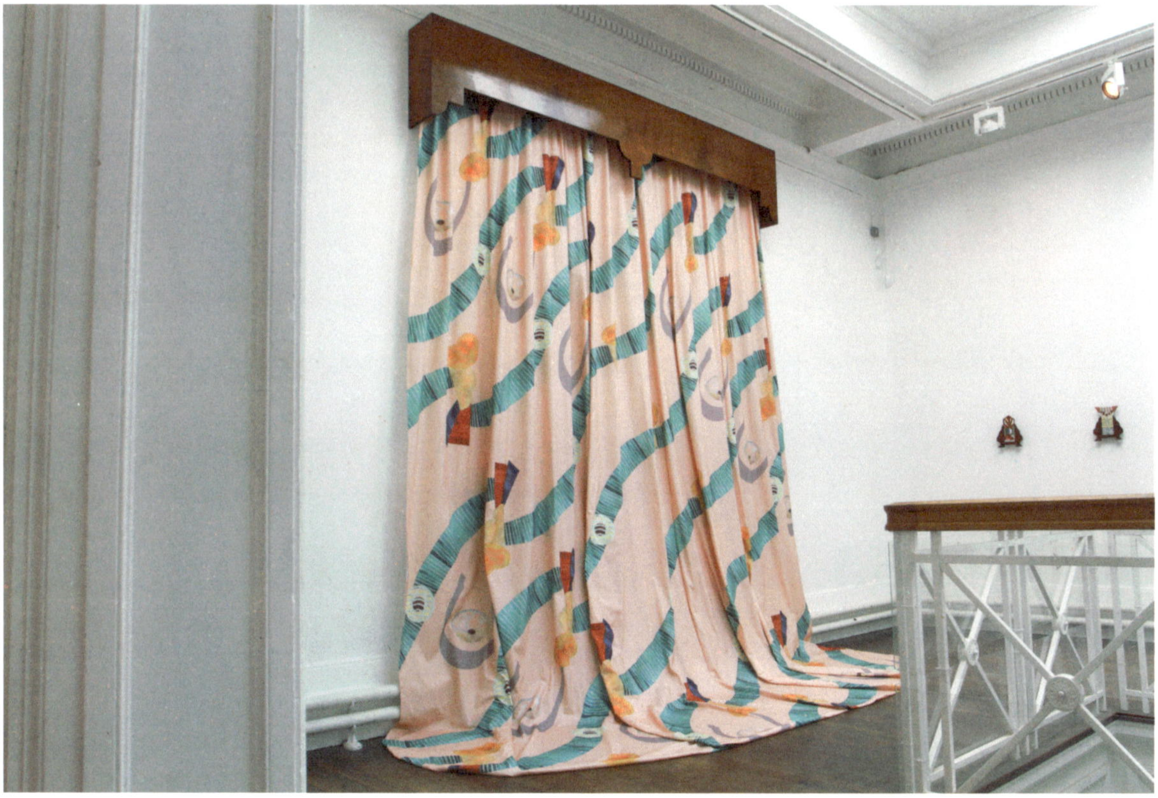

FIG 5

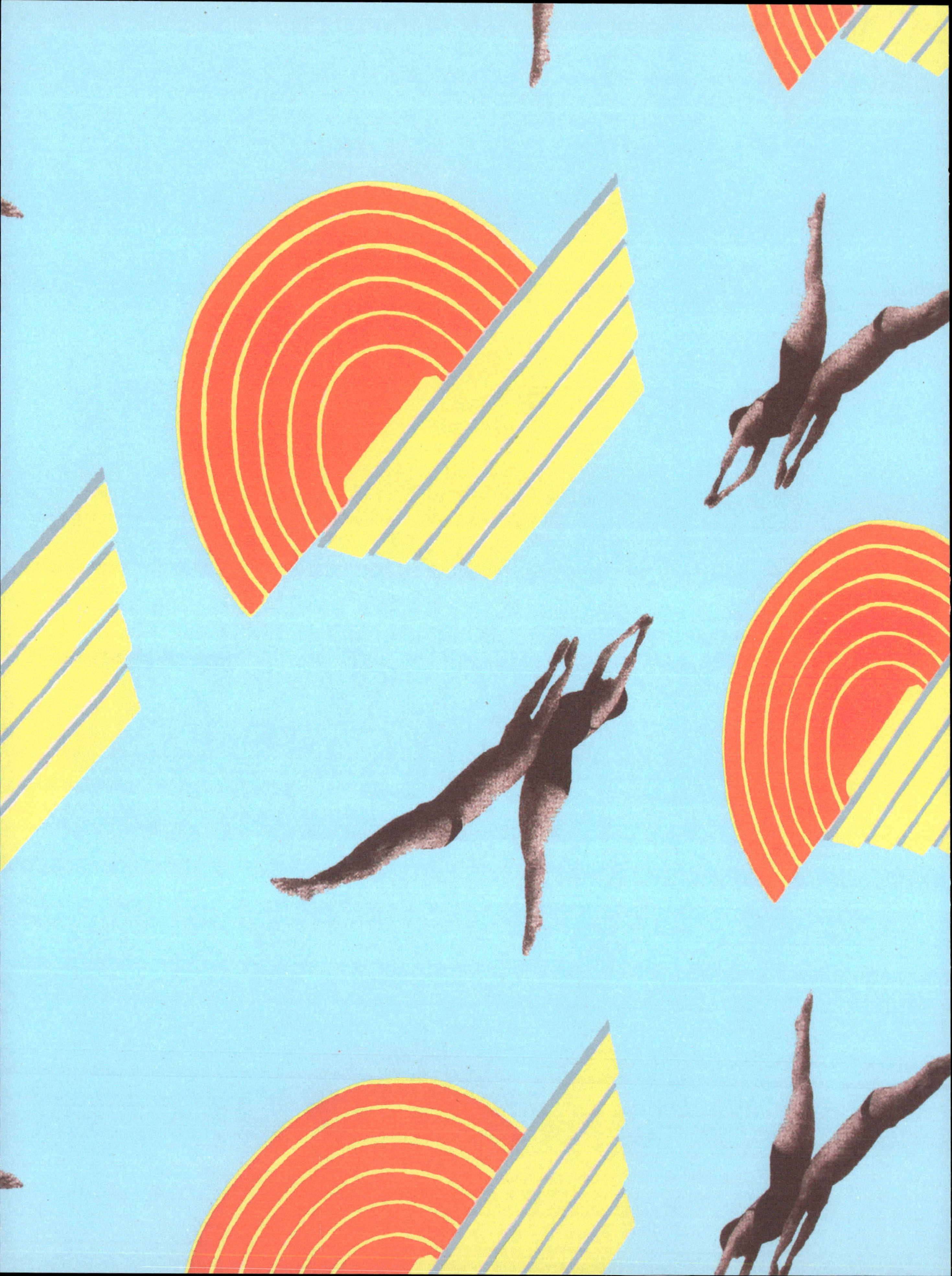

✦

References to nostalgia, in both its personal and collective form, evoked by experiences of seasideness, occur frequently in my work. I am interested in how experiencing nostalgia can have an uplifting effect on our wellbeing without naively viewing the past as a better version of our current life. The wallpaper, 'Over and Over Jump In!' responds to the architecture and archive of the Stonehaven Open Air Pool in Aberdeenshire, Scotland. My father visited the pool weekly as a child and took my sister and me as children. We now visit the pool as an annual family ritual with our spouses and children. The artwork uses architectural motifs from the building's colourful design, interspersed with divers from archival photographs. The title references the passing of time through generations, the repeated activities we undertake in the restorative environment of the pool and the importance of taking time to relax and recuperate during life's difficulties.

✦

Recovery at the seaside

As Jenny's work suggests, this bitter-sweet seaside nostalgia, which is strongly felt and can lift our mood and offer social connections, is often linked to notions of wellbeing. Any more substantial or long-term health benefits have not yet been proven. However, exposure to blue space (aquatic environments) more generally has been clearly linked to a feeling of restorativeness and seems to offer real health benefits (see Bell *et al.* 2015; White *et al.* 2010; White *et al.* 2013).

To some extent, seaside resorts have retained associations with wellness and recovery since they first developed in the industrial revolution when air pollution in cities was notoriously bad and the environmental benefits of the seaside were most obvious. Yet, resorts continued to market their health-giving properties well into the 20th century. If we take Morecambe as an example, the high quality of its air and climate were clearly extolled in various letters in the press throughout the 19th century (Grass 1972). Even in 1925, Morecambe girls were described as having 'clear eyes and clear complexions which only ideal surroundings can give' in marketing material (Bingham 1990: 185). The inter-war and post-war periods saw the height of seaside popularity, which was still concerned with health – especially swimming and exposure to the sun. During the second half of the 20th century, justified concerns about coastal pollution no doubt tempered this reputation, but the underlying association with health has remained (Hassan 2003).

OPPOSITE PAGE: FIG 6

With efforts to improve British beaches (largely due to EU regulations) and the recent confirmation by psychologists that blue space is good for us (see Foley and Kistemann 2015), the longstanding association with recovery may well be in recovery itself and this, in turn, can only be good news for British resorts. What is certain is that since the start of the 21st century, the British seaside resort has had a renaissance. Seaside towns around the country have seen numbers swell, not least due to recent changes in the value of the pound brought on by Brexit, but also through a growing demand for traditional holidays fit for modern consumers (*Financial Times* 2017). In 2015 seaside locations accounted for an impressive 39% of British holiday nights and this seems set to rise (Visit Britain 2017). The reasons for this are numerous, but resorts like Morecambe have become more fashionable. The designer Wayne Hemingway argues that there is a movement amongst young people to rediscover the coast and this is facilitated through a growing programme of coastal events (Hemmingway 2017), examples include Coastival in Scarborough and The Great Seaside Vintage Fair in Whitby. Indeed, Morecambe's nostalgia-fuelled Vintage by the Sea festival, associated with Hemmingway, now attracts 40,000 visitors compared with 6,000 only three years ago (Deco Publique 2017).

✦

The many layers of restoration and revival in relation to the seaside and its modern history fuel my making and research. My exhibition, 'This Building for Hope' at The Midland Hotel, Morecambe in October 2017, came from a desire to restore and highlight the optimism and exuberance evident in the original 1930s design of the building. The exhibition was also informed by research into Miami Seaside Moderne architecture, which I undertook during a visit to Miami Beach earlier that year. Following a hurricane in 1926, the majority of this resort, which had been swampland until 1885, was rebuilt in the Seaside Moderne style. Hundreds of hotels were built quickly and cheaply in the early 1930s, many of which referenced ship design, with features of masts, small windows and portholes. Horizontal racing stripes were also a common feature, suggesting movement towards a better and more progressive future.

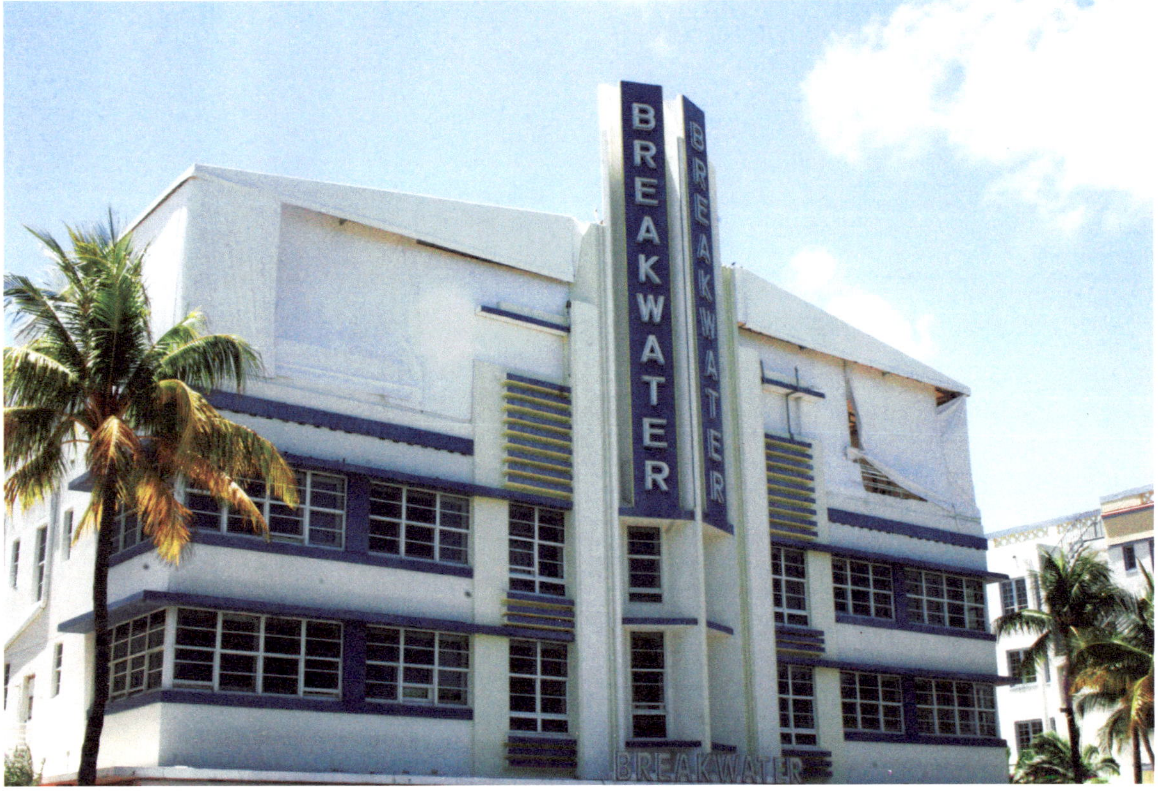

FIG 7

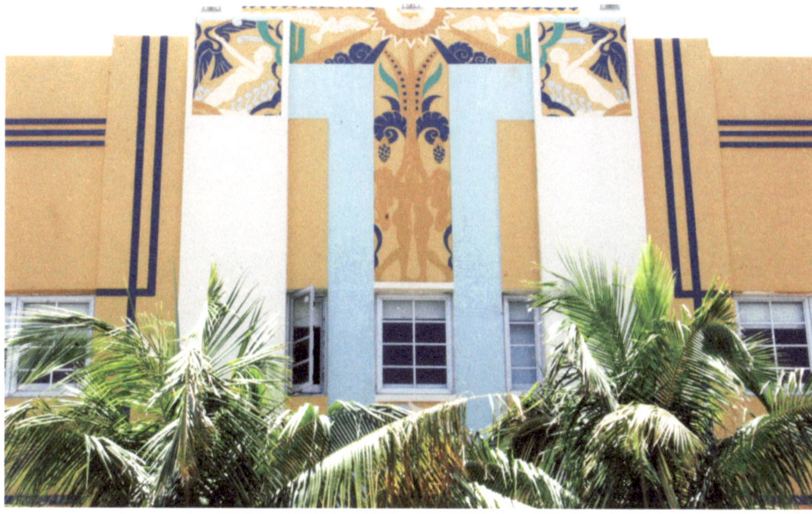

FIG 8

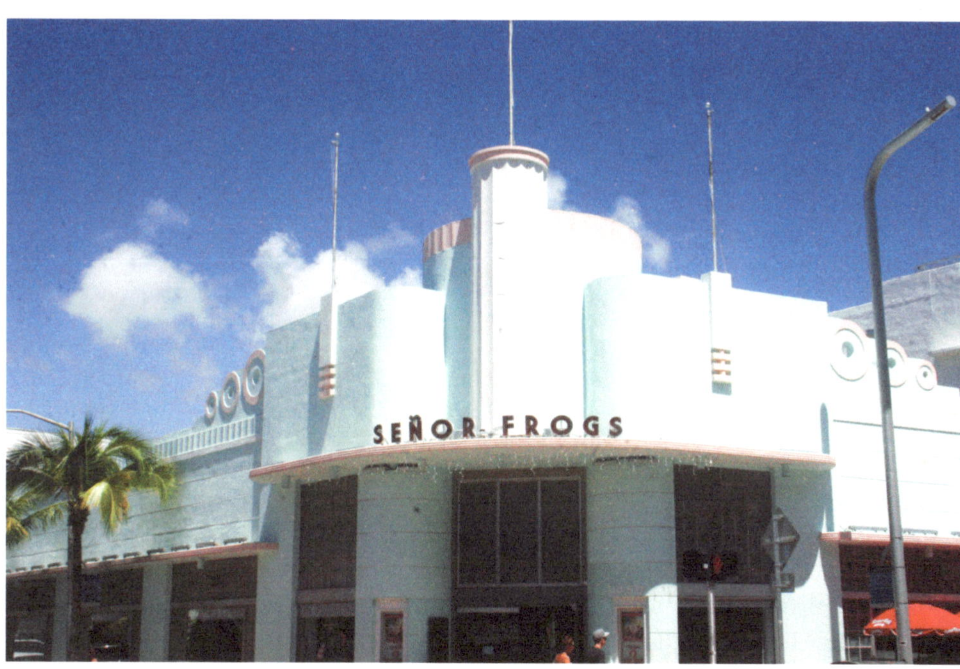

FIG 9

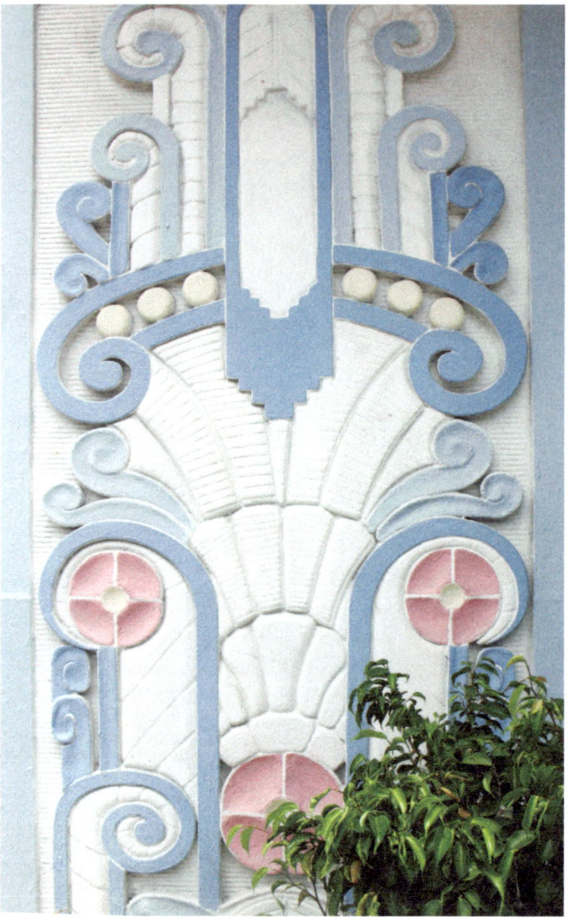

FIG 10

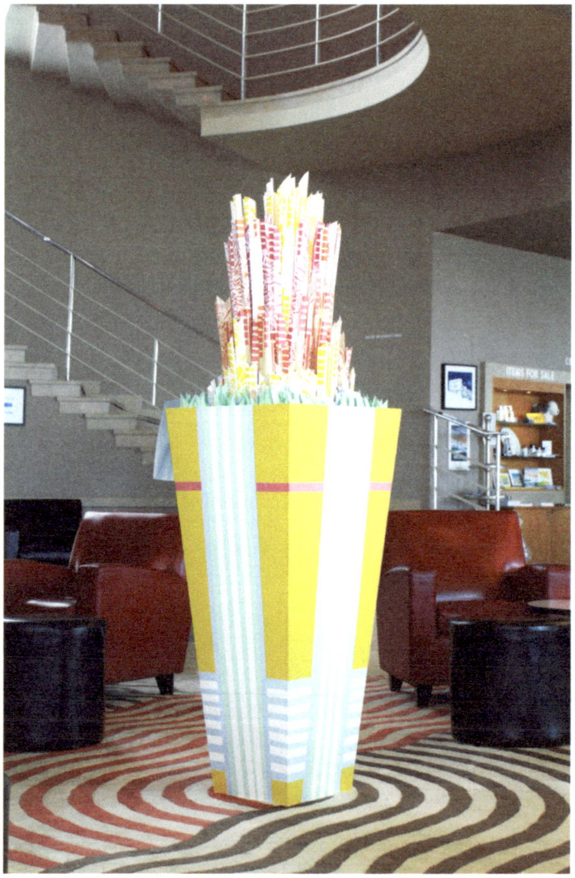

FIG 11

3. IN 1925, US PRESIDENT CALVIN COOLIDGE TRAVELLED TO THE PARIS INDUSTRIAL ARTS EXPOSITION AND WAS IMPRESSED BY EXAMPLES OF EARLY MODERNIST DESIGN AND ARCHITECTURE IN THE DESIGN OF THE PAVILIONS BY LOUIS DEJEAN AND ROBERT MALLET-STEVENS. COOLIDGE DECIDED THAT THE US WANTED TO ADOPT THIS FORWARD-LOOKING DESIGN IN NEW YORK, FURTHER SPREADING SOUTH TO MIAMI.

I installed a series of 'fountains' within the interior of The Midland, which referenced the recurring motif on the façades of the 1930s seafront architecture on Miami South Beach. The fountain motif, halted at the point of spouting upwards, features heavily as a plaster relief on the coastal architecture and acts as a metaphor for the social attitude of optimism during the building's construction. As a nation currently in the wake of austerity following financial crisis, and with considerable social and economic unease preceding the UK's separation from the European Union, the fountains suggest optimistic assurance that our country has recovered from previous trauma. Yet, just as the exuberance embodied by the original fountain motif was subsequently shattered by World War II, they also serve to remind us of how quickly the world can change.

The printed and painted fountains were temporary objects interspersed within the hotel's interior, suggesting an atmosphere of celebration and excitement through their shape, pattern and form. My aim was to enhance the atmosphere of revitalisation within the hotel's interior by connecting with its past and reviving the air of optimism and excitement which accompanied the building's original construction. In this way, the sculptures became new props within the existing stage set created by the original architect, Oliver Hill – an environment in which our main role is to enjoy ourselves.

The practice of taking and re-presenting architectural motifs, which may have gone unnoticed during our busy everyday lives, informs many of my artworks. I often reposition these motifs in new constellations to suggest an alternative narrative or a contribution to a larger history. Within the outdoor artwork, 'Not so Nautical a Divide', a 56-metre-long banner snaked along Morecambe's promenade separating the beach from The Midland and vice versa. The circular portholes in the work are motifs taken from both The Midland and examples of Seaside Moderne architecture in Miami, with the patterns and base line referencing the waterline of the ocean liners which carried the architectural style between the two continents.[3] The motifs, which otherwise adorn geographically distant buildings, are brought together to create one new artwork with an ambivalent shared history, which speaks of an international desire for optimism and release after the horrors of World War I but also the role of colonialism within the international development of modernist architecture.

The seaside in summary: resilience, reconnection, reverie and restoration

The seaside resort has proven itself to be resilient. A nostalgia-fuelled seasideness represents the long-standing sociocultural meaning of these places, but it is not as static as its adoption by the vintage movement indicates. This seasideness, which informs the cross-generational appeal of the resorts with their various traditions, featured in advertising campaigns in the 1980s, when the Isle of Man Marketing Board used the slogan 'Looking forward to going back' (Dann 1994: 75). In addition, the underlying appeal of the coastline as a place to 'reconnect' (primarily with nature) goes back at least as far as the early days of the Industrial Revolution and is now of great interest to environmental psychologists. Such reconnection not only occurs with natural and aquatic environments and coastal activities, but also involves the nostalgic past and our memories of seaside visits (Jarratt and Gammon 2016). Both forms of reconnection are now seen as experiences which can positively affect our mental state and wellbeing. So, the seaside is indeed a place of recovery through reconnection. As commentators such as Kenneth Lindley (1973) and Fred Gray (2006) have pointed out, and as I have discovered through my research, this nostalgic, perhaps romantic, sense of seasideness is facilitated by not only the liminal setting, but also the built environment. Despite the prevalence of 'dreary estates' along the coast (Lindley 1973: 20),[4] it is the seaside buildings and heritage of the seafront which really characterise these places and evoke a 'seaside image' (*ibid*: 19). Unique structures such as winter gardens, towers and piers, along with exotic architectural styles such as orientalism, all contribute to the 'otherness' of the seaside (Gray 2006).

✦

Of all seaside architecture, Seaside Moderne is the style which best reflects not only otherness, but also aspects of optimism, wellness and recovery with which the seaside is associated. This is one of the main reasons why I keep returning to this architecture in my work. It creates

4. LINDLEY IS REFERRING TO THE MID-20TH CENTURY GROWTH OF SUBURBAN HOUSING IN COASTAL RESORTS, WHICH BECAME INCREASINGLY POPULAR WITH COMMUTERS AND RETIREES. HE CRITICISED SPECULATIVE BUILDERS FOR THEIR LACK OF SENSITIVITY FOR THE LOCALE, SINGLING OUT BUNGALOWS AND SEMI-DETACHED HOUSES IN PARTICULAR.

the most joyful set of parameters within which we can escape our everyday lives and, no matter how fleetingly, enjoy ourselves. As Miami Modern architect Morris Lapidus famously said, 'If you create the stage setting and it's grand, everyone who enters will play their part' (Schellenbaum 2018).

This notion of architecture as a stage set for extraordinary activities and encounters is something which I'm particularly interested in. Seaside resorts are enhanced atmospheres, created for our enjoyment. As such, they could be, and often are, judged as false, frivolous and divorced from everyday life. The building façades of Seaside Moderne in Miami, built quickly and economically to be ready for the upcoming tourist season, were constructed from cheap plaster reliefs and intended to last for a maximum of 20 years. As with other seaside locations, the tropical paradise surrounding these buildings is also manufactured, with man-made sand dunes, imported palm trees and other exotic birds and foliage introduced to create an otherworldly environment. Yet, such artifice is what gives Seaside Moderne its power to enchant and enthral us.

The processes by which I make my work share a similar concern with façade; they are predominantly surface based – drawing, screen-print, painting and digital – and interventions, such as those within The Midland, are temporary and fleeting. 'The Tropical Garden', was a printed vinyl installation in the right-hand rotunda window of The Midland, which visually referenced the colourful and detailed façades of Seaside Moderne architecture in Miami. The work was influenced by photographs in the archive of The Wolfsonian of a 'Tropical Garden' in the Lincoln Road Mall, South Beach, Miami from the 1920s. The exotic garden diorama was lit up at night, as was my tropical garden, but, despite drawing people in to look, was physically inaccessible.

At the seaside there is always a tension between reality and artifice, the mundane and the fanciful, the everyday and escape – and this liminality is part of the seaside's genus loci (Gray 2006; Jarratt 2015; Jarratt and Sharpley 2017; Walton 2000). By whatever means we experience this optimism and exuberance, however transitory, superficial or rose tinted, seaside resorts provide an important release and new perspective on the everyday and ourselves. It is perhaps due to this very deficiency of depth that we are able to momentarily connect to a semi-idealised version of the world, through a 'tranquil reverie' (Bachelard 1971: 99) and feel uplifted.

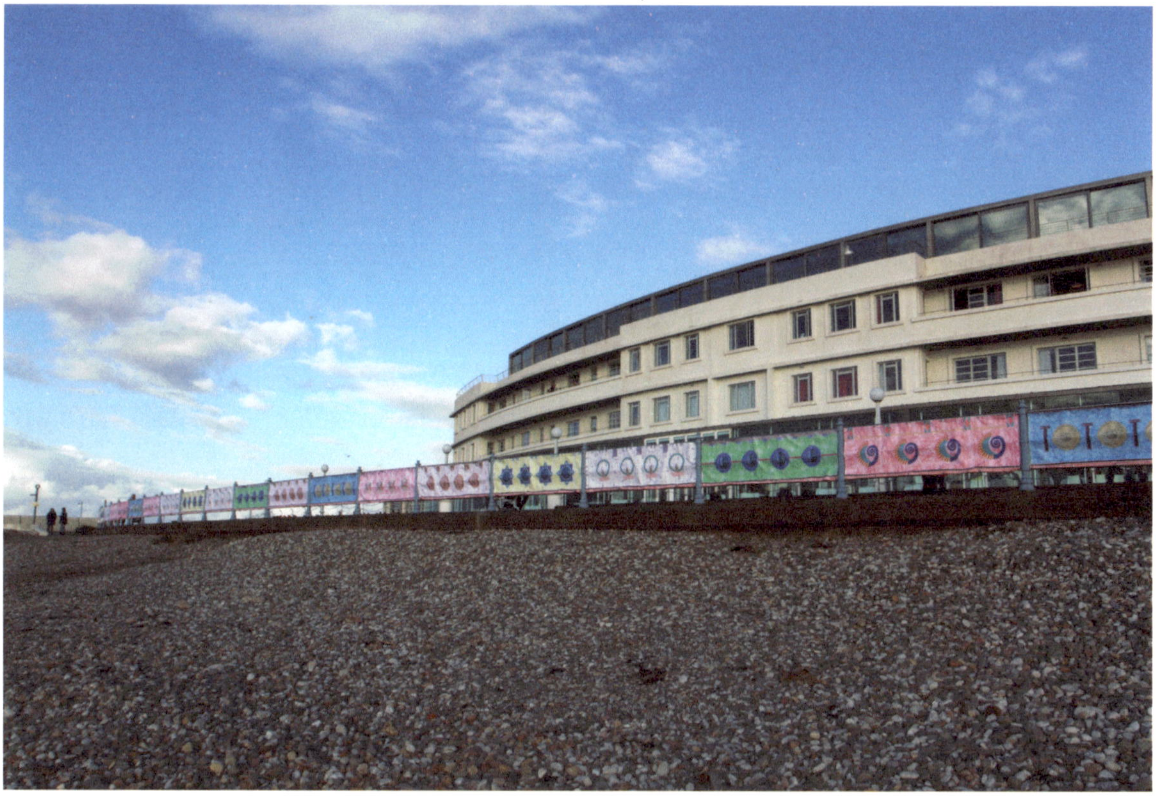

FIG 12

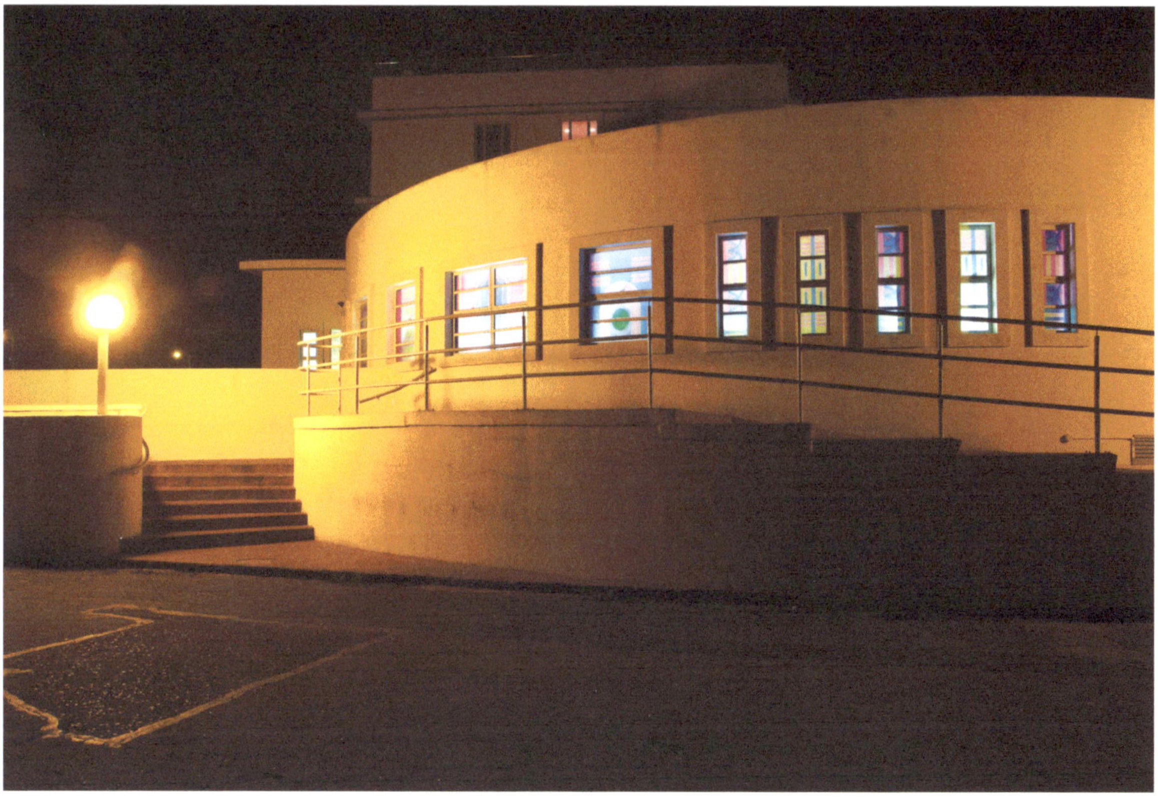

FIG 13

FIG 1 THE MIDLAND HOTEL
MORECAMBE, 1933.
–
ARCHITECT: OLIVER HILL
IMAGE: JENNY STEELE

FIG 2 ROTHESAY PAVILION
ISLE OF BUTE, SCOTLAND, 1938.
–
ARCHITECT: JAMES CARRICK
IMAGE: JENNY STEELE

FIG 3 STONEHAVEN OPEN AIR POOL
STONEHAVEN, ABERDEENSHIRE, 2015.
–
IMAGE: JENNY STEELE

FIG 4 + FIG 4A 'THE SEA BREEZE WAS THE CURE'
DIGITAL PRINT ON WALLPAPER
JENNY STEELE
GRUNDY ART GALLERY, BLACKPOOL, 2016.
–
IMAGE: DAVE BARTON

FIG 5 'A RESTORATIVE RESORT'
DRAWING AND PAINTING
DIGITALLY PRINTED ON COTTON
WALNUT BURL PELMET
JENNY STEELE
GRUNDY ART GALLERY, BLACKPOOL, 2016.
–
IMAGE: JOHN LYNCH

FIG 6 'OVER AND OVER JUMP IN!'
DIGITAL PRINT ON WALLPAPER
JENNY STEELE
IN CERTAIN PLACES, PRESTON, 2016.
–
IMAGE: DAVID BARTON

FIG 7 THE BREAKWATER
OCEAN DRIVE, SOUTH BEACH, MIAMI, 1939.
–
ARCHITECT: ANTON SKISLEWICZ
IMAGE: JENNY STEELE

FIG 8 POPPA & CICCIA ITALIAN RESTAURANT
COLLINS AVENUE, MIAMI BEACH, C.1930.
–
ARCHITECT: UNKNOWN
IMAGE: JENNY STEELE

FIG 9 HOFFMAN'S CAFETERIA (CURRENTLY SEÑOR FROGS)
COLLINS AVENUE, MIAMI BEACH, 1939.
–
ARCHITECT: HENRY HOHAUSER
IMAGE: JENNY STEELE

FIG 10 FOUNTAIN PLASTER RELIEF FROM THE CONGRESS HOTEL
OCEAN DRIVE, SOUTH BEACH, MIAMI, 1936.
–
ARCHITECT: HENRY HOHAUSER
IMAGE: JENNY STEELE

FIG 11 'THE FOUNTAIN - NORTH BEACH'
SCREEN-PRINT ON CARD, PRINT ON METAL
JENNY STEELE
THE MIDLAND, MORECAMBE, 2017.
–
IMAGE: DAVE BARTON

FIG 12 'NOT SO NAUTICAL A DIVIDE'
DIGITAL PRINT ON PVC BANNERS
JENNY STEELE
MORECAMBE PROMENADE, 2017.
–
IMAGE: DAVE BARTON

FIG 13 'THE TROPICAL GARDEN'
DIGITAL PRINT ON VINYL
JENNY STEELE
THE MIDLAND, MORECAMBE, 2017.
–
IMAGE: DAVE BARTON

BACHELARD G (1971)
The Poetics of Reverie.
Boston: Beacon Press.

BELL S, PHOENIX C, LOVELL R AND WHELEER B (2015)
'Seeking everyday wellbeing: The coast as a therapeutic landscape.'
Social Science and Medicine 142, 56–67.

BINGHAM RK (1990)
Lost Resort: The Flow and Ebb of Morecambe.
Milnthorpe: Cicerone Press.

BISHOP P (1995)
An Archetypal Constable: National Identity and the Geography of Nostalgia.
London: Athlone Press.

BOYM S (2001)
The Future of Nostalgia.
New York: Basic Books.

CRESSWELL T (2015)
Place: A Short Introduction.
Oxford: Blackwell.

DANN G (1994)
'Tourism and Nostalgia: Looking forward to going back'.
Vrijetijd en Samenleving 12(1), 75-94.

DECO PUBLIQUE (2017)
'Vintage by the Sea.'
Accessed on 15·6·18 at: decopublique.co.uk/vintage-by-the-sea-1

EAST J, RUTT N AND C20 SOCIETY (2012)
The Civic Plunge Revisited.
Accessed on 15·6·18 at: c20society.org.uk/wp-content/uploads/2013/03/2012-2403-CivicPlungeRevisitedlowres2.pdf

FAIRLEY S AND GAMMON G (2005)
'Something lived, something learned: Nostalgia's expanding role in sport tourism.'
Sport in Society 8(2), 182–197.

FINANCIAL TIMES (2017)
'Butlins woos cash-strapped vacationers in Brexit Britain.'
Accessed on 15·6·18 at: ft.com/content/176447ee-8986-11e7-bf50-e1c239b45787

FOLEY R AND KISTEMANN T (2015)
'Blue space geographies: Enabling health in place.'
Health and Place 35, 157–165.

GOULDING C (1999)
'Heritage, nostalgia and the grey consumer.'
Journal of Marketing Practice: Applied Marketing Science 5(6/7/8), 177–199.

GRASS J (1972)
'Morecambe, the people's pleasure. The Development of a holiday resort, 1880–1902.'
Unpublished MA dissertation, Lancaster University, Lancaster.

GRAY F (2006)
Designing the Seaside.
London: Reaktion Books.

HARVEY D (2000)
The Condition of Postmodernity: An Enquiry into the Origins of Cultural Change.
Cambridge, MA: Blackwell Publishers.

HASSAN J (2003)
The Seaside, Health and The Environment in England and Wales since 1800.
Aldershot: Ashgate.

HEMMINGWAY W (2017)
Interview with Wayne Hemmingway [TV programme].
BBC Breakfast – BBC1, 7 September.

HEWISON R (1987)
The Heritage Industry.
London: Methuen.

JARRATT D (2015)
'Seasideness: Sense of place at a British coastal resort: Exploring "seasideness" in Morecambe.'
Tourism: An International Interdisciplinary Journal 63(3), 351–363.

JARRATT D (2015)
'Sense of place at a seaside resort.'
In S Gammon and S Elkington (eds)
Landscapes of Leisure: Space, Place and Identities.
London: Palgrave Macmillan. pp.147–163.

JARRATT D AND GAMMON S (2016)
'"We had the most wonderful times": seaside nostalgia at a British resort.'
Tourism, Recreation Research 41(2), 123–133.

JARRATT D, PHELAN C, WAIN J AND DALE S (2018)
'Developing a sense of place toolkit: Identifying destination uniqueness.'
Tourism and Hospitality Research.
Accessed on 15·6·18 at: http://journals.sagepub.com/doi/10.1177/1467358418768678

JARRATT D AND SHARPLEY R (2017)
'Tourists at the seaside: Exploring the spiritual dimension.'
Tourist Studies 17(4), 349–368.

LINDLEY K (1973)
Seaside Architecture.
London: Hugh Evelyn.

LOWENTHAL D (2011)
The Past is a Foreign Country.
Cambridge: Cambridge University Press.

PATTERSON M AND WILLIAMS D (2005)
'Maintaining research traditions on place: Diversity of thought and scientific progress.'
Journal of Environmental Psychology 25, 361–380.

RELPH E (1976)
Place and Placelessness.
London: Pion.

ROUTLEDGE C, WILDSCHUT T, SEDIKIDES C, HART C, VINGERHOETS J, ARNDT J AND JUHL J (2011)
'The past makes the present meaningful: Nostalgia as an existential resource.'
Journal of Personality and Social Psychology 101, 638–652.

SCHELLENBAUM A (2018)
'In 1955, the Fontainebleau Hotel Was Irrepressibly Glamorous.'
Curbed.
Accessed on 15·6·18 at: curbed.com/2014/9/19/10044798/in-1955-the-fontainebleau-hotel-was-irrepressibly-glamorous

SHIELDS R (1991)
Places on the Margin: Alternative Geographies of Modernity.
Abingdon: Routledge.

URRY J (1997)
'Cultural Change and the Seaside Resort.'
In G Shaw and A Williams (eds)
The Rise and Fall of British Coastal Resorts: Cultural and Economic Perspectives.
London: Mansell. pp.102–117.

VISIT BRITAIN (2017)
The GB Tourist: Statistics 2015.
Accessed on 15·6·18 at: visitbritain.org/sites/default/files/vb-corporate/Documents-Library/documents/England-documents/gb_tourist_report_2015.pdf

WALTON JK (2000)
The British Seaside: Holidays and Resorts in the Twentieth Century.
Manchester: Manchester University Press.

WHITE M, PAHL S. ASHBULLBY K, HERBERT S AND DEPLEDGE M (2013)
'Feelings of restoration from recent nature visits.'
Journal of Environmental Psychology 35(1), 40–51.

WHITE M, SMITH A, HUMPHRYES K, PAHL S, SNELLING D AND DEPLEDGE M (2010)
'Blue space: The importance of water for preference, affect, and restorativeness ratings of natural and built scenes.'
Journal of Environmental Psychology 30(4), 482–493.

Place Pixelation: Interactions with the Fleshy Phantasmic

Victoria Lucas
/
Emma Fraser

This collaborative and experimental text has been informed by artist Victoria Lucas and sociologist Emma Fraser's shared interest in feminist readings of place. Their public event, *After Castle Market: Salvaging the Urban Obsolete*, explored themes of urban ruins and renewal, and included a screening of *After* (2013), a short film by Victoria, developed during her residency in Sheffield's Castle Market shortly before its demolition. This text combines themes of urban decay and failed utopias with the authors' current research around aspects of gendered space and digital cultures, and features images produced by Victoria during a research sabbatical in California during 2016.

ALL IMAGES FROM THE 'HYPERBOLIC ISLAND' SERIES, VICTORIA LUCAS, 2016.

I have reached an empty cabin. I sit on the wooden stoop and look out across the landscape that stretches towards the horizon. Apart from the wiry shrubs that flex in the light wind, the scene is still. On occasion I hear a single bird chirping and the odd insect clicking somewhere nearby. Mostly though, the only audible sound is the low, whining grumble of a rusty air duct that reluctantly dances in circles with the intermittent breeze.

The wasteland stands before me, rubble-strewn and open for exploration. Without another's gaze to intercept my path, I can wander as the flâneuse, unbound and beyond the usual rules of encounter. Place, here, is available to be made, unmade, remade, on a whim. Broken glass and disintegrating bricks shift beneath my feet as a harsh sun reveals an undulating scape of hidden information and fading memories.

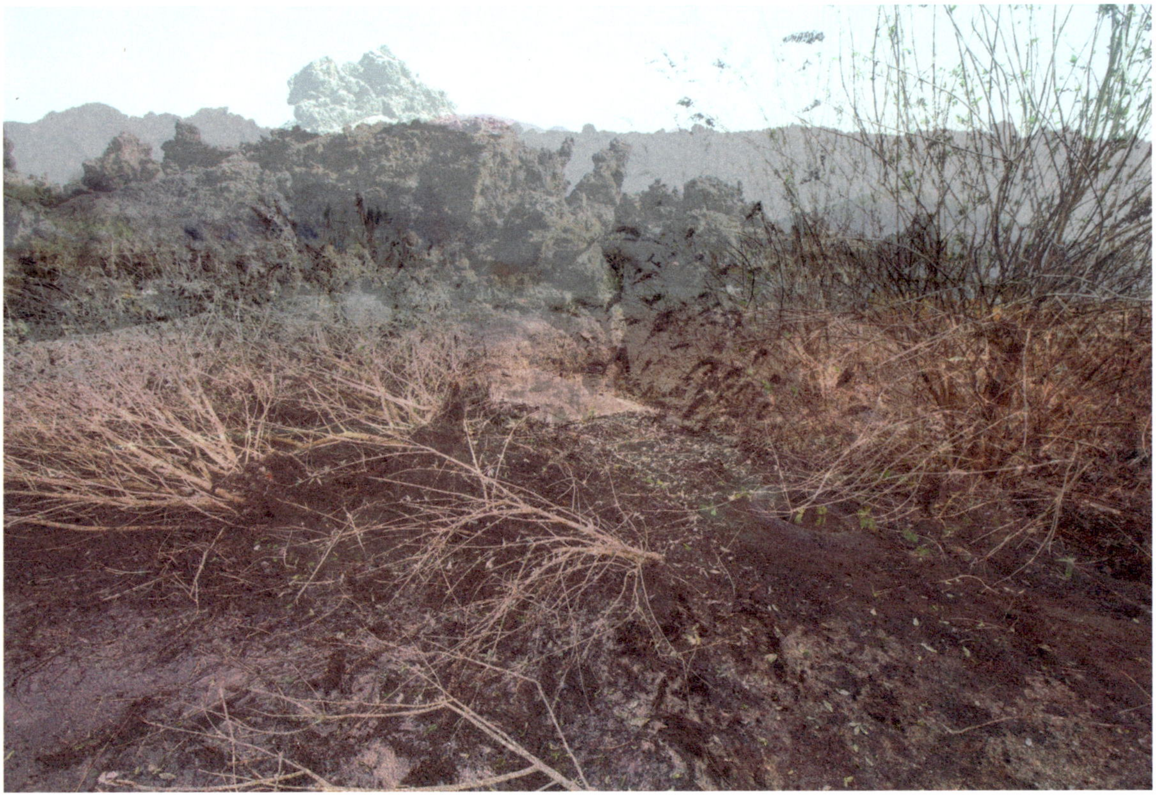

The wasteland, the ruin, the desert – these are material sites of paradoxical suspension (static, yet in the process of decay; atemporal and, simultaneously, symbolically indexing the passing of time; situated and embodied, yet also the abstract space of representation). The cinematic space captured through a camera lens encompasses a physical space yet also 'contains specific imaginary elements: fantasy images, symbols, which appear to arise from "something else"' (Lefebvre 1991: 311). The 'scene of cinema' (Burchill 2009) is an abstract representation of space, but the materialities of cinematic representation when situated in a familiar film location generate a slippage in the overall sense of reality and establish a sense of 'authority and prescriptive power in and through the space that underpins them and makes them effective' (Lefebvre 1991: 311). One can envisage the spectres of mainstream culture when walking through the cinema-scapes of westerns, horrors, road trip movies and science fiction narratives in the Alabama Hills – a rock formation that juts out of a valley just east of the Sierra Nevada in California. Through this representational power of space, augmented by the image of the ruin, wasteland or desert, the eerie and the strange (Fisher 2016) emerge from the landscape, generating a sense of distance and dislocation that repels, even as it welcomes.

This place, the ruinscape, is the liminal *Terrain Vague* (Solá-Morales 1995; Turner 1975). The liminal is an in-between space, it's not easily pinned down – it's the barren wilderness and wasteland, the rubble of an abandoned ruin, the shifting shoreline. It is perhaps closer to the floating virtuality of cyberspace, at once more and less real, more and less tangible, than everyday places of encounter. This liminal space, between the real and unreal, is where we find ourselves: two women in voids of our own making, Victoria's deserts, Emma's ruins. As we bring them together, they shift and fade, merge with dreamscapes, become virtual – strange transfigurations.

I stand on the top of a mountain, teetering on the edge whilst peering down towards the desert below. I have butterflies in my stomach – even though logically I know that there is no danger, my brain initiates a fear of falling that is difficult to ignore. I advance towards the horizon – quickly as if flying, but with no exertion. Effortlessly – gracefully – I drift through space, each subtle landmark falling out of view as I advance forward.

I feel the ground beneath my feet – it's soft, carpeted. It doesn't match what I can see. What's more, when I look down at my hands, they are not there... I look to my feet and instead I can only see the flatness of the ground. I drift higher, moving through space and time against the laws of physics. I look to the side of me and see the horizon, I see the line between the familiar sky blues and the unearthly blackness beyond, stars punctuating the emptiness as my eyes search for the familiar. I am an astronaut. I turn and see the Earth, I move along its rotation. I feel the weightlessness in my mind as I float – my eyes wide with an astounding sense of joy mixed with fear... fear of my own immortality, my insignificance, my small presence. I fall, but don't feel the full sensation of falling. I have complete control of gravity, I move forward and back at will. Even if I hit the ground, I can reverse the action or just stand, unscathed by my volatile movements.

In this realm, my cognitive perception stands before my body and leads my experiences. It is a reversal of reality, as if my mind has formed the outer shell of my being and my physical flesh is encased within, folded neatly and put to the side as an obsolescent entity. My body grows small, the new outer self growing in size, dwarfing my female form and becoming more than. My thoughts, my sense of self, reaches its full potential, like a fluid Möbius strip of energy – flexing and shifting.

The experience of the virtual and the ruin, in particular, share an affinity that goes beyond the conceptual – as the virtual fragments the real, the ruin detaches from the real the more it decays. Similar to the scene of cinema, the digital world brings forth abstract memories and material encounters, sitting on the cusp between representation and experience – what you see and what you feel – and what that means. The virtual world bleeds into the 'real'; the real is abducted by the images of imaginary spaces framed by technology. Virtual reality becomes an extension of our imagination that creates a permeability of bodily boundaries – a pastiche of sense and data, dissected sites and bytes representing a whole.

Encounters with liminal places take on a mediating effect; the journey through the ruins, desolate deserts and wastes evolves into a critical engagement with the situated self, which reveals a sympathetic relation between cyberspace, urban space and liminal space. Emma finds herself in a ruin – Victoria loses herself in a desert.

Walls are meant to contain but also to protect. They keep out heat, and dust, and wind, and rain. Brick by brick, stone by stone, they enclose, envelop, divide. Walls are forbidding. Hard surfaces, material barriers – walls tell you when you're not intended, when a space is meant for you or meant for someone else. They demarcate territories and zones; separate the liminal from the littoral, the threshold from the shore.

In this place, the walls are riven, they forget their duty. Here, a roofless ruin, knee deep in grit and detritus. The doors are gone, the windows gape and dust motes dance in the sunrays that beat down onto discarded stone. Built by human hands, this place has lost power over its inhabitants, scattered the patterns and habits of life, erased the myth of a history that fails to tell our story. Crumbling walls were once dividing lines and closed in sets, stages with their roles and plots. Containers gridded out for this or that – for him, for her, for one use or another. These walls constructed rooms, places, and neighbourhoods – but they also structured action and possibility... You can make what you want amongst the ruins, because the powerful sway of their forebears has begun to fade. Beneath the rubble there are no binaries or subjugations – just moments in which to reconfigure past and present, to persist amidst the dust and reimagine possibilities... I slip into a timelessness that is usually only present in dreamscapes.

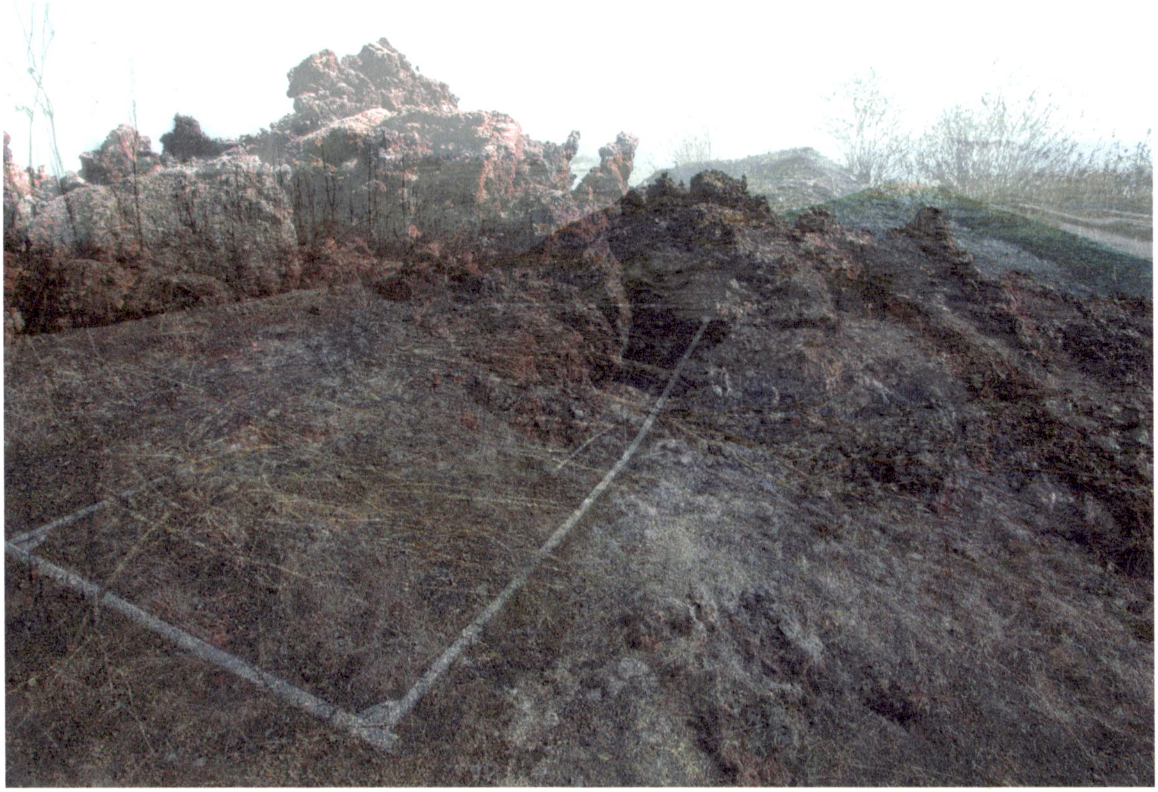

The city, as a dreamworld, is imbued with a ruinous transience – as Buck-Morss wrote at the close of the Cold War (1989; 1995) – tied to catastrophe, the image of which persists in the decaying and outmoded discards of earlier eras. The place that is discarded – whether the partially derelict Parisian arcades of Walter Benjamin's study (1999), the crumbling bunkers of the Cold War or the fields of ruin left by industrial mass-production – is evidence of utopian dreaming, liminal-scapes and zones that tell the body about how past people and cultures imagined the future. Dreams that now lie fallow in liminal dreamscapes.

Liminality speaks of exceptions, ambiguity and thresholds – and as such, in the spatial realm, is the stuff of ruins, deserts... and islands. Liminality, moreover, also tells us of the complex relationship between people and media – the threshold of meaning making, where an image starts to project beyond representation and into the lived world of those who perceive it. In liminality, 'It is as though all social structural statuses, roles, and rules cancel one another, leaving a liminal space that is at once pure act and pure potentiality, a zero that is all' (1975: 29). A liminal place stands adrift between the inchoate, chaos and fixity – a dusty desert, a fragmented architectural remnant, a bordered, yet infinite, island.

More than this, the liminal is about what can be said, done or felt. As Turner explains, 'We are provoked by silence, negativity, liminality, ambiguity, into efforts of extended comprehension' (1975: 33). An island is liminal because it is isolated, but also touched on all sides by the water, embodying the shifting and transient as the shore shifts and moves. Importantly, the liminality of the island makes us both think about the potential of space away from the entrenched patriarchal and capitalist systems that restrict certain social groups based on class, race and gender. Doreen Massey's feminist politics of space tells us that these complex power systems make many individuals feel 'quite simply out of place' (1994: 148). However, Massey was adamant that space is always open, and never closed; it is always becoming and there is always room for shifts to take place. We also think of Foucault's heterotopia (1986) – 'other spaces' that can't be categorised as sites of normal life. A heterotopia exists outside everyday space, as an exception to the usual ordering of the world – the cemetery, for example, is a heterotopia. Like Turner's liminal landscapes (1975), which occupy those uncertain spaces in-between fixed places, or Fisher's notion of the eerie (2016) as something unsettling or uncanny – the experiences of the world that are difficult to define, a heterotopic space doesn't properly fit anywhere; it will always be a bit peculiar. The subjective emplacement of the individual body (Foucault 1986), the constant shifting maelstrom of space – these are where the limits of what can be said or experienced are to be explored.

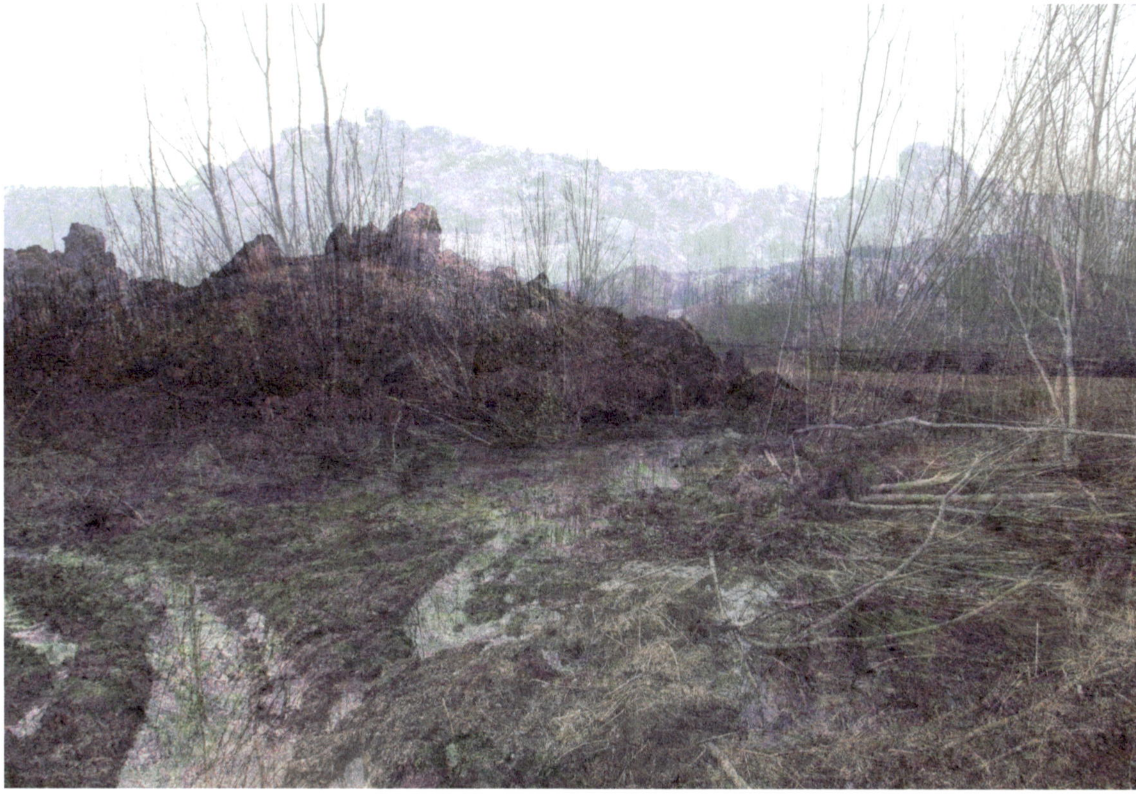

Liminality offers the possibility for heterotopic construction, providing new ground to traverse and utilise as an assertion of power in the face of elemental forces. Reclaiming and reasserting our rights over a space demands resistance, innovation and action. We start with nothing and, through a method of construction, arrive at a place that is suddenly imbued with significant value. This constructed reality forms a space in which to destabilise, subvert and radically reimagine established structures.

While internal space is phantasmic, shifting and contradictory, 'we do not live in a kind of void inside of which we could place individuals and things... we live inside a set of relations' (*ibid*: 23) that defines the specificity of space and also of power structures and encounters... The relationship of the sea with the shore, the ruin with the rubble, the self with the other. And yet, in this heterotopia, the dead's ruins that litter the landscape cease to be binding; they are outside or beyond – they are also *other*.

Between the real and virtual, the placed and emplaced, the wandering psychogeographer or flâneuse happens upon real and abstract fragmentation: bricks, concrete, stone – shards of metal and splintered plastic. Dust, scree, pebbles. These places are: 'counter sites, a... utopia in which... all the other real sites that can be found within the culture, are simultaneously represented, contested, and inverted' (*ibid*: 24). The inversion happens in the moment of contrast between the lived and structured world and the chaotic wasteland, desert, or ruin. Like Foucault's example of the cemetery, '(p)laces of this kind are outside of all places, even though it may be possible to indicate their location in reality' (*ibid*). Within the heterotopic is the possibility of space, even of the virtual, of the cyber – this is the moment of our encounter.

CYBERSPACE

In her manifesto for cyborgs, Donna Haraway (1983) describes a human hybrid comprising machine and organism as a 'prime resource to help imagine a different kind of material-semiotic world' (Schneider 2005: 62). Devised in a historic moment, when the militarisation of technology made it possible to blur the boundaries between human and machine, the image of the cyborg was presented by Haraway as a model that conceptualised the possibility of an emancipated, post-gender utopia.

Haraway argues that through a symbiotic relationship between social reality and imagination, 'antagonistic dualisms' that dominate the West, such as self/other, culture/nature, male/female, truth/illusion, can be challenged by 'high-tech culture' in the form of the cybernetic organism. This pre-internet theory provides a suitable model in which to critique the 21st century methods of learning and communication – as human beings become increasingly reliant on digital technology as an enhancing extension of the organic; as the pixelated image becomes space (Ash 2009); as utopias are found in cyberspace. Social media platforms provide individuals with the tools to present themselves as their digitally enhanced avatars, generating a utopian representation of the self. Addressing this shift, Amelia Jones (2006) states that the body now 'extends into and is understood as an image – but as an image understood itself, reciprocally, as embodied'.

Profound affective moments arise from the contact between self and image, at the intersection where the structures that form place begin to fall apart. The desert, the ruin... the island, the wasteland... as an image is pulled down into micro-parcels to be reassembled on-screen, so are sand and rubble the constituent parts of material encounter, reassembled through an embodied present in the virtual mirror of 'other' space – the transitory real, outside of all places.

Since Foucault's work on heterotopia, advancements in digital technology have initiated a transition in which the dualistic boundary between reality and representation is broken down, reshaping what we understand to be real, reducing the tangible social being to nothing more than a visual echo of one's existence. Social life and appearance are reduced to body contouring, fake tans, Botox, silicone implants – apparently normal augmentations of everyday reality, a phantom ideal – our bodies are starting to look less natural and more like our digitally enhanced avatars. Virtual and physical 'enhancements' feed between promoted and idealised images, strangers' bodies that are violently marketed as commodities by global billion-dollar industries. And yet, cyberspace has also made it possible for new mutable positionings to take place, breaking down fixed identities and structures, to make sense of and ultimately redefine identity outside of limiting, capitalist-driven frames. Digital space is infinite; as we look it makes room for #MeToo[1], for shifting cultural perceptions of gender inequality. How we work – where we work – what we can do. This collective effort is shaping policy and transforming the realities of women across the globe in a way that hasn't been possible before. For us, as this text is written into being, the very possibilities of life are reimagined, transgressing the liminal and virtual, what we see and what we know, enmeshing the real and the cyber.

1. THE #METOO TWITTER CAMPAIGN IS AN INTERNATIONAL MOVEMENT AGAINST SEXUAL HARASSMENT AND ABUSE THAT BEGAN IN OCTOBER 2017.

Cyberspace, in this context, reshapes the way we know place – and self, within place. Svetlana Boym, writing at the turn of the millennium, was especially sensitive to the strange flows of the cyber between the pre- and post-internet ages; she links the real and virtual to the ruin, but also the highway with the desert, through the linkage of the representational and the spatial. She says:

> The internet... took over elements of pastoral imagery and 'western' genres... the new media redefined the architecture of space with a 'superhighway', villages and chatrooms – all evidence that the internet foregrounds pastoral suburbia and the romance of the highway and domestic morality tales over the ruins of the metropolis.
> (Boym 2001: 348)

The ruined city of Boym's account is neither a literal ruin (though this age was defined by post-Soviet and post-industrial decay) nor an allegorical tale of a techno-apocalypse. Instead, it is the precise and fragmented site of our wanderer's encounter – in-between virtual and real; representation and experience; heterotopia and utopia. A void materialised in encounter, reimagined through image.

It is also the place in which we find ourselves – and lose ourselves.

UTOPIA

The vista I inhabit is a patchwork of paradise. Layers of rock, sand, dirt and ruinous concrete have been looted from the Earth, digitised and repositioned in a constructed utopia. Fragments of desert land are fused with volcanic island scenes, post-industrial brownfield sites, nondescript lakes and forests appropriated from across the globe. I walk towards the jagged, volcanic rock that juts out of the concrete slab. I graze my knee as I begin to climb, yet I do not feel the familiar sting as my skin is left behind on the hot black surface. I stand atop the rocky outcrop and survey the lay of the land.

DESERT / ISLAND

What is a utopia? Michel Serres finds these 'possible spaces' everywhere we have already been:

> Whether a city or an island, utopia, entirely spatial, also constructs another world: that of monumental construction, measured by string and compass, an architectural painting, a possible world, prepared, projected. A city-planner's plan or blueprint, Utopia masters space through representation. Conversely, because they project possible spaces, the architect and city-planner practice utopian trades. (Serres 2017: 52)

The utopian space of possibility presented by the wasteland is curtailed by the island. As the ruin is to the city (pushing it away and, in so doing, showing exactly what the city is made of), the island is to space – it both deconstructs it (by making a mockery of its perpetual openness, a horizon of infinite blue) and frames it (with a precise, yet wavering, border) at once. The monumentality of the architectural world, made for man, disintegrates in the waste, in the ruin – the architectonics of the utopian trade fall apart in the face of the ever-shifting island...

A colourful film distorts my view of the island. I touch it, and my hand slips through to the other side with little resistance, the oily patterns undulating along the screen surface in ripples all around me. My body becomes irrelevant as the iridescence of the landscape fragments my form, and I begin to float freely between layers of matter – my body stretched as the pixels that hold my image break down and reconfigure in order for me to achieve my full potential.

RUIN / VOID

For transience breeds hope – hope that there is another, alternative history to be built from the remnants... Boym saw this in techno-utopianism, the better world that will be built from cyberspace. This is proven to be a chimera – pixelated nothings that bring distorted mirror reflections, tortured flâneuses who fade in and out of being, frontiers that prove to be mirages. An abundance of realities, an infinitude of spaces, a perpetual breakdown into the liminal void.

Yet within the liminal, the transitory, the virtual and ruinous, there remains a utopian hope – from fragments new things can be assembled; in the wasteland life is more real; in cyberspace we can disappear, reappear and dream different selves into being.

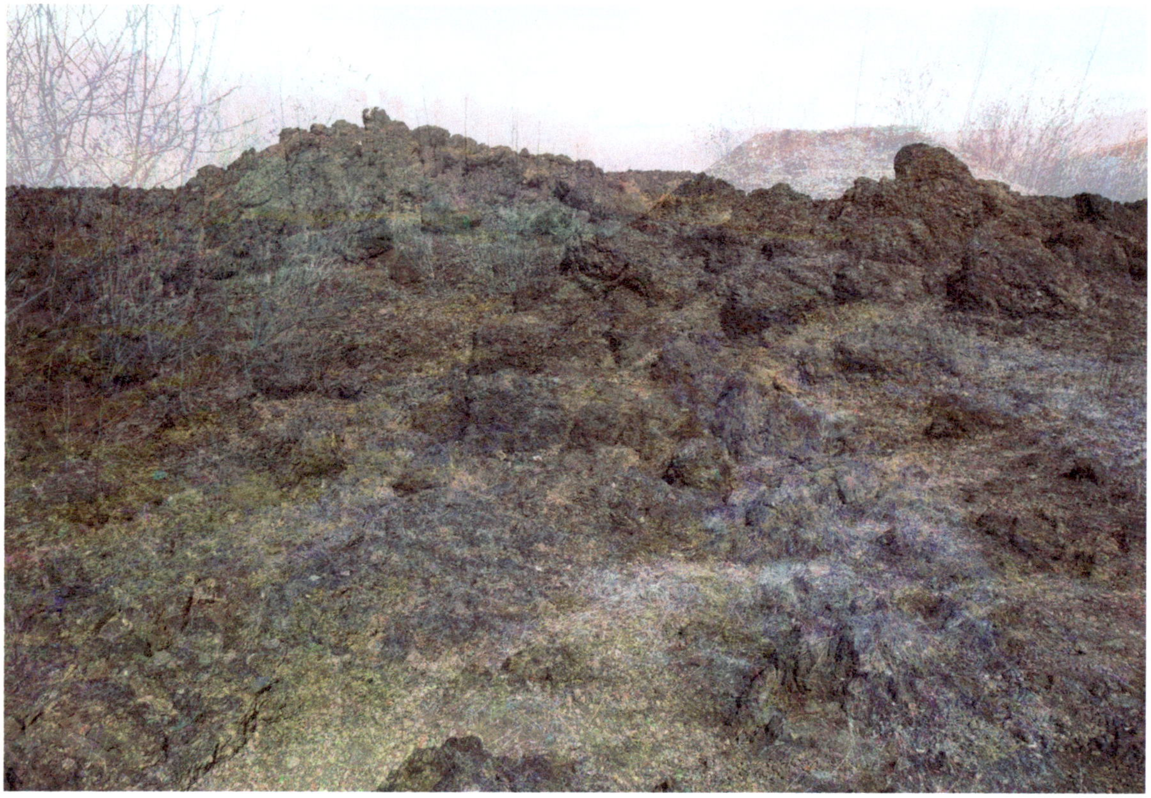

END

Just as metaphors of information superhighways and the politics of the non-real fragment the world into micro-parcels of human-machine relations, a fractured landscape deteriorates the (hu)man-made architecture, disintegrating centuries of lived encounter with place. Where the body encounters this disintegration – in ruins, in deserts – a transfiguration takes place; the heterotopia of the wasteland, the ruin, the island – these bring us closer in understanding our own connections with this world's, but also our two perspectives as they reverberate through different places, spaces, and frameworks.

The desert, the island, the ruin – these are places where each of us has been in reality, but also heterotopic spaces which offer glimpses of exception, states beyond the status quo, virtual existences and futures to be mapped. The magic of the transfigurative power of each site is felt through temporality, emplacement and subjectivity, and the liminal and utopian qualities of place translate the conditions of life for both of us, blurring boundaries between real and imagined, virtual and material until neither of us is sure where the other's account ends and our own begins.

As we wrote, we came to understand how the turbulent development of the cyber and the digital makes the construction of place increasingly weighted towards virtuality and transience, rather than materiality. The intercession of the digital image into everyday life and experience ultimately acts as a mediator of being in the realm of the (un)real, mirroring the experiences of being a woman, being an explorer in hostile worlds, being a body, being an artist and being a researcher. In the end, nothing quite seems real, and we lose sight of ourselves, only to be found again in these most abstract and unmoored places – on islands, in wastelands, in deserts and ruins.

ASH J (2009)
'Emerging spatialities of the screen: Video games and the reconfiguration of spatial awareness.'
Environment and Planning A 41, 2105–2124.

BENJAMIN W (1999)
The Arcades Project.
Cambridge, MA and London: Harvard University Press.

BOYM S (2001)
The Future of Nostalgia.
New York: Basic Books.

BUCK-MORSS S (1989)
The Dialectics of Seeing: Walter Benjamin and the Arcades Project.
Cambridge, MA: MIT Press.

BUCK-MORSS S (1995)
'The city as dreamworld and catastrophe.'
October 73, 3–26.

BURCHILL L (2009)
'Derrida and the (Spectral) Scene of Cinema.'
In F J Colman (ed) *Film, Theory and Philosophy.*
London: Acumen Press. pp.164–178.

FISHER M (2016)
The Weird and The Eerie.
London: Repeater.

FOUCAULT M (1986)
'Of other spaces.'
Diacritics 16(1), 22–27.

HARAWAY D (1983)
'A Cyborg Manifesto: Science, Technology, and Socialist-Feminism in the Late Twentieth Century.'
In *Simians, Cyborgs, and Women: The Reinvention of Nature.*
London: Free Association Books.

JONES A (2006)
Self/Image: Technology, Representation and the Contemporary Subject.
Oxon: Routledge.

LEFEBVRE H (1991)
The Production of Space.
Malden, MA and Oxford: Blackwell Publishing.

MASSEY D (1994)
Space, Place and Gender.
Cambridge: Polity Press.

SCHNEIDER J (2005)
Donna Haraway: Live Theory.
London: Continuum.

SERRES M (2017)
Geometry.
London and New York: Bloomsbury.

SOLÁ-MORALES ID (1995)
'Terrain Vague.'
In CC Davidson (ed.) *Anyplace.*
New York: Anyone Corporation.

TURNER V (1975)
Revelation and Divination in Ndembu Ritual.
London: Cornell University.

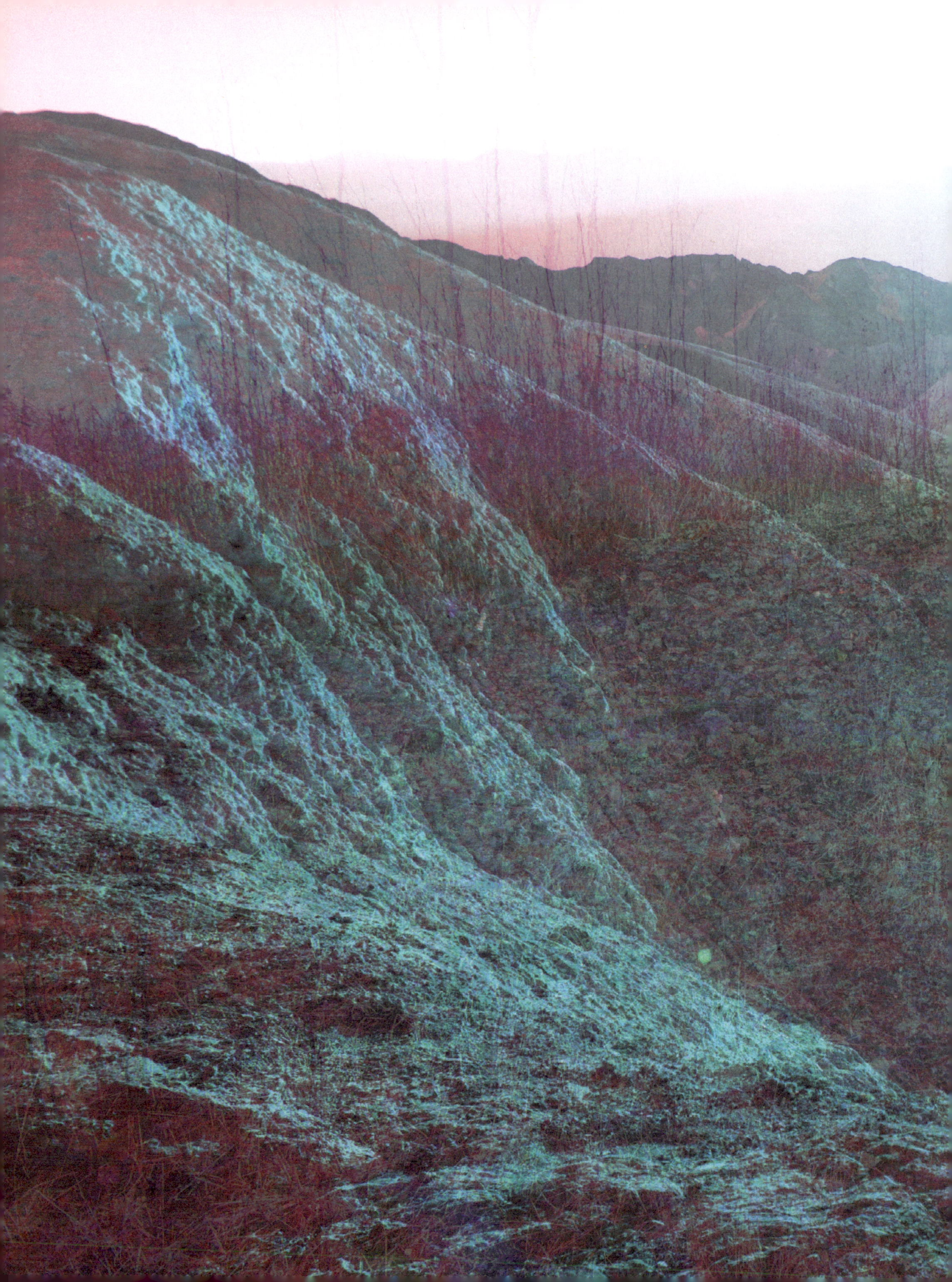

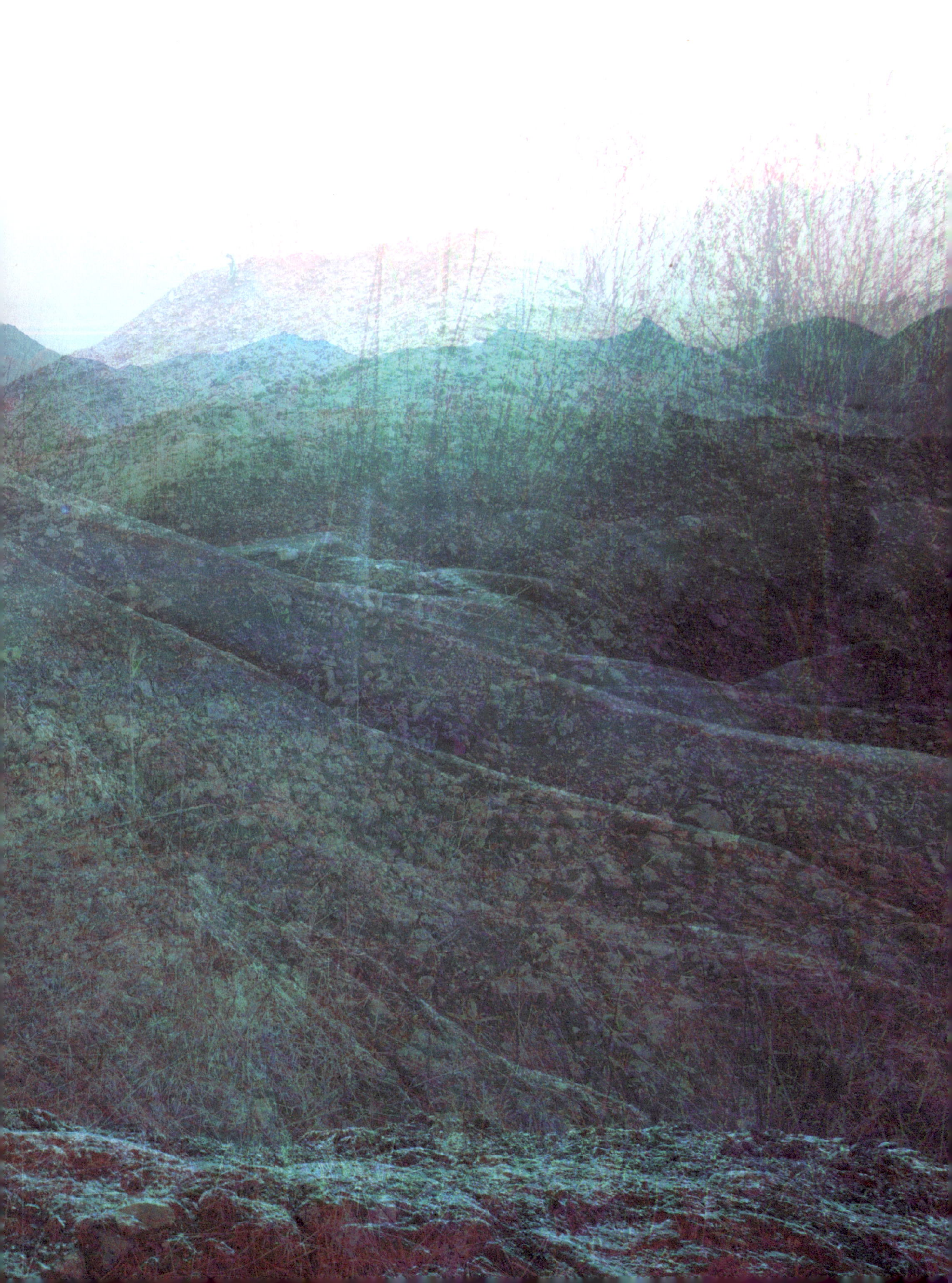

As a collaborative project, this book has been a true pleasure to work on. Each author has shown a huge amount of enthusiasm for the project, and I would like to thank them for their creativity, generosity and patience. I also owe a huge amount of gratitude to Sarah Auld for her invaluable help in navigating the publishing process, and to Mike Collier at Art Editions North for his guidance and encouragement. Bonnie Craig and Deborah Stevenson's attention to detail, and the resourceful creativity of Vicky Carr and Chris Shearston at Textbook Studio have also been vital in making the book a reality. Finally, I would like to thank my In Certain Places colleagues Rachel Bartholomew and Charles Quick for their ongoing support, and Lubaina Himid for planting the seeds of this project in my mind during our conversations many years ago.

REBECCA CHESNEY'S practice examines our complex relationship with the natural world by engaging with issues of culture, politics and power. Her artworks, which take the form of installations, films, interventions, drawings, maps and walks, are often created in response to specific places and are underpinned by environmental research. Recent projects include *Alla Breve* (2018) at Museo Casa Rurale di Carcente in Italy, a Lucas Artist Fellowship (2016/17) at Montalvo in California USA, *Snapshot* (2016) residency and commission by Peak with Brecon Beacons National Park Authority and *Death by Denim* (2015) Harris Museum, Art Gallery & Library.

DAVID COOPER is a Senior Lecturer in English at Manchester Metropolitan University where his teaching and research focus on contemporary place writing and geographical thought.

He has published extensively on the literature of the Lake District and has a particular interest in the ongoing legacies of the Romantic poetics of place. Alongside this, he works on the relationship between literature and (digital) mapping and is currently Co-Investigator on *Chronotopic Cartography: Mapping Literary Place, Space, and Pace* (Arts and Humanities Research Council, 2007–2010). He is also a founding co-editor of *Literary Geographies*: an international, open-access journal dedicated to the publication of interdisciplinary research.

David is also interested in the synergies and tensions between critical and creative approaches to place. At Manchester Metropolitan University, he supervises a range of creative–critical doctoral projects and leads on the MA/MFA in Place Writing. Creativity is also becoming increasingly integral to his own, frequently collaborative, research.

AMELIA CROUCH is an artist who lives in West Yorkshire. She uses media including print, moving image and installation to produce work for both gallery and site-responsive, public-realm locations. Her artwork is underpinned by an interest in the relational and mutable nature of meaning and usually begins with words as either content or inspiration. Outcomes range from simple acts of wordplay – such as semiotically inspired text animations – to more elaborate, performative videos.

Recent commissions and exhibitions include: The Tetley, Leeds (2017); Castlefield Gallery, Manchester (2016); Coventry Artspace (2016); and Pavilion, Leeds (2015). Amelia holds an MA Fine Art from Manchester Metropolitan University and a BA Fine Art from Leeds University. She works as a Fine Art Lecturer at Leeds Arts University.

EMMA FRASER completed her PhD in Sociology at the University of Manchester in 2018, which was focused on video games, digital space and imaginaries of urban decay. Emma's most recent work is focused on 3D and digital worlds in terms of meaning production, urban play and visual media. Emma's work broadly considers regeneration, urban exploration and modern ruins, and has focused on fieldwork and embodied experience in Detroit, Chernobyl, Berlin, Paris, New York, Sydney, Christchurch (NZ) and elsewhere. Emma is a member of the Playful Mapping Collective.

LUBAINA HIMID lives and works in Preston. Forthcoming solo exhibitions in 2019 include New Museum, New York, and Frans Hals Museum, Haarlem. Himid has held solo exhibitions in a number of institutions recently such as Harris Museum, Preston, and Musée régional d'art contemporain Occitanie / Pyrénées-Méditerranée, Sérignan – 2018; Badischer Kunstverein, Karlsruhe, Spike Island, Bristol, and Modern Art Oxford – 2017. Group exhibitions include Berlin Biennale, BALTIC, Gateshead, and Glasgow International – 2018; South London Gallery, Nottingham Contemporary, and Walker Art Gallery, Liverpool – 2017; as well as Van Abbemuseum, Eindhoven – 2016. Her work is held in several public collections including Tate, Museum Ludwig, National Museums Liverpool, British Council, Arts Council Collections, UK Government Art Collection, Birmingham Museums, Rhode Island School of Design, Middlesbrough Institute of Modern Art, Victoria & Albert Museum and Wolverhampton Museum.

Himid is Professor of Contemporary Art at the University of Central Lancashire where she runs the Making Histories Visible archive and collection. She is the winner of the 2017 Turner Prize.

DAVID JACQUES studied Muralism at the Chelsea School of Art and gained an MA in Public Art at the Duncan of Jordanstone College of Art and Design in the late 1980s. His current practice involves a diversity of media and deals with varied approaches to narrative and the construction of mythologies. His projects are underpinned by prolonged periods of research into prevalent socio-political issues. He deploys metaphor and allegory in scripted, conflated tales that generally revolve around historiographic, speculative and 'weird' outcomes.

In 2003 he won the Firestation Artists Studio Award in Dublin and was commissioned by Dublin Port Authority in 2005 to produce a year-long socially engaged public art project. In 2010 he was shortlisted for the Northern Art Prize and won the Liverpool Art Prize. His video work has been screened at film festivals across the world and he has shown internationally in numerous group and solo exhibitions.

DAVID JARRATT lectures in Tourism at the University of Central Lancashire (UCLan). Recently, he has been researching sense of place as experienced by visitors to the traditional British seaside resort or seasideness. He has written for a number of tourism journals and contributed to books such as *Landscapes of Leisure: Space, Place and Identities* (Palgrave Macmillan, 2015). David is currently researching other elements of the tourist experience, including nostalgia.

BOB JOHNSTON is a Senior Lecturer in Landscape Archaeology in the University of Sheffield. He researches histories of landscapes in Britain, with specific interests in the uplands, boundaries and prehistoric field systems. He is currently working in Wales: the western fringes of Snowdonia and Skomer Island, Pembrokeshire.

JOANNE LEE is Senior Lecturer in Graphic Design at Sheffield Institute of Arts. She is an artist, writer and publisher of the Pam Flett Press, a serial publication essaying everyday life. Her research, pursued through written and photographic investigations of place, focuses on the surfaces of post-industrial sites, explores vague, difficult-to-classify locations in Northern England and attends to the spatial metaphors at work in thinking/making.

Publications include 'Vaguely Northern: In between in England', a chapter for the book *Northern Light: Landscape, Photography and Evocations of the North* (Transcript Verlag, 2018) and 'On Not Staying Put: Georges Perec's "Inter(in)disciplinarity" as an Approach to Research', an article for the journal *Literary Geographies* (2017).

RUTH LEVENE'S work is driven by a curiosity about and concern with the complex infrastructure systems we live by and how we manage our natural resources. She is currently working with Arts Catalyst on a three-year project called Test Sites, researching water governance in relation to human health and wellbeing and the resilience of communities and ecologies.

DUNCAN LIGHT is Senior Lecturer in the Department of Tourism and Hospitality at Bournemouth University. A human geographer by background, he worked for 20 years in Liverpool before moving to Bournemouth. He has research interests in urban landscapes, particularly in Romania (a country he has visited regularly for more than 20 years). In particular, his research has explored the efforts to remake the 'official public landscape' created by Romania's communist regime in the post-communist period. He has published papers on these issues in a range of journals (including *Europe-Asia Studies, Journal of Historical Geography, Annals of the Association of American Geographers, Transactions of the Institute of British Geographers* and *Human Geographies*) and has also contributed chapters to a number of recent edited volumes about post-communist change.

VICTORIA LUCAS'S artwork is often initiated by a physical encounter with a place, site or landscape. She is specifically concerned with the chimerical potential of space; documenting, fabricating or reconstructing places using digital and sculptural means as a way to reposition socially constructed identities. Her work has been exhibited internationally, including solo exhibitions at Grizzly Grizzly, Philadelphia; Airspace Gallery, Stoke-on-Trent and Chiara Williams Contemporary at London Art Fair. Group shows include Casa Maauad, Mexico City, Millennium Galleries, Sheffield and The Front, New Orleans. Victoria won the SOLO award™ in 2016, and has artist book works in the Tate Archive, the MOMA New York and the V&A collection amongst others. Victoria is an artist, Senior Lecturer of Fine Art at the University of Central Lancashire and current PhD scholar at Sheffield Hallam University.

JAMES G MANSELL is Associate Professor of Cultural Studies in the Department of Cultural, Media and Visual Studies at the University of Nottingham and Co-Director of the Nottingham Sensory Studies Network. He is the author of *The Age of Noise in Britain: Hearing Modernity* (University of Illinois Press, 2017), a history of everyday sound and hearing in early 20th-century Britain. He works mainly in the field of sound studies and has contributed chapters to books such as *Sounds of Modern History* (Berghahn, 2014) and The Routledge Companion to Sound Studies (Routledge, forthcoming). He is a Research Associate at Science Museum, London, where he has collaborated on projects about sound, collections and exhibitions. He is Book Reviews Editor of the journal *The Senses and Society*.

IAN NESBITT uses art to create spaces for exchange that are beyond the everyday. His social practice examines ideas of commonality, working alongside citizens and communities to offer new readings of the territories we inhabit. His work has recently been shown at Abandon Normal Devices, Nottingham Contemporary, Millennium Gallery Sheffield and Flatpack festival, Birmingham.

LES ROBERTS is a Senior Lecturer in Cultural and Media Studies at the University of Liverpool. Interdisciplinary in scope, his work explores the broad intersection between space, place, mobility and memory. He is author/editor of eight books, including *Deep Mapping* (MDPI AG, 2016), *Locating the Moving Image* (Indiana University Press, 2014), *Liminal Landscapes* (Routledge, 2012), *Film, Mobility and Urban Space* (Liverpool University Press, 2012) and *Mapping Cultures* (Palgrave Macmillan, 2012). His most recent book, *Spatial Anthropology: Excursions in Liminal Space* (2018), is published by Rowman & Littlefield as part of their Place, Memory, Affect series.

ROSEMARY SHIRLEY'S research centres on everyday life and visual culture, with a particular emphasis on contemporary rural contexts. She is interested in how the English landscape might be explored through notions of national identity and discourses of modernity. This has led her to write about topics as diverse as litter, motorways, folk customs and scrapbooks. She is also interested in how contemporary artists engage with landscape as a place that is lived in rather than simply looked at or visited.

In 2017 she co-curated the large-scale exhibition *Creating the Countryside* at Compton Verney (March–June 2017), which featuring over 100 works of art from the 17th century to today and was accompanied by a publication of the same name. She is the author of *Rural Modernity, Everyday Life and Visual Culture* (Routledge, 2015).

EMILY SPEED is an artist based in the North West. Speed works in sculpture, installation and performance and her work is concerned with the relationship between the body and architecture. Recent projects include The Happenstance as part of Scotland + Venice at La Biennale di Venezia, a new commission for Knole House (National Trust) and a new dance work for Look Again Festival, Aberdeen. Recent exhibitions include Exeter Phoenix; TRUCK, Calgary; Fort Worth Contemporary Arts, Texas; Plymouth Art Centre; g39, Cardiff; Oredaria Gallery, Rome; Laumeier Sculpture Park, St Louis, USA; Yorkshire Sculpture Park; and Musée Cantonal des Beaux-Arts, Lausanne, Switzerland. Emily's work is held in the Arts Council Collection and Tate Artist Books Collection and her artists' books are held in numerous libraries in the US including Yale, Library of Congress and MIT. In 2014/15, Speed was resident at the British School at Rome as the Derek Hill Foundation Scholar (drawing).

ELAINE SPEIGHT is a Research Fellow in the School of Art, Design and Fashion at the University of Central Lancashire, where she also lectures on the MA Fine Art programme. Her curatorial practice is concerned with the capacity of art to interrogate, mediate and critique the connections between people and place, and the relationship between art practice and research. Since 2005, she has co-curated In Certain Places, an artistic research project, which explores new and creative ways of informing the future of places through an ongoing programme of artistic interventions within the city of Preston. Elaine has written about place-based art and curatorial practice for various publications including *Engage* (2015), *Public Art Dialogue* (2017) and *The Everyday Practice of Public Art* (2015, Routledge).

MAGDA STAWARSKA-BEAVAN is a multi-disciplinary artist primarily concerned with the evocative, immersive qualities of sound, while combining a moving image and printmaking practice. She is interested in how soundscape orients us and subconsciously embeds itself in our memories of place, enabling us to construct personal recollections and offering the possibility of conveying narrative to listeners who have never experienced a location.

Her site-specific and outdoor installations have been shown as part of the TONSPUR programme in MFRU, Foundation Son:DA, Maribor Old Town Hall, Slovenia (2017); Kapelica Gallery Ljubljana, Slovenia (2016); 28th Exposition of New Music Brno Festival (2015); MQ21 TONSPUR passage/Q21 MQ, Vienna (2013); and Preston City Centre through a commission by In Certain Places (2011). Other exhibitions include *Sounds Like Her*, New Art Exchange, Nottingham and UK touring (2017–2018); TIES, Toronto Electroacoustic Symposium (2017); Kinokophonography Night at The New York Public Library for Performing Arts (2015, 2014).

JENNY STEELE is an artist whose research-led practice is motivated by 20th century architecture, most recently coastal mid-war architecture and design. She is interested in this period of modernist design which demonstrated a social emphasis towards renewal, and she seeks to revive elements of its ebullient, restorative qualities through sculpture, printmaking, drawing, textiles and site-specific artwork. Recent projects include *This Building for Hope*, The Midland Morecambe (2017), *Too Much is Never is Enough*, The Breakwater, Miami, USA, *This House for Building* residency and exhibition at The Tetley, Leeds (2017) and *An Architecture of Joy*, Grundy Art Gallery, Blackpool (2016).

PAUL WILSON is a researcher, typographer and writer whose work explores the intersections of language, landscape, community and communication. His current research involves the production of designed narratives of community and place and, in particular, investigates the potential for critically engaged typographies and language-acts, focusing on sites of class experience and situated knowledge at moments or points of change or transition. Much of his work orbits ideas and ideals of utopianism found in manifestations of the utopian action and has resulted in a broad range of activities: surveying the noticeboards found in the interior landscapes of working-men's clubs; mapping the route of the march which marked the closure of Britain's last deep coal mine; exploring the post-Brexit significance of the Esperanto-English dictionary held in Keighley Library, West Yorkshire. He is a Lecturer in the School of Design at the University of Leeds.

First published in 2019 by Art Editions North
in an edition of 1,000 copies.
-
Art Editions North is an imprint of
the University of Sunderland.
-
Editor: Elaine Speight
Design: Textbook Studio
Printed by: Pression Creative Print and Finishing
Copy editor: Bonnie Craig
Proofreader: Deborah Stevenson
-

Practising Place is an In Certain Places project,
based in the School of Art, Design and Fashion
at the University of Central Lancashire.
incertainplaces.org

Contact:
aen@sunderland.ac.uk / info@incertainplaces.org

A British Library CIP record is available

ISBN : 978-1-906832-35-3

Distributed by Cornerhouse Publications
HOME - 2 Tony Wilson Place
Manchester M15 4FN
England

Tel: ++44 (0)161 212 3466 / 3468
publications@cornerhouse.org
cornerhousepublications.org

Supported using public funding by
ARTS COUNCIL
ENGLAND